Broken China

Broken China

How the Economic Miracle Shattered and What it Means for the World

Logan Wright

polity

Copyright © Logan Wright 2026

The right of Logan Wright to be identified as Author of this Work has been asserted in accordance with the UK Copyright, Designs and Patents Act 1988.

First published in 2026 by Polity Press Ltd.

Polity Press Ltd.
65 Bridge Street
Cambridge CB2 1UR, UK

Polity Press Ltd.
111 River Street
Hoboken, NJ 07030, USA

All rights reserved. Except for the quotation of short passages for the purpose of criticism and review, no part of this publication may be reproduced, stored in a retrieval system or transmitted, in any form or by any means, electronic, mechanical, photocopying, recording or otherwise, without the prior permission of the publisher.

ISBN-13: 978-1-5095-7067-6

A catalog record for this book is available from the British Library.

Library of Congress Control Number: 2026930332

Typeset in 11.5 on 14 pt Adobe Garamond
by Cheshire Typesetting Ltd, Cuddington, Cheshire
Printed and bound in Great Britain by CPI Group (UK) Ltd, Croydon

The publisher has used its best endeavors to ensure that the URLs for external websites referred to in this book are correct and active at the time of going to press. However, the publisher has no responsibility for the websites and can make no guarantee that a site will remain live or that the content is or will remain appropriate.

Every effort has been made to trace all copyright holders, but if any have been overlooked the publisher will be pleased to include any necessary credits in any subsequent reprint or edition.

For further information on Polity, visit our website:
politybooks.com

For Bridget and Keira

Contents

Introduction

Du Liang slumped against the temporary wall, clutching a water bottle in his left hand. As he looked up once more, a semicircle of tormentors shouting slogans stared down at him, becoming more and more agitated as the day continued. A woman lay with her eyes shut on a pillow to Du's right, already exhausted from the ordeal after reportedly passing out from exasperation and fatigue, while a nearby demonstrator fanned her. Sitting directly to Du's left, another woman in a hat still had the energy to continue screaming into his ear. The protesters in the lobby of the headquarters of Evergrande, China's largest property developer, occasionally broke up their chants and shouts to sing the national anthem. Some took videos with their phones, and a few photographers recorded the scene on that afternoon of September 13, 2021.[1] But at its core the conflict was easy to understand. The demonstrators wanted their money back. Du, the general manager and legal representative of Evergrande's wealth management division, could not explain how they would get it.

Given the Chinese Communist Party's obsession with maintaining political and social stability, protests are highly unusual in China. Most protests that do occur are in smaller cities or rural areas, focused on minor or local grievances, directed against lower-level officials and local governments. But the demonstration that took place in Evergrande's lobby in downtown Shenzhen, one of China's largest cities, was a rare exception.

These were not disgruntled homeowners complaining about problems in the construction of their apartments. The people demanding their money back were investors, many of whom were Evergrande's own employees. They had placed portions of their salaries and their savings in investment vehicles called wealth management products offered directly by the developer. The products basically consisted of loans to the company and promised returns as high as 8 to 10 percent, much higher than standard bank deposits. Not all were willing investors either, as some employees were told that they would lose their bonuses for the year if they refused to invest in the company's products.[2]

Evergrande was experiencing a bank run, even though it was not a bank. Du found himself in the unenviable position of George Bailey in the classic Frank Capra film *It's a Wonderful Life*, explaining that the money people wanted to be repaid could not be found right away. As conditions in China's residential property market had weakened over the previous months, Evergrande's own employees had suddenly lost confidence in the company's ability to service its debts, which included repaying the high-interest products in which they had invested their savings. They were demanding the money back, which in many cases included their own salaries and bonuses. Soon after the September 13 demonstration, contractors and suppliers to Evergrande followed with protests of their own, concerned that they too would not be paid.[3] In the end, very few employees and contractors received their money.

As China's property sector boomed in the 2010s, Evergrande had become a behemoth, borrowing more and more over time until debts reached an astonishing $310 billion at their peak, an amount close to the gross domestic product (GDP) of Finland.[4] This single Chinese company had taken on debt equivalent to that of an entire medium-sized country. The company's obligations at the time of the September 2021 protests were not only to its employees and investors in its wealth management products, but to offshore bondholders, to Chinese banks, and to around 1.6 million homebuyers who were still waiting for houses they had already paid for to be actually completed and delivered.[5] In China's property market, it was increasingly common for homebuyers to make mortgage payments on homes years in advance of the houses actually being completed, because the prices had always risen even during construction. Evergrande's woes were indicative of the activities of many other Chinese property developers, who had been essentially borrowing money from future homeowners (and their own employees) in order to build houses for which people had already paid. To repay the investors in the wealth management products, they would need to sell even more houses before they could be built. And then they would need to figure out how to finance the construction of those homes by borrowing even more from future buyers.

For years, Evergrande and other property developers in China had few problems borrowing large sums of money to make even larger investments in land, confident that prices on the completed properties would always continue rising. The high-margin and highly competitive property business justified taking these risks, as they had always paid off in the past, and any developer in China that was unwilling to take the same risks would likely find themselves out of business. It was the Chinese equivalent of former Citigroup CEO Charles Prince's infamous line ahead of the 2008 global financial crisis, "As long as the music is playing, you've got to get up and dance."[6]

But the music had stopped for Evergrande. Soon it would stop for most of China's private property developers, and the consequences would be felt throughout the banking system, local governments, and the entire Chinese economy. Property was the most important asset for most Chinese households, making up 60 to 80 percent of citizens' total net worth. The activities of the industry represented around one-quarter of China's entire economy at its peak. The story of why so many people in China would pay for the promise of houses that developers were planning to build – and start making payments on mortgage loans for those houses years before construction was complete – is the story of how China's multi-decade economic miracle shattered between 2018 and 2023. At its heart, it is about financial overextension, fueled by a political system pushing for national rejuvenation and willing to cover up the economic costs of those policy choices.

The End of Rapid Economic Growth

No individual event marked the end of three decades of rapid economic growth in China. However, the protest at Evergrande's corporate headquarters in September 2021, which accelerated the company's default and eventual bankruptcy, was an important inflection point. When China's largest firm within its most important sector became unable to service its debts, questions naturally arose about what would replace property construction and sales as a driver of growth in China's economy.

The forces ending China's decades of strong economic growth were much broader than the property sector and were fundamentally about the end of an unprecedented credit bubble, which had driven the breakneck expansion of China's financial system over the previous two decades.

The property sector and local government investment were the primary beneficiaries of that expansion, but bubbles in these sectors had resulted from the political priority to maintain high rates of economic growth regardless of the financial risks that credit growth generated.

At the same time, changes in China's political system contributed to the economic slowdown. The centralization of authority under Xi Jinping altered the nature of economic and financial risk in China. Under a more consensus-driven leadership in the 2000s and early 2010s, policy changes were gradual and incremental. Most lenders and investors assumed that under a consensus-driven system, any significant losses on loans or investments would face resistance from the political interests behind those investments, and hence, actual losses were unlikely. Financial risks accumulated for the system as a whole but risks for individual investors were low.

Under a more centralized political system, however, Xi Jinping's campaigns in the service of "common prosperity" disrupted the operations of some of China's most important Internet platforms and technology firms, as well as education and tutoring firms. The new challenge for investors under Xi's leadership was to avoid any type of asset that might become politically targeted, because there was no consensus-driven policymaking process that would constrain Xi's decisions. Financial risks for individual investors in China were now much more acute, with some facing enormous losses overnight as informal financial institutions collapsed or government policy changed individual firms' prospects. Investors in trust products promising returns triple those of bank deposits found themselves protesting on the streets of Shanghai in 2020 as those investment products defaulted. As investors and banks became more cautious, the slowdown in credit growth weakened China's overall economy and created new financial risks, with many more types of assets suddenly capable of defaulting.

The emergence of both systemic financial risks and risks of losses for individual investors in China has been a new phenomenon over the past eight years. For most of the four decades that Beijing calls the period of "reform and opening" after the death of Mao, catch-up economic growth papered over most of the inefficiencies generated by China's policy choices and reliance upon a state-directed financial system. But following the global financial crisis in 2008, China's banks embarked upon the largest credit expansion the world had seen in at least a century, adding credit equivalent to one-third of *global* economic output in only eight years, within a single country. China's banks basically lent out the equivalent of the entire US banking system's assets in less than a decade. That expansion of credit funded the rapid investment growth – particularly in residential property and infrastructure investment – that drove China's world-beating economic performance. With this much money moving out the door, financial risks to any individual asset were limited, as there was always new money available to cover the bad loans of the past.

The slowdown in China's economy today is the result of the bill for all of that past lending finally coming due. China's credit growth has fallen by half since 2018 and slowed even more significantly since 2022, placing more assets at risk of default, such as the wealth management products offered by Evergrande and the bonds issued by other property developers. The challenge China now faces is how to decide which lenders and investors will be repaid, and which will face financial losses and potential bankruptcy. The politics of scarcity have returned. While there are some market-based mechanisms involved in allocating losses across the economy, this is fundamentally a political decision, as Soviet leaders discovered at a similar fork in the road in the early 1960s.[7] After many years in which a rising tide lifted all boats, China's leaders must now decide which sectors of their economy will take up the limited seats on the lifeboats available.

More recently, the trade war between the United States and China has added new complications for China's economic future, threatening to cut off one of the most important sources of demand for China's export manufacturing sector. China's economic distress started well before Donald Trump imposed 145 percent tariffs on Chinese imports in April 2025, the equivalent of an overnight trade embargo. Those economic woes will persist even as threatened tariff rates have come down from those punitive levels. But the collapse of China's credit bubble weakened domestic demand in China, making the economy even more vulnerable to US tariffs, as well as trade defenses from other countries. China now needs foreign demand for its exports more than ever before, and while China can and has retaliated against the United States, Beijing still must sell Chinese manufactures somewhere. Without improving the health of China's domestic economy, diversifying trade will eventually involve even more countries pushing back against a flood of Chinese goods. Beijing has offered no long-term solution to this economic bind.

A Broken Model

This book offers a different interpretation of recent events in China's economy than the conventional wisdom, which argues China will retain its economic vitality in the years ahead, even if a modest slowdown in growth to 4 to 5 percent per year continues. Most analyses claim that China can still control its economic future and only needs to make the right policy choices to change its trajectory. In this prevailing view, the problems currently evident in China's economy are tied to individual sectors, or to the property sector or local government debt, and are not a byproduct of the structure of China's financial system. The conventional wisdom either underestimates the magnitude of China's current economic problems, labeling the current slowdown as cyclical, or attributes them to past policy mistakes such as the zero-COVID restrictions on people's movement. This view also implies that China still has the capacity and resources to manage its most pressing economic problems, because China's leaders have always successfully muddled through in the past and maintained strong rates of economic growth over the past four decades.

In contrast, the fundamental argument of this book is that China's economic model is broken, and the slowdown in China's economy is inextricably linked to the problems in China's financial system, creating a structural and long-term decline in economic growth. The old policy tools no longer work, and they cannot be repaired without a wholesale restructuring of China's economy and its financial and fiscal systems. It is impossible for China to maintain future rates of economic growth even close to the 7.7 percent rise in real GDP per year seen over the last decade (the 2010s) without accepting a much sharper economic decline as a short-term cost of adjustment. Even the government's recently targeted rates of 5 percent are beyond China's current reach, and 2 to 3 percent growth is more realistic, in line with the actual trajectory of China's economy since 2022. The trade war is only one of the logical and predictable consequences of this broken economic model and the weakness in China's domestic demand.

As a result, the key questions confronting Beijing at present are whether they view the political costs of a restructuring of China's financial and fiscal systems as far too high, or whether embarking upon such a restructuring would imperil the Chinese Communist Party's survival. So far, the default choice from Beijing has been inaction, which has only created further decay in China's economic policy tools.

In auto racing terms, China's economy has suffered from a significant mid-race collision sometime over the previous few laps. The car is losing speed, leaking fuel, and the engine might catch fire the longer that it keeps running. Staying on the road is an option, but there is no longer a realistic chance of racing as the car keeps slowing down. A pit stop would only confirm how many problems need to be fixed. The whole vehicle needs to come off the road and be replaced with a different one, but someone has to make the call to exit the race. The metaphor is overextended, of course, and economies do not function like automobiles, but the choices that Beijing now faces are stark. Strategic competition between China and the United States becomes far more difficult for Beijing when facing a long-term economic slowdown and no straightforward path to return to past growth rates. Stopping the race and moving toward a longer-term economic détente with the United States is certainly one of the options China's leaders will eventually consider. Focusing on entirely different objectives from economic growth is another option, such as dominance in advanced manufacturing techniques or technologies such as artificial intelligence. The trade and economic war currently underway makes these choices even more difficult for Beijing.

China's economic difficulties are self-created. They are intrinsically linked to the operations of China's financial and fiscal systems and the domestic political forces directing those systems. China's slowdown is not attributable to Western pressure on China's economy, new tariffs on Chinese exports, or policy changes limiting China's access to advanced technologies. None of those factors forced China's banks to extend one-third of global GDP in new credit in only eight years. Even if US export controls on China's technology industries intensify in the years ahead, they may influence China's progress in certain industries but will not have any meaningful impact on China's macroeconomic trajectory.

China certainly benefited economically from joining the World Trade Organization (WTO) and a more benign economic environment of rapidly growing global trade flows, but the recent changes in China's external circumstances are minor compared to the adjustments in domestic credit and investment conditions.

Some analysts have contended that China was always destined for a confrontation with the West. This book argues instead that China's economic trajectory changed significantly from the promise, even if distant, of an eventual convergence with a Western economic rules-based order to an increasingly divergent course from global economic norms and practices. These changes in China's economic reform trajectory were not inevitable. China's strategic competition and confrontation with the West in the 2020s emerged from multiple policy choices in Beijing in the 2010s. Most of these shifts have occurred even after Beijing outlined a comprehensive agenda for structural reform of its economy in 2013, which took place after Xi Jinping assumed power. The shift in China's approach depended upon choices that Beijing made to maintain rapid economic growth despite the difficulties in sustaining that growth and decisions to slow or reverse necessary reforms when the economic consequences of those choices and the resulting market volatility appeared. Some Western business executives and politicians were naive about Beijing's political intentions and prospects for economic liberalization changing the nature of China's authoritarian political system, but most were not. China's economy was legitimately reforming in the 2000s, and there were strong reasons to believe that reforms in line with global economic practices would continue into the following decades as well, even without significant political liberalization.

The Financial Explanation of China's Economic Slowdown

Global perceptions of China's economy have changed quickly since the COVID-19 pandemic and the property market's collapse. As late as January 2021, the impact of the pandemic on the US economy and China's control of the disease were expected to *accelerate* the timeline on which China would overtake the United States as the world's largest economy. Rob Subbaraman of Nomura argued at the time, "We believe that on reasonable growth projections the size of China's economy in

USD terms will overtake the US in 2028."[8] He went on to argue that if the currency continued strengthening, China could move ahead of the US even earlier, in 2026.

Yet by August 2023, less than three years later, *The Washington Post* was publishing an editorial page compendium of views entitled "What just happened: Storm clouds loom for China's economy," that contained no fewer than seven separate accounts from its columnists and outside authors of what was driving China's economic slowdown and the implications of those changes.[9] The editorial page of one of America's most important newspapers clearly did not believe China's official GDP statistics that showed that the Chinese economy was recovering in line with officially targeted growth rates around 5 percent and would eventually exceed those targeted rates at 5.2 percent for 2023. Instead, the columnists identified the factors most closely associated with China's economic slowdown today – demographics, youth unemployment, the property market's collapse, and declining foreign investment – and painted a darker picture of China's economic and political prospects. This was a jarring and sudden dislocation in the conventional wisdom surrounding the world's second-largest economy, and it cries out for a coherent explanation.

The thread that ties together all of the factors contributing to China's long-term slowdown is the overextension of China's financial system to shield Beijing from the political consequences of its economic policy choices. Demographic changes in China were important contributors to slowing growth, along with the rising external resistance to Chinese exports and the massive overbuilding of residential property. These factors have slowed China's potential growth, and economic policy in Beijing should have readjusted the goals of China's leadership. But for several years following the global financial crisis, China was able to use its financial system as a shock absorber to insulate its economy from the problems produced by the excesses of its investment-led growth model. The financial system expanded quickly and drove faster rates of investment than China's economy would ever be able to justify based on its own fundamentals. The political logic was to keep new money flowing out the door to prop up unproductive firms and investments in order to minimize losses, unemployment, and bankruptcies.

Eventually the risks that China had accumulated – substituting financial risks for the political risks of a slowing economy – started to become independently dangerous for political and economic stability. Since 2018, the slowdown in the growth of the financial system itself has reversed China's economic momentum. Now, the decay within China's financial system constrains economic growth and limits the options that Beijing has to restore the economy to its previous growth rates above 5 percent per year. The decisions of the past are strangling the future.

The problems in China's financial system, as well as their spillovers into China's fiscal system and government finances, explain why the country's economic slowdown is now a long-term, structural phenomenon. This contrasts with a shorter-term cyclical period of weakness in an economy tied to the regular changes in the business cycle. Low rates of growth around 2 to 3 percent per year are here to stay, with global cyclical conditions occasionally pushing China's economy slightly faster or slower than that range. China's long-term slowdown is intrinsically linked to the exhaustion of the investment-led growth model that Beijing has used to maintain rapid economic growth throughout the twenty-first century. China can neither redirect credit toward more productive and efficient borrowers nor control problems like widespread local government debt without changing the entire structure of its economy.

A financial system clogged with undeclared non-performing assets cannot be easily repaired, particularly one valuing its own banking system's assets at $60 trillion in 2024, or over half of global economic output. The fact that Beijing has control over all of the critical actors involved in its financial system is actually the core problem for China, not a path to a solution. Shifting state resources among entities to support unproductive companies and banks involves restructuring the economy, which means that one set of actors that used to benefit from access to credit and state support will suddenly lose that access. Writing down the values of some of the assets of financial institutions is an intrinsically political process that strikes at the heart of the Communist Party's legitimacy and its levers of control over the economy. Can the Party turn its back on the workers in its own local governments and state-owned enterprises, even if they are at the center of the current economic slowdown?

This book also offers a different account from many descriptions of the recent slowdown in China's economy, centered on discrete events such as the property market's collapse and zero-COVID policies, and more recently on the trade war between Beijing and Washington. Most of these explanations emphasize that Beijing remains largely in control of its economy. Throughout the adjustment in China's property sector, analysts at the time pointed to Beijing's goals in controlling the growth of the sector, arguing that Beijing was proactively bursting the property bubble before it became even larger. China's COVID controls are often described as a temporary policy mistake that should not have had any fundamental impact on China's long-term economic prospects once the controls were lifted.

A financial system-centric view of China's slowdown reveals a different perspective. With the end of the credit bubble, China's overextended residential housing sector could no longer serve as a driver of growth. China's property sector was always going to decline, because speculation on housing – funded via the financial system – had accelerated the pace of construction far beyond the level of demand from people who actually intended to live in these homes. With credit growth slowing, the correction in China's housing sector was underway well before the most stringent controls were imposed by Beijing – the "three red lines" limiting developers' leverage in late 2020 – and was tied to the slowdown in China's informal banking system. Evergrande and other property developers' woes were fundamentally linked to the imbalances between supply and demand in the property market as a whole, which had widened because of the financial system's expansion of credit to households and developers.

The collapse in credit growth removed some of the shock absorbers Beijing had relied upon to insulate the economy from the inevitable slowdown in property construction. As a result, the decline in the property industry occurred far faster than anyone in Beijing could have expected. Chinese authorities were never in control of the pace of the property bubble's expansion on the way up, nor the pace of the contraction on the way down. As of the end of 2024, China's new housing construction had declined by 69 percent in annualized terms in only three and a half years, a rapid and historic collapse. The same level of correction had taken around fifteen years in Japan's housing market.

Zero-COVID policies and restrictions on citizens' movement similarly acted as an accelerator of China's economic woes, rather than an independent cause of them. The widespread restrictions contributed to weaker consumer and business confidence and suppressed demand for credit. The policies also slowed property sales just when developers were attempting to recover, exacerbating their financial difficulties and leading to a collapse in buyers' confidence in developers' capacity to complete apartment construction. Beijing had not provided households with stimulus-related checks or transfers during the pandemic, so there was no real recovery in consumer spending after pandemic-related restrictions were lifted in late 2022.

Looking at developments in the financial system, the critical turning point in China's economic trajectory over the past decade was the deleveraging campaign that attacked China's shadow banking system starting in late 2016. Once the effects of that campaign became apparent in 2018, the slowdown in China's credit growth produced escalating pressure on different types of financial institutions in China, gradually moving closer and closer to the central levers of Beijing's control of the economy. When peer-to-peer lenders defaulted in 2018, these failures had little impact on the system as a whole but started to chasten individual investors in those riskier products. Then smaller banks started to fail, along with investment firms known as trust companies and property developers such as Evergrande. Corporate bonds also started to default, even those issued by state-owned companies. Eventually local governments themselves were at risk. The institutions that had benefited during China's credit expansion were now perceived by investors as increasingly risky as credit slowed. The weakness in China's economy after the pandemic was driven by this reversal of the drivers of growth before the pandemic.

As a result, China cannot and did not easily return to its past rates of economic growth simply by reversing its policies toward the property sector or lifting the restrictions on movement that had been enforced under zero-COVID policies. Even if Beijing had done everything differently and had relaxed credit limits on property developers early in 2021 and never imposed draconian restrictions on residents' movements during the pandemic, China's economy still would have slowed dramatically. Now that credit demand has weakened because financial losses are tangible to individual lenders and investors, it is simply far more difficult to maintain the pace of credit and investment growth from the years of China's rapid expansion.

Beijing does have policy options available, and Chinese authorities can always take incremental steps to support consumer spending or attempt to boost fiscal spending or local infrastructure investment. But those policy tools are simply less effective within an impaired financial system. The problems facing China's economy are structural in nature, and fixing them requires changing the ways in which the financial and fiscal systems operate. For the financial system, this means changing who receives loans and how lenders price credit risks. For the fiscal system, this means collecting more taxes from consumers, while also reallocating fiscal transfers to households. Those potential solutions are costly in terms of short-term growth and will jeopardize Beijing's other political objectives, such as Xi Jinping's "great rejuvenation" (*weida fuxing*) of the Chinese nation or expanding China's international power and influence.[10] The decisions on when and how to restructure China's impaired fiscal and financial systems are intensely political, because they will sharply reduce China's economic growth to even lower rates. The key questions facing Beijing at present concern which types of political costs China's leaders are willing to bear.

China's push for dominance in advanced technologies and manufacturing techniques will not resolve these structural economic imbalances, and may actually exacerbate them. Producing things more efficiently with new manufacturing technologies in capital-intensive industries does nothing to improve Chinese households' incomes or purchasing power. Beijing must still restructure China's fiscal system to boost household incomes and domestic consumption more sustainably. A slowdown in China's economy can still occur alongside significant technological and industry-defining achievements from Chinese firms, both state-supported and fully private. Even though they have far smaller pools of funding than state-directed companies, Chinese private high-tech firms can still access venture capital and other forms of financing for faster development. None of these individual corporate successes is inconsistent with deteriorating macroeconomic conditions in China overall, nor will rapid technological advances in certain industries change the structural constraints on China's economic growth. DeepSeek-type developments in artificial intelligence can still deliver Beijing positive headlines about specific innovations, even while the foundations of China's historical drivers of economic growth remain under pressure.

Even if China's industrial policy efforts and promotion of technological innovation in strategic industries succeed beyond Beijing's wildest ambitions, this will not change the need to restructure the financial and fiscal systems. As long as China's policy tools to support domestic demand are ineffective, overseas consumers will still be required to provide the marginal demand for the products emerging from China's new technological achievements. The larger problem Beijing faces is the cost of shifting away from the old economy, which continues to limit the growth of the new.

The deterioration of China's economic policy levers is not a harbinger of a "crisis" or the "collapse" of China's economy: these are terms loaded with implied analogies to recent events and are not the most effective descriptors of China's current economic challenges. The closer description is the breakdown or extended decay of Beijing's levers of control over the economy, namely, the direction of credit toward state policy objectives and the usage of fiscal policy to fund investment at the local level. This decay can only be reversed by stark changes that strike at the core of the Communist Party's political constituencies and are therefore not presently on the horizon. Since 2021, there has already been a notable shift from China's previous economic trajectory and a meaningful downgrade in China's future economic prospects. The policy measures that China is deploying at present are merely trying to engineer a cyclical turnaround, which will leave these structural problems unaddressed.

This Was Not Part of the Plan

One of the most persistent myths about China's political system is that its leaders are unique among modern politicians in developing complex long-term plans and strategies to achieve Beijing's political objectives. The idea of China engaging in a "hundred-year marathon" is only one of the more extreme expressions of this view. It is common to hear that China's leaders think in terms of decades, while Western leaders are beholden to the pressures of short-term electoral cycles, preventing them from making long-term strategic investments in their national interests.[11] The publicity surrounding the Belt and Road Initiative in particular is often viewed as evidence of China's long-term strategic planning to expand its global power and influence.[12] Henry Kissinger may have been one of the first proponents of this view of China's leaders and a reason for its resilience in Western circles, as he argued consistently that China's historical global power and influence was the driving force behind long-term strategic plans to restore the country's previous position in global affairs.[13] His famous invocation of Zhou Enlai's response in 1972 when asked what he thought of the French Revolution – that it was "too early to tell" – reinforced this perception of the long-term thinking of China's leadership. Never mind that Zhou actually thought the question was referring to the more recent 1968 demonstrations in France.[14]

It goes without saying that a long-term slowdown in China's economy was not part of any strategic plan that Beijing had created over the past four decades. Moreover, Beijing obviously had no intention of triggering a decline of two-thirds of its residential property construction, the country's most important industry that represented around one-quarter of its economy. Therefore, there is a strong tendency among the Party's propagandists to downplay the significance of China's economic slowdown, or to describe it as cyclical.

Economic growth has been the foundation of the popular view that China would continue to rise inexorably in global power and influence. Yet China's most important policy decisions influencing its economy over the past decade were largely reactive to events rather than proactive in shaping them. China's deleveraging campaign marked the end of an unprecedented credit expansion, but it was a reaction to the unruly and dangerous enlargement of China's shadow banking system. Supply-side structural reform in 2016 and 2017 was a clunky response to deflationary pressures in China's heavy industries. Similar measures are now being discussed in 2025. Even the Belt and Road Initiative was partially driven by the need to find additional overseas markets for industrial sectors in which China was facing excess capacity relative to domestic demand. Spending hundreds of billions of dollars in an unsuccessful attempt to prop up the stock market in 2015 clearly did not fit a long-term strategic plan to develop China's capital markets. Through the lens of China's financial system, very little in recent economic history appears to have been planned, including the recent fallout of defaults and rising credit risks.

The more prosaic reality is that while Beijing may develop long-term economic plans, the objectives China's leaders pursue often conflict with one another. The reversals in China's approach to first encouraging the growth of its financial technology firms and then later aggressively regulating them in the service of common prosperity starting in late 2020 suggested conflicting political objectives, rather than long-term strategic planning. Some of those political objectives have been easily abandoned when it is expedient to do so, or the consequences of pursuing them are too economically painful. For most of the reform era, China's leaders have been pragmatic and flexible, but this does not suggest a strategic design around specific long-term economic goals.

The most important example of such a change in economic priorities was the structural reform agenda outlined in the 2013 Third Plenum's "Decision of the Chinese Communist Party Central Committee on Several Major Questions About Deepening Reform," which was a wide-ranging and clearly articulated long-term strategic economic plan that placed markets in a "decisive" role in resource allocation in China's economy. Yet by Xi Jinping's third term as general secretary of the Chinese Communist Party in 2023, most of the reforms that had been promised in 2013 had either stalled or had been actively reversed, given the costs of pursuing them or the resulting market volatility.[15] The eagerly anticipated subsequent Third Plenum meeting in 2023 did not even occur on time and was delayed for still unexplained reasons until July 2024. When that meeting finally took place, the decisions revealed an entirely different long-term economic strategy for China from what Beijing had promised in 2013: an agenda focused on innovation in advanced manufacturing and other technologies, with little emphasis on domestic consumption and continued reliance upon exports to power growth. China's declared long-term economic strategies had changed completely over eleven years, after notable setbacks to the 2013 iteration.

This was not evidence of executing a long-term economic plan, and these reversals in China's priorities have had significant consequences for China's economic relations with the rest of the world. Rather than contributing to an expanding pool of global demand, China is now essentially trying to grow its share of a shrinking pie through additional exports, making China more vulnerable to tariffs and other forms of trade protectionism. This result is also difficult to reconcile with an effective long-term strategy to expand China's global influence.

China's policymaking will continue to be far more reactive to economic and financial stress and foreign economic policies, rather than proactively setting an economic agenda in the years ahead. The most important question now facing China's leadership is why the Party is still trying to maintain rapid economic growth around 5 percent per year even now, despite the clear pressures on the credit and investment-led growth model. While most now agree that China's official economic data are manipulated or fabricated to some extent, the economy is still officially hitting all of its most important economic targets, with GDP growth reaching 5.2 percent in 2023 and exactly 5 percent in 2024. However, since 2023 Beijing has actually set economic policy as if a full-blown economic crisis is underway, by cutting interest rates, unveiling new consumer subsidies, adjusting its fiscal targets and budget allocations mid-year, instructing its central bank to purchase government bonds (or "quantitative easing"), and providing retroactive raises for civil servants. All of this occurred well before Donald Trump started raising tariffs on Chinese exports to the United States. The disconnect between Beijing's policy actions to support the economy and its official macroeconomic data has continued to erode the credibility of both the official statistics and China's preferred narrative that stable and rapid economic growth is driving the "great rejuvenation" of the country. In politics, when you're explaining, you're losing. And the reason Beijing continues to cling to the narrative of its inexorable economic rise is fundamentally political, rather than resting on a solid economic foundation.

Plan of the Book

This book attempts to explain the most important factors that have contributed to the long-term slowdown in China's economy and the rapid change in global perceptions of China's economic health. The first chapter outlines the reasons that optimism about China's economic trajectory in the 2000s persisted so long into the next decade. China was making genuine substantive reforms to its economy at that time, and there was a realistic promise that this trend would continue, supported by pragmatic and technocratic leadership. Neither a collapse in economic growth nor a path toward confrontation with Western economies was inevitable; these were the byproducts of policy choices that Beijing made.

The second chapter explains the central role that the expansion of China's financial system played in its economic growth. Following the global financial crisis, China's banks launched an unprecedented credit boom, which fueled rapid rates of investment growth and financial speculation. As the risks of this expansion accumulated, China's leaders attempted to control them with a concerted deleveraging campaign that ended up significantly slowing credit growth. The weakness in China's economy since that campaign reflects the slowdown in credit and investment, while new credit risks for lenders and investors and the size of China's financial system now prevent Beijing from replicating the credit growth seen since 2008. Continuing to pay for the costs of bad loans made at the direction of the state prevents China from redirecting its financial system toward lending to more efficient private sector firms or toward more productive advanced technologies.

In addition to the slowdown in credit, changes in Chinese politics have impacted economic growth, primarily driven by the concentration of decision-making power under Xi Jinping. The third chapter describes the impact of the evolution of economic policymaking in China from a consensus-driven system powered mostly by economic technocrats to a top-down process guided by Xi's smaller leading groups of officials. This context explains some of the sudden campaigns against China's Internet platform companies, education and tutoring companies, and the financial system itself. The change in political structure introduced new forms of financial risks in China and reduced confidence among both domestic entrepreneurs and foreign investors in the country's economic prospects.

The fourth chapter attempts to explain why views of China's economic prowess remain so resilient, despite recent setbacks. While China's economic data are increasingly suspect, there is no obvious alternative measure of economic activity that is equally reliable. The result is a competition of narratives about the future of China's economy, but the "authority bias" of most neutral observers and international financial institutions lends an implicit credibility to Beijing's official narrative, even if that is unwarranted. Beijing actively propagates the narrative of China's inexorable economic rise for both ideological and strategic purposes. This competition of narratives produces contested visions of China's economic future across the world.

The structural economic slowdown will severely constrain China's economic growth and Beijing's policy options in the years ahead. The fifth chapter explains the fallout of the end of an unprecedented credit expansion for China's domestic economy and politics, including weaker investment growth, deflation, an impaired fiscal system, and slow growth in household consumption. Beijing has policy options available to restructure the financial and fiscal systems, but they necessarily involve even slower economic growth in the short term and an entirely different growth model after reform. Moreover, while decay in China's financial and fiscal systems erode their power gradually, decay is comforting to China's leadership, because it produces no immediate crises. Reform is difficult because China's economy and financial system are most vulnerable to crisis when leaders decide to repair the system and pare back government guarantees.

The final chapter explains what China's structural economic slowdown means for the rest of the world. Imbalanced Chinese economic growth has produced widening trade surpluses in China and exports of excess industrial production to global markets. This trend has galvanized political forces arguing for trade defenses against these exports, not only in the United States and Europe but also in developing economies. The costs of China's external lending to developing nations continue to accumulate, as China is facing pressures to provide debt relief. A different perspective on China's economic trajectory should drive a changing view of the nature of China's military and strategic threat to the United States and the Western world. But the intellectual bubble surrounding China's economic prowess may take much longer to burst, even after the end of China's investment-led growth model.

1

The Promise of China's Economic Development

Learning about China's economy involves visiting some unusual classrooms. One of the least conventional was the Starbucks in the rear annex of the Parkson department store at the Fuxingmen intersection in western Beijing. For most of the 2000s, this was the closest coffee shop to the People's Bank of China (PBOC), China's central bank, and the most convenient spot for officials there to meet outside of their offices. The officials whom I met from the central bank and the banking regulator, which was also located nearby on Jinrong Jie or Finance Street, were generally happy to speak with an American graduate student asking questions in faltering Chinese about the difficulties of their jobs and what they were trying to achieve. In 2003, I had started research for a dissertation concerning how China considered the reform of its exchange rate policies, which were both an indicator and enabler of market-driven reforms in China's overall economy.

It took me a while to establish some level of trust with these officials, but one meeting often led to a recommendation to speak with someone else or address a larger group. I gradually discovered that most of these officials in the central bank knew one another very well, knew most of the professors in Chinese academia working on similar issues, and maintained informal discussion circles and dinner groups. Occasionally I would be invited to one of these meetings or to conferences at the Chinese Academy of Social Sciences (CASS). Most of the mid-level officials working in China's financial institutions and academic think tanks were only around five to ten years older than me. They were generally frustrated with the political structures in which they operated and were critical of their own system, but they also resented foreign criticism of their methods. They could explain to me, over time, how they were trying to make changes within their system and how they thought they could push reforms forward, even from a relatively weak institutional position within China's bureaucracy.

The meetings and conversations in the 2000s were mostly technical in nature and were generally unremarkable, except in hindsight. At the time, the Chinese system was quite open and actively welcomed foreign input and consultations. These officials were not particularly suspicious of the motives of people meeting with them and were perfectly willing to share their opinions about their system. There was nothing unusual at all about a foreign graduate student trying to understand the activities of China's central bank: they seemingly hoped I would be followed by dozens more. After all, China would only become more important for foreign graduate students and economists to understand as the economy grew in global influence.

Given the dramatic changes in Chinese society and politics over the past decade, particularly since Xi Jinping's tenure began and the public sphere became far more restricted, the idea that China's system was largely accessible to foreign researchers may appear completely unbelievable to some readers. But anyone living or doing business in China in the 2000s could easily attest to the fact that the dominant view on the ground was that China was becoming stronger and more powerful *because* it was opening up to the world. China's economic reforms were moving forward while political liberalization was not, but there was still a general hope that reform would continue to proceed in a "two steps forward, one step back" fashion. There were notable and outspoken proponents of structural economic reform within China's political leadership, particularly Zhu Rongji, who served as premier from 1998 to 2003. And even without the hope of political pluralism or hints of democratic liberalization in China, there were realistic views that China's economy and regulatory systems were gradually converging toward the norms and rules practiced in the rest of the world. Hosting the Summer Olympics in 2008 was reflective of China's new global influence, but also its openness.

This environment was particularly evident in regulatory changes in the economy and the financial system. Chinese institutions such as the banking regulator would often explicitly conduct studies of foreign approaches to particular problems and then use a version of one of these models or a mixture of them. The approach not only allowed Chinese officials to benefit from foreign expertise, but to attract foreign investment as well, because the models of regulation that China was using appeared so similar to those elsewhere in the world.

The curiosity and openness of China's economic technocrats reinforced confidence that economic reform would continue. Structural market-oriented reform was not an esoteric concept in China at the time. Chinese officials sitting in meetings would concretely explain to foreign officials and foreign investors how they were trying to change the system and to make the economy operate based on market forces and more in line with global practices. Joerg Wuttke, the former president of the European Chamber of Commerce in China, commented on the role of foreign businesses in this process: "We were part of [the] opening up of China. And we got good feedback [. . .] and there was real engagement. [. . .] Ministers came in, we could chit chat, they gave a speech, they waited for us to approach them, there was a real conversation and policy debate going on."[1] Officials' goals were explicitly to make the Chinese economy stronger, but there was no aversion at the time to speaking openly to Western diplomats and businesspeople about their methods and about how foreign influence could help.

At the same time, China's economy was still highly inefficient and riddled with waste and corruption. State-owned enterprises dominated most sectors and absorbed most of the credit from the banking system. With real GDP growing at an average annual rate of 10.4 percent during the 2000s, China was still in a phase of "catch-up" growth and most investment was profitable and reasonably productive. The constraint was access to bank capital to fund new investment. Prices on loans and deposits were still fixed administratively. State-owned enterprises could access credit as they were considered safe bets by loan officers at state-owned banks, but private enterprises would struggle to expand or access capital. Industries in which foreign investors could take majority stakes in firms were the exception, rather than the rule.

The economy was still primarily driven by investment and the export sector, particularly after China joined the WTO in 2001, opening several global markets to its products and providing cheaper manufacturing bases for global firms. For many Chinese firms, it was much easier to be paid in foreign currency from an overseas client rather than to expand inside the Chinese market, where one had to compete against several local governments, all protecting their own industries against both domestic private firms and foreign companies.

Bureaucratic resistance to reform was entrenched as well. China's political system is best characterized as a one-party state, in which the Chinese Communist Party controls all sources of political power and the institutions of the state itself. However, centralization in a party structure does not necessarily imply policy agreement among China's leadership. Reformers have always faced resistance from conservatives in attempting to change the economy. In the 2000s, the transition from the leadership of Jiang Zemin as general secretary of the Communist Party to Hu Jintao's administration created a nine-member Politburo Standing Committee (previously seven members) and a focus on consensus-driven leadership. The search for consensus among these nine members and within the broader Politburo often came at the cost of decisive action, as more difficult reforms were stalled by vested interests within the Chinese system, usually represented by one of the Standing Committee members.

Even as reform moved forward in the 1990s and early 2000s, the successors of the state planning agencies at the National Development and Reform Commission (NDRC) were heavily involved in investment decisions within the economy, approving projects to be implemented by state-owned enterprises and local governments. Five-Year Plans were still published with targets for all of China's important industries. The financial system was generally viewed as a tool to serve the political interests of the Party, prioritizing political objectives and stability rather than efficiency or the market pricing of capital. The PBOC was only a ministry within the system, and one voice among many at the State Council, rather than an independent central bank like most of its international peers. To the extent the central bank had a policy agenda, it required approval from China's leadership even for adjustments to interest rates and banks' required reserve ratios, which are common monetary policy tools usually set independently by central bankers.

Foreign naivete about China's prospects was also rampant. Many multinational corporate investors had rushed in during the 1990s and had struggled to make any meaningful inroads into China's markets, drawn only by the size of the potential consumer base and the idea that over one billion Chinese people would eventually buy what they were offering.[2] Business bookshelves were littered with stories of companies that had seen their intellectual property stolen or their joint venture partners engaging in outright theft of their business models to compete with them in the Chinese market and overseas. James McGregor, a veteran executive in China for over three decades and former chair of the American Chamber of Commerce in China, commented, "You can't imagine how many companies had their shit stolen, and wouldn't talk about it."[3] Some multinational firms exited the China market very early, before WTO accession, while others maintained a cautious stance.

But despite the obvious problems of China's economy and political system, the lure of directional change had created significant optimism that reform would continue and most of these problems would become far less pressing in the future. Or alternatively, many believed that even if China did not change significantly, the growth of the economy itself would still be significant enough to offer meaningful opportunities for profit and development. The direction of travel was a far more powerful narrative force than clarity about the destination.[4] Even if Western analysts disagreed about the objectives of Chinese policymakers or the extent of change that was underway, no one was seriously questioning the reform progress that China had made, and no one was anticipating the reversal of those reforms. Wuttke argued, "The backdrop was there were hardly any laws, so let's help the Chinese to define the laws. So we felt we were part of the reform program, very strongly. Zhu Rongji stood for it."[5] China would grow stronger and more powerful, and its economic growth would underpin that inexorable rise, even if there were disputes about the speed of these shifts and the bumps that might be encountered along the way. These beliefs were widely held, both inside and outside China. And even if they sound overly optimistic in hindsight, they were hardly outlandish views throughout the 2000s and even in the early 2010s.

The Case for China's Long-Term Economic Potential

The view that China would enjoy strong long-term economic performance and would continue to reform and become a significant source of global demand was well supported throughout the 2000s. The foundations of this optimistic view of China's prospects rested on several arguments about the Chinese economy and political system. Many of these views are still held today to some extent, but they were vitally important in anchoring global perceptions of China's economic prospects at the time.

Structural drivers of economic growth. The clearest case to believe in China's long-term economic prospects was anchored in the country's potential. The world's largest population of 1.3 billion people (in the early 2000s) had been essentially held back from economic development by decades of policy mistakes and relative impoverishment during the Maoist era. After the death of Mao, Deng Xiaoping's reforms started to open China's economy internally, and then subsequently to the rest of the world. China was able to grow rapidly throughout the 1980s by simply removing some of the obstacles that central planning and campaign-style economic governance had put in the way. The labor force was growing after a Mao-era baby boom, delivering additional support to economic growth. People responded to the "directional liberalism" of that era, noting the changes underway in the economy and society, even if objectively conditions were not friendly to entrepreneurs or businesses relative to other economies.[6]

Structurally, China's economy was always going to grow under these conditions. State-directed credit facilitated new investments in infrastructure, which enabled new forms of economic activity. China's relative underdevelopment compared to other economies provided conditions for perhaps three decades of catch-up growth. Economic growth per year averaged 9.3 percent in the 1980s, 10.5 percent in the 1990s, and 10.6 percent in the 2000s. This was a remarkable and unprecedented record, but it also reflected the extremely low level of development in China in the late 1970s after Mao died. Following the global financial crisis, China deployed even more state-directed credit via the same investment-led model, focusing on new projects such as the world's largest high-speed rail network. Most economists understood that these investments would eventually reach a point of diminishing returns, but anyone looking at China in the 2000s or early 2010s could easily make the case that structurally, China had many more years of growth ahead, even if cyclical economic conditions changed. It was hard to know when the investment-led model would run out of steam.

Long-term planning. It was commonly argued that while Western democratic systems were beholden to election cycles and could not maintain political agendas beyond those limited timeframes, the Chinese Communist Party thought in decades, and was always focused on a longer-term political and economic agenda. Throughout the 1990s and 2000s, large projects and plans were frequently introduced with end dates in the 2010s or 2020s, emphasizing officials' far-sightedness. The typical ten-year tenure of Chinese leaders before Xi Jinping's rule helped to reinforce these arguments. Short-term problems in the economy were viewed as temporary, because China's long-term plans to develop and open the economy further were more important. These views of China's planning capacity were typically overstated, but they were widely held.

State capacity and technocratic competence. Alongside long-term planning was the view that China's leaders were fundamentally technocratic, as many within the Politburo throughout the 2000s had engineering backgrounds. China's leaders were seen as capable because they were solving problems within the economy pragmatically, rather than ideologically. The political system in the early 2000s was elevating members of the Communist Youth League over the "princelings" who primarily claimed authority because of their family relationships to China's past leaders. In 2001, the Party itself started admitting entrepreneurs and businesspeople as members of a party that had historically represented workers, soldiers, and peasants, based on the logic that the Party needed to represent "advanced productive forces" in the economy.[7] More and more of these Party leaders attempted to travel to Western countries and study there as well, and training programs were established with foreign universities. In combination with the administrative powers of the Chinese state, the perception of a capable, flexible, and technocratic leadership created strong confidence in China's economic future.

Openness to foreign investment. Many developing economies attempt to attract inbound foreign investment, but China's system encouraged foreign capital like few others. Local governments offered generous incentives, including tax holidays in specific development and industrial zones, and the localities themselves competed with one another to attract inbound investment. This openness to foreign capital was obviously viewed as beneficial to China, and it often came with requirements to transfer technology and certain intellectual property. But the broader stance of openness to foreign companies, in combination with the stated development plans for the country, created a ready impression of a government interested in working hand-in-hand with foreign firms and offering them a share of the benefits from China's development.

Those assumptions were tested mightily throughout foreign firms' involvement in China, but many had clear-eyed views about the potential benefits of investing relative to those risks. As McGregor argued, "In the early 2000s [. . .] even stupid foreign companies were doing really well." But even after Hu Jintao and Wen Jiabao replaced Zhu Rongji and they started placing additional roadblocks to foreign companies' operations in China more selectively, "I never met anyone who was delusional [and] thought China would become a democracy and everything would work out fine. They thought it would become a member of the world and conform with its economic norms and then would use its influence to change the international system more in line with their way of thinking. And that was actually fair enough."[8]

A strong track record of reform. China had engaged in meaningful economic reforms throughout the 1980s, breaking from the ideological constraints of Maoism to gradually introduce market forces into the economy. Under Deng Xiaoping's leadership, pragmatic steps to introduce changes to the state-directed system encouraged rapid growth, confidence, and additional investment. Deng's remark that "It doesn't matter if the cat is black or white; if it catches mice, it's a good cat" was generally viewed as a pragmatic corrective to ideological rigidity in characterizing ideas, people, or class labels as black or white. After the Tiananmen Square massacre, China's conservative forces shut down economic reforms again, until Deng's trips to booming Shenzhen in 1992 (his "Southern Tour") re-catalyzed political momentum toward the liberalization of the economy and society. This track record of reform was real and tangible for Chinese citizens, as well as foreign observers and investors.

Moreover, China was able to boast a strong record of reform in the face of economic headwinds in the late 1990s and the high domestic costs of opening the economy further to foreign influence. Accession to the World Trade Organization involved wrenching transformations of legacy state-owned enterprises in China's northeast, and massive unemployment resulted as workers lost their cradle-to-grave benefits at these enterprises. Yet China's leadership had pushed on with the reforms, essentially offloading some of the political costs of this adjustment and overcoming bureaucratic opposition by pointing to the external requirements of WTO membership.

Similarly, following the Asian financial crisis in the late 1990s, China had taken aggressive steps to restructure its financial system and reduce the risks of the same types of financial threats that had engulfed Indonesia, Thailand, South Korea, and other regional economies. Despite facing market pressure to depreciate its currency, Beijing maintained the stability of the renminbi (RMB), intervening in foreign exchange markets and selling reserves in order to do so. This helped to prevent another wave of competitive currency devaluations in the region, stopping a further escalation of the financial crisis. China then restructured its central bank into several regional offices to resemble those of the Federal Reserve, providing a modicum of international credibility to the new structure. Beijing established the China Banking Regulatory Commission (CBRC) as a new banking regulator to separate monetary policy and financial regulation and created a financial stability department within the central bank.[9]

The more difficult work was tied to the banking system itself. Over a period of five years, beginning in 1998, the Ministry of Finance injected capital into the banking system, while the central bank provided additional liquidity to the largest state-owned banks by cutting reserve requirements aggressively. Fixed deposit rates and lending rates ensured banking system profitability and established a foundation for China to grow out of its bad debt problems from the previous decade. The central bank then used a portion of its foreign exchange reserves, totaling $60 billion, to recapitalize the banks, offering a positive signal to foreign strategic investors, who then were invited to deliver not only capital of their own, but additional expertise and risk management tools.[10] After the recapitalized banks then sold shares in Hong Kong and Shanghai equity markets, most of the foreign investments in these banks became highly profitable in a very short period of time.

The financial restructuring of the banking system after the Asian financial crisis was costly to the state, but generally considered successful, even if the underlying operations of the banks had not changed considerably after the restructuring. The question that any critic of China's reform progress needed to confront throughout the 2000s was: If they were faced with the same type of problem in the future, why could Beijing not simply deploy the same methods again? And why would they not do so, given their past successes? China had developed a strong track record of embarking upon difficult reforms even in the face of economic challenges, and of relaxing a degree of political control in order to maintain China's economic momentum. There was little reason to question whether the same logic would hold in the future.

Foreign Investment and Joining the World Trade Organization

Throughout the 1980s and 1990s, foreign investment played an important role in kickstarting China's economic growth. China's low labor costs and large population provided the conditions under which Chinese firms could manufacture consumer and intermediate goods more cheaply than in other countries and could export them overseas at enormous cost advantages. But many countries could offer global manufacturers low labor costs at the time. The rest of the logistical infrastructure that was necessary for global exporters and manufacturers to thrive – modern container shipping ports, railways, roads, and trucking capacity – was still absent and took time for China to build.

Special economic zones (SEZs) that helped to attract foreign investment played a critical role in this process. The export-oriented industries that emerged first were those in southern Guangdong province, near the border with Hong Kong, which already had a modern container port engaged in shipping to the rest of the world. Foreign-invested enterprises started to emerge throughout China's Pearl River Delta region, in Shenzhen, right on the border with Hong Kong, Dongguan, around 50 kilometers north, and Zhuhai, on the border with Macau. When Deng Xiaoping needed to point to a success story of foreign investment to restart economic reforms on his Southern Tour in 1992, Shenzhen was the obvious choice. China's foreign trade surged from $41 billion in 1980 to $475 billion in 2000.

However, foreign investment in China still faced important political headwinds, in the form of uncertainty over the liberalization of China's trade system and potential trade barriers to Chinese exports in the rest of the world. China still imposed considerable restrictions upon foreign investors, requiring joint ventures with Chinese partners and limiting ownership stakes in foreign-invested firms. Foreign-invested enterprises were largely using China as a final destination for processing and assembling exports, so there was limited value-added within the domestic economy, and limited technological development of industries within China itself.

In the United States, China had been subject to an annual review of its Most Favored Nation (MFN) trading status ever since the normalization of US–China relations in 1979. MFN status allowed imports of most Chinese goods to receive the lowest-level tariffs available, but the annual review process always created the uncertainty that these conditions might change in the future, which would result in significantly higher tariffs. Membership in the WTO and permanent normal trading relations (PNTR) were seen as essential for China, not only to drive China's economic growth, but to integrate one of the world's largest trading nations into the most important global trade arrangement.

Most of the requirements that China faced for WTO membership involved more aggressive liberalization of China's domestic economy. The promises China made to open critical sectors in agriculture, finance, and telecommunications, with lower tariff barriers for many sectors, marked dramatic changes. China's own leadership viewed WTO membership as a way to catalyze reform within the domestic economy, as reformist Premier Zhu Rongji commented in a press conference with President Clinton, "The competition arising will also promote a more rapid and healthier [*sic*] development of China's national economy."[11] The resulting transformations of China's domestic industries that started even before WTO accession faced considerable political resistance inside China and created widespread unemployment, particularly in China's "Rust Belt" northeastern provinces that were dominated by state-owned enterprises.

There is now a commonly held view within the United States that allowing China into the WTO was a mistake at the time, based on the idea that China had never intended to comply with the rules and standards of global trade and would simply use lower trade barriers elsewhere in order to increase its own export market shares and develop at the world's expense.[12] At the time that WTO membership was negotiated, however, this argument would have been difficult to understand. Most other export markets were already relatively open to Chinese goods. The promise of WTO membership was designed to liberalize China's domestic markets and to include a major trading nation in WTO rules to manage future trade disputes. China had to make far more concessions to the rest of the world regarding market access in the short term in exchange for becoming part of the global trading system, particularly by reducing tariff barriers in critical sectors. President Clinton described the arrangement as "the equivalent of a one-way street. It requires China to open its markets – with a fifth of the world's population, potentially the biggest markets in the world – to both our products and services in unprecedented new ways. All we do is to agree to maintain the present access which China enjoys. Chinese tariffs, from telecommunications products to automobiles to agriculture, will fall by half or more over just five years."[13]

However, the legitimacy paid off for China, as WTO membership reduced many of the perceived political uncertainties tied to global trade with China and catalyzed a new and much larger wave of foreign investment. Inbound foreign direct investment (FDI) jumped from an average of $43 billion per year in the five years before WTO accession to $78 billion per year in the decade after. In addition, from 1995 to 2005, China had a de facto fixed exchange rate against the US dollar, in which the currency barely moved around the level of 8.276 RMB per dollar. This created stability in external pricing of China's goods in dollars. When the dollar fell in global markets against the euro and other currencies starting in 2001, China's cost advantages in exporting to the rest of the world became even more pronounced, providing a further boost to trade growth.

China started to benefit from a virtuous cycle, in which new foreign investment created clusters of manufacturing and industrial capacity, which made it easier for even more foreign investors to consider deploying capital in China. The foreign currency inflows that came from that foreign investment created conditions in which Chinese banks could lend more money for new domestic investment, most of which took place in the export industry, which raised China's trade surplus further. That new investment was also profitable as long as China's currency remained relatively weak, which it did. The cycle continued for most of the decade, from China joining the WTO in late 2001 to the global financial crisis in 2008, and allowed China's export-oriented manufacturing industry to thrive.

Overall, however, China's WTO membership made it far easier for multinational corporations as foreign investors to argue to their shareholders and home governments that while they may be shifting investment to China in the short term, the long-term benefits of those investments would pay off in the form of selling into China's rapidly growing domestic consumer markets. And they had a good point. These looked like aggressive but highly sensible investments in one of the fastest-growing economies in the world. James McGregor summarized many of these views among American businesses: "Some companies were arrogant and full of themselves and thought they could conquer China. Others were naive and gullible and kind of taken in and played. But as an overall business community, the big multinationals really learned, and they were very clear-eyed about what China was up to . . . And they were making a lot of money."[14] Companies had to be active in China, because their competitors were active in China. Experience in China became an important qualification for promotion to C-suite jobs at multinational companies. There was plenty of naivete among foreign investors as well, but the Chinese economy itself was providing ample justification for optimism about business prospects and the need for new investments, enmeshing China more firmly within the global economy.

The 2008 Olympics and the Global Financial Crisis

Two events in the same year were indicative of both the hopes for China's eventual integration into the global economy and the risks of China's unreformed financial system, with vastly different consequences for the country's future: Beijing hosting the 2008 Olympic Games, and the eruption of the global financial crisis starting in the US housing market.

The history of China in the twentieth century contains numerous references to mass protests, demonstrations, revolts, and expressions of public discontent with the end of the imperial era, the period of warlord rule, the Nationalist administration of Chiang Kai-shek, and the rule of the Chinese Communist Party. But only two weeks after I arrived in China to live for the first time, something entirely different happened: a mass spontaneous party, all over the city of Beijing and the country. On the evening of July 13, 2001, the International Olympic Committee announced that Beijing would host the 2008 Summer Olympic Games.

Tens of thousands of people poured out into the streets of the capital late in the evening after the decision in Moscow was broadcast, with traffic clogging the wide avenues and motorists honking their horns loudly throughout the night. Thousands flocked to Tiananmen Square and climbed the lampposts more closely identified with the suppression of the demonstrations twelve years earlier. The sentiment on the streets was almost entirely new: that China had finally made it in the world.

The preparation for the Olympics consumed China, and Beijing in particular, over the next seven years. Taxi drivers were given English-language instructional cassette tapes (generally discarded after a few months), and a wave of projects and events were launched to demonstrate the seriousness of China's commitment to assuming a prominent place within the global order. But importantly, the significance of China's effort to host the Olympics was that it reflected a political priority to be seen as aligned with the rest of the world and to build up China's global political influence or "soft power."[15] The slogan of the 2008 Olympics was "One World, One Dream," and while it is easy to dismiss as internationalist pablum after the fact, it remained consistent with the broader thrust of Chinese economic policymaking at the time.

China's commitment to host the Olympics was viewed as evidence of the country's broader integration into the global economy. China's Olympic teams featured foreign coaches and managers – twenty-eight of them to be exact – showing that China was open to more foreign influence over even its most important performances.[16] (The last Chinese men's soccer team to qualify for the World Cup, in 2002, also featured a foreign manager, Serbian Bora Milutinovic, so this trend was seen as entirely consistent.) Foreign brands were eager to sponsor the Games, given the possibilities of China's consumer market. A new airport terminal in Beijing was unveiled just in time for the Games to begin, designed by the architect Norman Foster. The Olympic Stadium and the nearby National Aquatic Center (colloquially called the "Bird's Nest" and the "Water Cube") were architectural showpieces for both domestic and foreign audiences. Three new subway lines to carry passengers to the venues opened over the summer of 2008. The total infrastructure buildout was estimated to cost over $40 billion at the time.[17]

It was widely acknowledged that China's leadership was using the Olympics as an advertisement for China's one-party political system and style of government, despite considerable international criticism of China's human rights record, following a crackdown on demonstrations in Tibet earlier in 2008. But the Olympics signified that China was still intent on joining the rest of the world with the Communist Party at the helm and that China was becoming stronger because of its opening to the world. The convening power of the Games was significant, with more than eighty state leaders or members of royal families joining the opening ceremonies, including George W. Bush and Vladimir Putin.[18] China's sporting success at the Games – winning the most gold medals of any country – only reinforced the sense of China's inexorable rise. The Olympic Games provided tangible evidence to the rest of the world of the dramatic change within China that had occurred over the past three decades.

Shortly after the Olympics concluded, of course, the global economy plunged into crisis as the fallout from defaults on subprime mortgage-backed securities and derivatives spread around the world. As global credit conditions contracted sharply, governments launched unprecedented interventions in support of national banking systems, including direct state capital injections into privately held banks and guarantees on deposits and other assets. Borrowing by consumers and businesses collapsed, and asset prices – particularly housing – followed shortly thereafter. As the crisis intensified, US officials asked China not to amplify market stress by selling its US securities, particularly bonds issued by the US housing agencies Fannie Mae and Freddie Mac, or US Treasuries.[19] While there was some uncertainty over Beijing's response, China's central bank and the State Administration of Foreign Exchange (SAFE) generally held firm.

Nonetheless, the global financial crisis was an important inflection point in China's relationship with the United States and Western economies more broadly. The instability that occurred shattered many long-held impressions of US technocratic competence and the superiority of Western market-based systems. If these systems could produce such significant losses and instability, many Chinese analysts and policymakers began to question why China was trying so diligently to replicate Western methods and practices. Wuttke shared an anecdote in which a reformist official made the argument that Western practices had been discredited: "What he told me was that we reformers lost our support from you guys being an example. We could not tell anyone in the system that it works for them, so it might work for us."[20]

China was not immune to the fallout from the crisis, which included a dramatic drop in exports to the United States and Europe, as well as a significant tightening of global trade credit, most of which was denominated in US dollars. China's exposure to tighter US dollar liquidity conditions led PBOC governor Zhou Xiaochuan to propose new arrangements for global trade, with the International Monetary Fund-issued Special Drawing Right (SDR) as a foundational reserve currency, and more of China's own trade denominated in its own currency, the renminbi.[21] China's economy was impacted by both falling exports and weakening domestic demand, given the ongoing impact of tightening monetary conditions, higher commodity prices, and a slowing property market.

In November 2008, the global economy was confronting a dramatic contraction in overall demand, and governments began to collectively brainstorm how to provide the requisite stimulus that could restore the global economy to health. The problem for countries collectively agreeing on stimulus measures, of course, is the risk that any country's fiscal policy support for their own economy might spill over into generating demand for imported goods rather than supporting domestic employment. Everyone can agree that fiscal policy support for the economy is necessary, but no country wants to be the only one providing it. Amidst all of these challenges, China appeared to be in one of the best positions to provide new sources of demand for the global economy. Beijing had a state-owned and state-directed banking system and still heavily relied upon investment rather than household consumption to power growth. Therefore, at the time, the constraint on investment-led stimulus was simply the willingness of government to instruct banks to lend and local governments to borrow for new investment projects.

To counteract the effects of the global financial crisis, China announced a "4 trillion yuan" stimulus plan in November 2008, which was designed around a rough level of 10 percent of GDP.[22] The central bank cut interest rates by 1.08 percent at once in late November, and in total reduced benchmark interest rates by 2.16 percent. Banks started making new loans in large volumes. Eventually this would produce significant imbalances in China's economy and set the stage for the structural slowdown currently underway, but at the time, this was exactly what the world wanted to see. Unlike other developed economies that would struggle to incentivize private actors to borrow as the economy weakened, China could simply direct borrowers to do so. Large-scale public infrastructure projects such as a new high-speed rail network took center stage within these initiatives. Localities dusted off their own investment plans, and in 2009 a construction frenzy began.

The actual size of China's post-crisis stimulus was far larger than the initial 4-trillion-yuan price tag, but most of it was funded by the domestic banking system, rather than direct fiscal spending. However, the overall significance of the effort was felt globally, as China emerged from the crisis faster than any other major economy. By 2010, China had officially overtaken Japan to become the world's second-largest economy, measured via GDP. And more significantly, the post-crisis stimulus worked in the same direction as the messaging from the Olympics. Beijing could reasonably argue that China was being a responsible global economic citizen by contributing to global demand and deploying credit, investment, and fiscal resources so that the entire world could recover.

Stimulus, Response

Over the four years following the global financial crisis, China's economy appeared to be fulfilling the dreams that its political leaders and foreign investors had anticipated for decades. As loans flowed out of the banking system in massive volumes, with aggregate credit rising by 32 percent in 2009 and a further 24 percent in 2010, virtually everything boomed. GDP growth reached an astonishing 9.4 percent the year after the global financial crisis, 10.6 percent in 2010, and 9.6 percent in 2011. While this was unsurprising in retrospect given the volume of money flowing at the time – the country's money supply grew by 79 percent in just three years – the investment frenzy that was underway created widespread expectations that China's underlying economic strength could continue, even if the post-crisis stimulus ended.

Investment boomed around the country, particularly in the property sector, and within China's so-called third- and fourth-tier cities, those much smaller than provincial capitals. Local governments set up new companies to kickstart projects with clean balance sheets. This was the time in which entire "ghost cities" or new but empty districts were created, with the logic being that if these areas were built, people would eventually move there. After all, this had been the pattern in all of China's development zones so far. High-speed rail projects launched all over the country, eventually creating the largest network in the world.

China also started expanding overseas investments during this time, led by the China Development Bank under Chen Yuan, the son of Chen Yun, China's most prominent economic official from the Mao era. The China Development Bank would make extensive loans to developing countries, with some to be repaid directly with commodity exports – those to Venezuela and Russia in exchange for oil were prominent examples during this time.[23] China's investment in Africa exploded in the late 2000s and early 2010s, with state construction companies following the lending of Chinese banks. At first, before the Belt and Road Initiative was formally unveiled, these loans were usually designed around specific infrastructure projects, or to increase China's investment in commodity extraction and exports. Loans would flow from China's state-owned banks to third-party borrowers, on the condition that the money would be spent to contract with Chinese firms, often at above-market prices. The results would be a no-bid contract awarded to a Chinese firm or consortium of firms, usually state-owned. The debt would be held by the third government, often repayable in US dollars, other foreign currencies, or commodities shipments. In many cases, the direct benefit to the developing economy borrowing the money was mitigated because Chinese firms sent their own workers and imported their own construction materials, paying for them in RMB. But the net effect of these loans, even before the launch of the more prominent Belt and Road Initiative, was to significantly expand China's external economic influence. China had arrived and was now making significant outbound investments and loans in developing countries.

At the same time, the volume of lending underway within China produced significant short-term costs. When the money supply expands by 79 percent in just three years, the probable result is inflation, and this occurred in short order in China. Inflation was not just limited to goods prices but asset prices as well. The consumer price index started to rebound in late 2010, and by 2011 had reached 6.5 percent, with the rising prices concentrated in food. Property prices skyrocketed from late

2008 to 2010 and started to create widespread concerns about social mobility in China, as large numbers of newly married couples struggled to afford houses for themselves, while cash-rich investors bought empty apartments and left them unoccupied, anticipating further price appreciation.

The central bank started raising interest rates in response to rising inflation in October 2010, and authorities unveiled administrative controls on housing purchases, while increasing down payment requirements on mortgages for second and third home purchases. In general, these failed to contain the popular frenzy for property purchases, which were based upon realistic expectations that prices would keep rising because local governments would need to sell more land in order to maintain investment and economic growth at the same rates. However, rising interest rates did meaningfully slow credit demand among private borrowers in China, while state-owned borrowers maintained their access to credit. Though an old phenomenon when monetary conditions were tightened in China, it was now labeled "*guo jin min tui*" (the state advances, private firms retreat). Banks faced credit quotas as authorities tried to limit the overall volume of loans after the excesses of the previous few years. The PBOC unveiled a new measure of credit growth in 2011, called "total social financing" or "aggregate financing for the real economy" that included additional measures of lending outside of bank loans, including some forms of "shadow" or informal borrowing. The central bank published this new measure seemingly to reveal the surprisingly large volumes of lending in the years immediately following the global financial crisis and to build political support for finally limiting credit as inflation and asset prices rose. Shadow or informal lending had proliferated, particularly among property developers, as a way of circumventing the formal quotas on loans.

At the end of 2011, China's economy faced a new set of challenges as problems in a different financial system began to impact China's export manufacturing sector. As a result of Europe's sovereign debt crisis, several European banks cautiously pulled back their own lending activity around the world. The net effect was that Chinese institutions borrowing US dollars for trade finance purposes indirectly through Hong Kong suddenly faced calls on their loans and needed to repay them. This placed pressure on China's currency to depreciate, as Chinese companies and banks needed to find dollars quickly. The currency depreciation was only a few percentage points and helped China's exporters modestly, but global demand also appeared to be weakening.

By late 2011, the post-crisis stimulus surge was ending. China's drivers of growth following the global financial crisis – infrastructure investment and property construction – were running out of steam without significant new volumes of credit to fund them. Household incomes had increased, and household consumption activity had improved, but the economy's rapid growth rates were still heavily driven by investment and exports. Overall, the Chinese economy still appeared highly imbalanced, even though the post-crisis stimulus effort had helped China to lead the world out of recession, providing around 30 percent of global economic growth from 2009 to 2011. But as the end of General Secretary Hu Jintao and Premier Wen Jiabao's administration of China loomed in 2012, calls for fundamental reform were growing louder, related to the structure of the economy and its dependence upon state credit, as well as social ills such as rising inequality and corruption. Stimulus would not maintain growth forever. China's technocratic leadership had reformed its economy before and was being called upon to do so again.

The Third Plenum of 2013

The year 2012 was tumultuous in China. The transition to Xi Jinping's administration was interrupted by political scandal. Chongqing Party Secretary Bo Xilai, considered a contender for a top position in the next leadership, was expelled from the Party after he attempted to cover up his wife's murder of a British businessman. Rumors of a coup circulated around the capital in March 2012, and security chief Zhou Yongkang was eventually ousted from the Party after seemingly throwing in his lot with Bo.[24] Xi Jinping himself disappeared from public view for ten days in September without any official explanation.[25] The Eighteenth Party Congress, which would officially announce the Communist Party's next leadership, would usually be held in October, but as September and October passed, no date for the meeting was announced. The stock market declined sharply as uncertainty mounted, with the Shanghai Composite Index reaching lows unseen since the global financial crisis.

Finally, the Congress date was set for November 8, with the new leadership to be unveiled on November 15. Xi Jinping walked out on stage leading the seven members of the Politburo Standing Committee, a smaller number than the nine that had been leading China through the previous ten years from 2002 to 2012. As will be discussed in much more detail in chapter 3, the slower pace of economic reform during the Hu Jintao years was the byproduct of several factors, but particularly the consensus-oriented approach to leadership, which essentially allowed individual members of the Politburo Standing Committee to thwart reforms that could have damaged their own personal financial interests or control of certain industries or sectors. As Xi Jinping took control, hopes rose that a stronger executive leadership style could break through some of the deadlock around structural economic reform that had characterized the late Hu–Wen era. Many prominent voices at the time anticipated that Xi Jinping would be an aggressive reformer.[26]

The Chinese Communist Party had previously unveiled major economic reforms in the course of the Third Plenary Session of a Party Congress that was typically five years in duration. This was the venue for Deng Xiaoping's dramatic economic reforms in 1978 and the revival of reforms following Deng's Southern Tour in 1992. These meetings did not often promise specific policies but outlined the clear direction of government efforts, which would then be implemented over the following five years. The schedule of any Third Plenum meeting could be flexible but would usually occur in October or November of the year following the convening of the Party Congress, which in this case meant the autumn of 2013.

The stakes for the Third Plenum meeting in 2013 were high, and Chinese officials had been raising expectations for a fundamental structural reform package throughout the year. Most of the political energy of Xi Jinping's first year was absorbed by a wide-ranging anti-corruption campaign; Communist Party cadres were warned against extravagant spending, and several high-profile officials were arrested. The campaign can be viewed as an extension of the scandals of 2012, but the important point was that Xi seemed to be operating differently from Chinese leaders in the past and taking on powerful interests. The mounting expectation was that, when it came to economic reform, the same type of political momentum would start to break down opposition from vested economic interests in China.

The document that resulted from the Third Plenum meeting in 2013 was entitled "Decision of the Chinese Communist Party Central Committee on Several Major Questions About Deepening Reform," and contained sixty separate "decisions" with several subcomponents. It was a detailed blueprint for structural reforms over the next decade, setting a 2020 deadline for most changes. The headline pledge was for market forces to play a "decisive" role in allocating resources in the economy. Promised reforms included aggressive efforts to scale down the business activities of state-owned enterprises outside of their core functions (to stop operators of power plants from owning hotels and developing property, as just one example) and to introduce market-based interest rates and exchange rates into the financial system. Other highlights were reforming the balance of central and local government revenue and spending responsibilities and increasing rural incomes by making homestead land rights for farmers subject to market forces, allowing rural residents to sell or rent their land for additional income.[27]

Most of the specific elements of the reform agenda had been discussed by Chinese officials in the past. But now they were being structured within a larger comprehensive framework that had been used to enable decisive reforms in previous decades. One could question the political will to implement that agenda or the appropriate diagnosis of China's economic problems, but the fact that such a structural reform agenda now existed and had emerged from China's bureaucratic system was indisputable. Noted China economist Daniel Rosen commented in his extensive discussion of the reform plan: "The program's redefined mission statement for government and nine major clusters of regulatory overhaul are consistent with advanced-economy notions of economic governance."[28] The respected economic analyst Arthur Kroeber noted: "The basic reform idea – giving the market a 'decisive' role in resource allocation – is potentially very significant, and should not be dismissed as mere semantics."[29] Moreover, the critique of China's pattern of development outlined within the Third Plenum communique was also consistent and coherent, arguing that China's existing pattern of investment and export-led growth was unsustainable. The Third Plenum agenda pledged to provide a decisive role for markets and to reduce the role of the state in resource allocation outside of specific areas. It promised to rebalance China's economy toward household consumption and away from investment and exports, and therefore to contribute to global demand rather than further expanding China's trade surpluses. There were skeptics of China's intention to reform at the time, but those concerns were also weighed against the case for China's continued growth. China's working age population was still expanding in 2013 and would hit its peak around the same year. Foreign investment was still pouring in, and China's outbound economic footprint was expanding rapidly. The Third Plenum's announced reform program anchored expectations that China was prepared to pare back state control once again for the sake of continuing China's economic growth for another decade or more.

Technology Firms and Financial Innovation

One of the more concrete manifestations of China's ongoing reforms was underway in the financial sector of the economy, where new financial technology firms were encouraged to challenge the staid business models of the state-owned banks. Over the 2010s, these firms – Tencent, Alibaba and its affiliate Ant Financial, and others – became some of China's largest and most dynamic consumer-facing businesses, and emblematic of Chinese innovation and ongoing growth prospects. In 2012, China's banks were conservative institutions with fixed deposit rates and limited flexibility in setting lending rates. They still prioritized lending to state-owned enterprises or to local government companies that could back their loans with fixed assets, while private companies lacked this collateral or implicit government guarantees.

Yet the financial bureaucracies, including the central bank and the banking regulator, were still considered among the most reform-oriented in China, and they had been looking for ways to change how China's banks operated. China's economic and financial technocrats often consulted their counterparts overseas. They were led by the governor of the People's Bank of China, Zhou Xiaochuan, an English-speaking and academically minded official who conversed easily in the language of central bankers and finance officials. PBOC and China Banking Regulatory Commission (CBRC) officials became regulars at the international conferences and meetings of the International Monetary Fund (IMF) and World Bank. They outlined their intentions to reform China's financial system, including the liberalization of interest rates, market-driven and flexible exchange rates, and openness to international capital flows. Western governments started to view empowering the PBOC as a critical step toward enabling financial reform and breaking down the resistance of vested interests within the Chinese system.

Zhou's unlikely career path may have had a decisive role in financial technology firms' evolution in China. Most Chinese officials at the minister level (the status of China's central bank governor) only stay in those positions for a five-year term, and two full five-year terms is generally considered the outer limit of a minister's tenure. Zhou was appointed as governor of the PBOC in December 2002 and was widely expected to retire in 2012, with a new PBOC governor to be appointed for 2013 to 2018. The lineup of the Communist Party's Central Committee, announced in November 2012, did not include Zhou's name, reinforcing expectations that a leadership transition at the PBOC was underway. Yet for reasons that still remain unclear, Zhou survived and was reappointed as PBOC governor for a third term. He was designated a deputy state leader in order to bypass normal restrictions tied to the retirement age of ministers. Zhou's reappointment also helped to reinforce foreign perceptions of policy stability and that financial reform in China would continue.

A series of coincidental events in 2012 and 2013 helped to kick-start the rapid rise of China's financial technology firms. Alternatives to deposits at state-owned banks already existed in China, known as "wealth management products" or WMPs. These products were typically offered by banks as ways to circumvent quota-based restrictions on lending. Rather than banks making a loan to a company directly, the bank was simply investing the WMP funds in an investment product with a similar return to a loan. The caveat was that because these were being used by banks to bypass regulations on interest rates, they were not explicitly authorized and therefore regulated by any specific bureaucracy in China. That offered new financial technology firms an opportunity to market their own WMPs to retail customers. Instead of needing a large initial sum of 10,000 to 50,000 RMB to invest in a product at a bank branch, ordinary people could invest much smaller amounts in similar products on their smartphones, which were becoming far more common in China in the early 2010s. The most popular product was Alibaba's Yu'ebao, meaning "leftover treasure" or more colloquially, "loose change," and it advertised interest rates on small deposits much higher than those available from banks.

How was Alibaba able to offer its customers higher interest rates than banks? Some luck and the timing of the launch came into play. In early 2013, Chinese regulators became increasingly concerned about the volumes of WMPs being issued by banks and the level of shadow banking activity underway. As a result, in June of that year they attempted to engineer a squeeze in interbank money markets, to force banks to reduce their shadow banking exposures. The net result was a dramatic overreaction, as authorities had underestimated the extent to which banks depended upon WMPs as a funding instrument. When interbank rates started rising, banks started to panic. With fewer lenders available, on June 20, 2013, the entire financial system basically froze. But one of the new funds looking for higher returns that was willing to lend to banks for months at a time at rates above 5 percent was Yu'ebao, and the fund could then provide higher returns to its investors. These types of offerings allowed Yu'ebao to quickly expand, attracting 100 billion yuan in investment by the end of 2013 and an astonishing 500 billion yuan by May 2014.[30] By 2017, Yu'ebao was the largest mutual fund in the world.[31]

The capacity of these funds to attract depositors from large state-owned banks naturally raised questions about how they should be regulated. In a more conservative regulatory environment, these financial innovations may simply have been curtailed by more aggressive prudential measures. After all, they were highly risky, as many peer-to-peer lending products proliferated from 2012 to 2018 and defaulted in large numbers after regulatory pressure intensified. But the PBOC under Zhou and the broader community of financial regulators generally viewed these innovations as effective mechanisms to break down the oligopolistic structures of the larger state-owned banks and drive lending to the more innovative private sector of China's economy. If banks needed to compete with Internet-based money market funds for deposits and make more productive lending decisions to justify higher rates, all the better, even if it entailed some risks along the way.

In early 2013, at the Chinese Academy of Social Sciences (CASS), I presented arguments to a small group of economists that shadow banking activity as it was occurring in China had severely eroded China's capacity to control its financial system. At the same time, the growth of WMPs was contributing to expanding income inequality, as the wealthy were capable of receiving higher returns on their WMPs by pledging larger sums for investment, while these returns were not available to lower-income investors. The responses from the CASS economists generally acknowledged the point but argued that the reform potential of WMPs outweighed any negative consequences. If the PBOC and others tried to regulate the new WMP offerings or Internet funds more aggressively, these CASS economists argued, then there would be basically no chance to change the operations of the state banks in the future. While imperfect, WMPs were viewed as an instrument of reform in the system.

Over time, this light regulatory touch allowed the Internet platform companies to expand their service offerings rapidly. The sudden availability of consumer-focused financing options on smartphones facilitated the development of other financial service offerings, including online payment systems. The popularity of services such as Alibaba's Alipay and Tencent's WeChat Pay combined with the rapid spread of individual payment wallets made China the center of a global shift toward online retail payments and financial services. For years, China's financial system remained heavily dependent on cash-based payments, even for large consumer purchases such as automobiles, because of the lack of consumer financing options and even basic services such as credit cards. The absence of an existing payments infrastructure focused on credit cards or other alternatives allowed firms such as Alibaba and Tencent to create an entirely new system of electronic payments. In less than a decade – by the end of the 2010s – China's retail economy had become almost entirely cash-free.[32] These dramatic changes in consumer finance reinforced global public perceptions of China's dynamism and the economy's capacity for innovation, even if there were important constraints stemming from China's older investment-led growth model.

RMB Inclusion in the IMF's Special Drawing Right Basket

China's evolution within the global financial system was not limited to technologies for its own retail consumer market. In 2014 and 2015, officials from the PBOC worked on an aggressive campaign to include China's currency, the RMB, in the International Monetary Fund's Special

Drawing Right (SDR) currency basket, which is a unit of account based on different weights of commonly used currencies for executing transactions with the IMF itself. The significance of including the RMB in the SDR basket for China was that it would provide an external validation of the currency's potential usage as a "reserve currency," or one whose assets might be held by global central banks within their foreign reserves.

Of course, nothing prevents any country from holding another country's currency or assets within its foreign exchange reserves, and several countries running trade surpluses with China at the time, such as Russia, Malaysia, and Thailand, were already holding RMB-denominated assets as reserves before China's inclusion in the SDR basket.[33] But the IMF's imprimatur would mark China's currency as roughly equivalent in status to the other currencies in the SDR basket: the US dollar, the euro, the Japanese yen, and the British pound sterling. That international recognition would likely make it easier for China to encourage additional capital flows into its own equity and bond markets from a wider base of foreign investors. In turn, the PBOC officials pushing for this recognition saw it as a way to accelerate liberalization of China's controls on cross-border capital flows. After all, for other countries to be willing to hold RMB-denominated assets within their foreign reserves, these investors would need to be able to move money both into and out of Chinese markets. That would require China's barriers to these capital flows to come down over time, permitting greater international influence over China's domestic financial conditions.

The United States continues to exercise considerable influence over IMF decisions and could have easily mounted opposition to including the RMB within the SDR basket. But there were also perceived benefits to including China in this architecture. At the time, China had just proposed the creation of a new multilateral Asian Infrastructure Investment Bank (AIIB), as a parallel to the Asian Development Bank (ADB) and an alternative lender to the World Bank for global infrastructure projects. The AIIB was associated with China's Belt and Road Initiative, a large-scale program of outbound investment activity. When the United Kingdom expressed interest in joining the bank in early 2015, the United States struck a far more cautious tone, and early signals indicated a reluctance to join.[34] The general fear was that China was starting to create new international institutions of its own, as a challenge to the US-led

Bretton Woods-era institutions that were created following the end of World War II.

Even as China was creating the AIIB and Belt and Road Initiative, it was simultaneously petitioning the IMF to be included within the current system of international financial governance, rather than setting up an alternative. Approving the RMB's inclusion in the IMF's SDR currency basket was essentially a costless gesture for the Fund and for the United States. If the move promised to integrate China more completely into the existing global financial architecture, then inclusion was seen as advantageous, rather than driving China to push for the creation of different international structures altogether. If this did little to advance China's reform, it would merely change a small volume of transactions between central banks and the IMF.

As a result, the IMF included the RMB within its currency basket in a decision in late November 2015, with a weight in the currency basket of 10.92 percent. This occurred despite the fact that the onshore version of China's currency would probably not have qualified as "freely usable" under the IMF's standards for inclusion, and the Fund needed to instead cite trading characteristics of the CNH, China's offshore currency – rather than the onshore CNY – in order to justify the RMB's addition.[35] The timing was also somewhat surprising, as 2015 was a dramatic year in China's financial markets, with a historic boom and bust in the equity market and a shock depreciation of the currency in August, which catalyzed considerable capital outflows and caused widespread concern about the reformist intentions and competence of Chinese officials. Nobel laureate Paul Krugman famously entitled a column in July of that year "China's Naked Emperors" and questioned the logic of the equity market bailout. About China's leaders, Krugman declared: "Forget everything you've heard about their brilliance and foresightedness. Judging by their current flailing, they have no clue what they're doing."[36] Those concerns became a broader refrain in financial markets that year, particularly following the currency depreciation and resulting panic in August. China's reform-oriented financial technocrats were reluctant to speak out publicly and criticize the central leadership, and many were notably silent in 2015.

But importantly, these concerns about China's short-term actions were still largely dismissed. The logic of including the RMB in the SDR basket was a long-term bet on China's future and on the capacity of a technocratic leadership to correct China's course. That same bet had seen China grow in international influence and economic heft throughout the past two decades, and it still looked to be a strong one for the 2020s and 2030s. The eventual inclusion of the RMB in the SDR basket did drive some central banks to purchase Chinese assets within their foreign reserves. The IMF's decision also likely expedited the addition of Chinese assets to global bond and equity indices and facilitated more passive purchases of Chinese stocks and bonds on global markets. That process fulfilled one of the PBOC's underlying objectives, by driving additional capital flows into China.

A Changing Narrative

In his important review of China's economic resilience published in early 2020, *China: The Bubble That Never Pops*, Tom Orlik of Bloomberg Economics makes the point that China's technocratic leadership has demonstrated the capacity to overcome economic challenges. He writes, "If China's leaders appear confident in their abilities, there's a reason for that."[37] Obviously, the narrative concerning China's economy changed quickly following the collapse of China's property market and the overall economic slowdown in recent years. I highlight this view not to disparage it with the unfair benefit of hindsight but to point out how reasonable it was at the time, and how views of China's technocratic competence, long-term planning, and structural drivers of growth were fully mainstream. Joerg Wuttke added that foreign businesses were similarly willing to give China's leadership the benefit of the doubt: "Business has a tendency to always look in the rear-view mirror. Extrapolation was the word. It worked, and it will work again."[38]

The rapid change in China's economic narrative since 2022 has upended several of the underlying assumptions about China's fundamental economic strength. As this chapter has argued, these views of China's state capacity and history of reform were both strongly held and reasonably grounded. These views may have ultimately been disappointed, but the causes of China's slowdown were not inevitable; they resulted from specific economic and political decisions from Beijing. China's recent change in economic fortunes has been the result of policy choices, not irreversible trends. Foreign investors and observers may have been overly optimistic, but they also had sound reasons for optimism about China's prospects. Widespread naivete and delusion is not a compelling explanation for why impressions of China's economy have now changed so rapidly.

The chapters that follow will outline more concrete explanations of how China's economy hit the wall, starting in 2018 rather than with the collapse of the property market in 2021 or the zero-COVID policies of 2022. The reversal of several of the structural economic reforms promised at the Third Plenum played a prominent role, as China's leaders became alarmed by the potential consequences of reform and the resulting market volatility. Politically motivated crackdowns against some of China's most vibrant consumer-facing industries, such as the Internet platforms and education and tutoring services, also contributed to weaker confidence among entrepreneurs and private businesses. The centralization of power and decision-making under Xi Jinping undermined several of the foundations of China's technocratic governance, as will be discussed in chapter 3. But the fundamental cause of China's rapid economic reversal in recent years was the end of the unprecedented credit bubble emerging from China's financial system.

2

The Rise and Stall of China's Financial System

On the morning of August 6, 2018, Beijing witnessed a financially motivated protest – entirely different from the demonstration at Evergrande's headquarters three years later – as large numbers of people filled the streets near China's banking regulator on Finance Street on the west side of the city. The protesters were demanding the return of their investments in failed peer-to-peer (P2P) lenders, which had started defaulting in large numbers earlier that year after new regulations targeted these online lending platforms. The demonstrators hoped that if enough people could communicate their anger at financial losses on these investments, the central government would have no other option but to compensate them and make them whole. In the past, other demonstrators acting in large numbers had been successful in negotiating some recompense for their losses. However, these particular protests in August 2018 fizzled out quickly, as they had been organized on WeChat and other online platforms, enabling them to be monitored by security services who were alert to signs of unrest.[1] Most of the demonstrators were quickly put on buses that had been arranged by security forces in advance, detained for a while, and then sent back to their hometowns, often in other provinces. Few, if any, reported receiving compensation after investing in the failed P2P companies.

While the protests at Evergrande's headquarters in September 2021 indicated an inflection point in the state of China's property sector, the August 2018 protests on Beijing's Finance Street marked an earlier and far more significant shift for China's economy: the end of implicit government guarantees on Chinese financial assets. Chinese authorities never had any intention of repaying the large and growing number of investors in riskier P2P lending platforms, just as there was no plan for Beijing to repay investors in Evergrande's WMPs. But the demonstrators did not know that at the time, because they assumed collectively that China's leadership wanted to avoid the perception of political instability and public expressions of unrest. The protesters assumed that China's leaders valued that perceived political stability over the limited cost of compensating them for financial losses, so it made sense to go to the streets.

The demonstrators did not make a mistake when they organized on WeChat, because they *wanted* to be noticed. Forcing the security services to take note of the size of their collective action was the mechanism by which they hoped to receive compensation for their investment losses. Many of the investors in these P2P products likely recalled the government's bailout of the stock market in 2015, just three years prior. At that time, Chinese authorities became alarmed about the rapid fall of the equity market and deployed as much as $250 billion in purchases of stocks from state-owned entities, funded in part by the central bank.[2] Demonstrators on the street in Beijing could be forgiven for thinking that the losses at P2P lenders in 2018 were small change compared to what Beijing had disbursed in 2015, allowing stock investors to cash out at higher prices. But the August 2018 protesters went home empty-handed, and after they did, they were far more likely to be cautious and conservative with their money in the future, rather than investing in products offering unreasonably high returns. That made it far more difficult for informal or "shadow" lenders to continue operating in the years following these P2P defaults. As more and more P2P lenders and informal banks started defaulting, riskier private sector businesses were unable to borrow, and low-income households lost many of their financing options, including access to mortgage loans to buy houses.

In the 1990s and 2000s, state-owned banks had been reluctant to lend to both private sector firms and lower-income households. Financial repression was the term typically used to describe a system in which households had no other option besides state-owned banks to place their savings, and those banks made low-interest loans in line with government objectives. As financial reform had progressed in China, private P2P lenders and shadow banks would lend to private firms and households, but they would charge higher interest rates. China's financial system had expanded rapidly in the 2010s by deepening access to financial services to new types of borrowers with new types of lending, as informal lenders took risks that state-owned banks would not. But as that deepening process continued, it also meant lending to new borrowers that would have problems repaying the loans, much like the expansion of subprime lending in the US housing market in the 2000s. The expansion of any financial system requires balancing the potential benefits of deepening access to new types of financial services against the potential rise in credit risks, as these usually go hand in hand.

The protests in Beijing in August 2018 occurred during a sea change in Beijing's approach to managing these financial risks, which was a critical turning point in the overall direction of China's economy. Starting in late 2016, Chinese authorities launched a deleveraging campaign to reduce systemic risks within China's financial sector. This meant cracking down on shadow lenders, many of which had been lending to property developers and firms in China's real economy, in addition to making riskier speculative investments. The result of this deleveraging campaign was far slower credit growth for the economy as a whole. The pace of lending fell by half starting in 2017, which also produced slower investment growth. But importantly for the protesters who had poured into Beijing anticipating that they could obtain compensation for their losses, the deleveraging effort also meant that China would take a far more rigid approach to bailing out riskier lenders and investors. After several years in which it was extremely difficult to lose money investing in virtually anything in the Chinese financial system, investors suddenly needed to tread cautiously, because perceived government guarantees were no longer what they seemed.

The change in China's approach to regulating financial risks in 2017 and 2018 coincided with a notable slowdown in China's economy, well before China's property bubble finally burst or the consequences of the COVID-19 pandemic manifested. China's economic growth relied heavily upon investment, which depended upon large volumes of new credit every year. Most of China's investment was led by local governments, property developers, and state-owned firms. Cutting credit growth in half across China's economy meant that significant numbers of borrowers needed to reduce investment or output, and to cut back on hiring and paying workers.

The story of the rise and eventual stagnation of China's financial system is a story of multiple rounds of unintended economic consequences of Beijing's policy choices, with little evidence of long-term design or strategy. Policymakers were slow to correct obvious excesses within the financial system, forcing them to use increasingly blunt and costly measures when they finally responded. Those excesses in credit expansion and the policies used to correct them produced the economic slowdown China is facing today.

The End of a Historic Credit Bubble

The protests in front of China's banking regulator in Beijing in August 2018 and those at Evergrande's headquarters in September 2021 were linked to the same complaints and had the same ultimate cause: the end of China's globally unprecedented credit expansion. China's economic growth since the global financial crisis depended upon the rapid growth of China's financial system. Beijing is currently trying to manage the economic consequences of the slowdown in credit growth that has occurred since 2018 but is struggling to do so. The pace of credit growth to China's firms and households has slowed to less than 6 percent in early 2025 from an average of 17.5 percent per year during the boom years from 2009 to 2016.[3] The financial system remains inefficient and bloated with non-performing loans from the past surge in lending, so it cannot maintain the same pace of investment as in the past. China's long-term economic growth depends upon the long-term health of the financial system that will be needed to fund new investment in the years ahead.

This chapter will explain why China's economy has slowed so dramatically in recent years and why Chinese authorities will struggle to maintain economic growth in the future. China's economic slowdown is directly related to problems that have developed within China's financial system. In contrast to the prevailing view that China follows long-term economic plans and has powerful policy tools to steer its economy, this book argues that Beijing currently has little control over its economic future, given that its primary tools to influence credit growth and fiscal spending are highly impaired. Business as usual in China no longer holds, and the economy is already falling short of Party leadership's long-term plans and goals. China does have some policy options available to change this trajectory, but they involve even slower economic growth in the short term, and uncertain prospects of success given the likely resistance within China's political system. The critical arguments within this chapter can be summarized as follows:

- The expansion of China's financial system was the most important and underappreciated contributor to China's rapid economic growth over the past two decades. The end of that unprecedented credit and investment growth is the most significant factor contributing to China's current economic slowdown.
- The financial system now acts as an important constraint on China's economic growth. China's banks can no longer serve as a shock absorber for the real economy, which means they cannot mitigate the political consequences of unemployment and defaults.
- China cannot reallocate credit within the financial system toward advanced technologies or more productive private firms without a significant recapitalization and restructuring of its banking system. But any such recapitalization or restructuring would by necessity slow investment growth and the overall economy significantly.
- Similarly, China cannot shift patterns of economic growth away from investment and toward domestic consumption without structural reforms to its fiscal and tax systems. Those changes would need to significantly increase long-term income growth for Chinese households.
- There is little evidence of long-term planning in China's most important economic policy decisions over the past two decades. This rapid credit expansion did not follow a long-term plan for China's development. The expansion of China's shadow banking activities was similarly unintended, along with the sudden need to control informal finance in China starting in 2016. Yet the fateful decision to limit these forms of credit growth was one of China's most important economic policy choices of the past decade.

As a result of these factors, China's leaders have far less control over the country's economic future than conventional wisdom suggests. Even an ideal economic reform program to make China's economic model more sustainable would likely produce far slower rates of future economic growth than China's current targets.

Every credit bubble features an expansion phase, an inflection point where risks start to become apparent, and a contraction phase. This chapter chronicles all three of those stages in China's recent economic history. The record-breaking credit boom following the global financial crisis was sustained by widespread moral hazard and implicit guarantees on financial assets, as well as the growth of China's shadow banking system. The risks developing within the informal financial system started to become readily apparent in 2015 and 2016 with a proliferation of financial bubbles. Finally, the consequences of slowing credit growth started to emerge after China launched its deleveraging campaign from 2016 to 2018, and then rippled through the property sector and local government finances in the 2020s.

The Growth of China's Financial System

As the rest of the world was struggling to recover from the global financial crisis, China's economic growth was remarkable, with the economy averaging 8.3 percent GDP growth from 2009 to 2016.[4] Even more astonishing was the rate of expansion of China's financial system over the same timeframe, adding $25 trillion in bank assets and averaging 17.5 percent credit growth per year (figure 2.1). While all countries responded to the global financial crisis with some combination of monetary easing and fiscal stimulus, China's policy response was simply far larger than any other economy's. Over these eight years after the financial crisis, China's banks extended credit equivalent to an astonishing one-third of *global* economic output. This was the largest expansion of credit in a single country over a similar timeframe in more than a century. China's total credit expansion from 2009 to 2016 was around *five times* the size

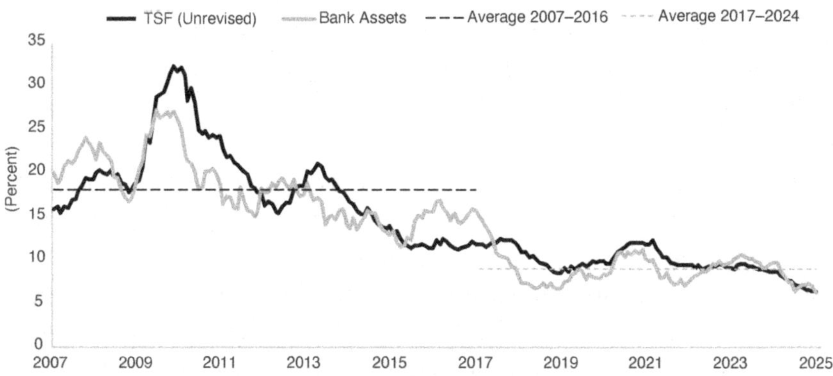

Figure 2.1 Measures of credit growth in China, 2007–2025.
Data source: People's Bank of China.

of the expansion in US consumer credit that had driven the subprime mortgage crisis in US dollar terms, although this is not a perfect apples-to-apples comparison.

It may appear unusual at first glance to describe the recent economic history of a country as large and diverse as China through the narrow lens of the evolution of its financial system. But finance has always had a disproportionate impact on economic growth in China, and particularly over the past two decades. China's economy has been investment-led, and the credit to fund that investment has been sourced primarily from state-owned banks, rather than through the profits of private enterprises. Understanding the operations and incentives of those banks is therefore important for comprehending the evolution of investment trends, and therefore economic growth. Most of the lending in China's economy is extended to state-owned enterprises and local governments, where operating cash flows from their underlying businesses are weak. In the absence of profit and cash flows from their business and investment activities, the economy relies upon new credit, every year. Therefore, the volume of new credit extended, the forms and prices of that credit, and the stability of the financial system extending those loans all become important vectors through which Beijing influences the direction of the economy. The slowdown in China's annual credit growth from an average of 17.5 percent from 2009 to 2016 to stalling at an average of only 9 percent starting in 2017 had a significant impact on investment growth and thus China's overall economic growth.

By itself, an expansion of a country's financial system and the capacity of that financial system to intermediate savings into investment are generally desirable and beneficial to economic growth. But not all forms of lending are equivalent or productive, even when funded by the government for public infrastructure projects. A multi-year loan to build a bridge across a river connecting two cities likely unleashes significant productivity gains, with the long-term economic benefits likely exceeding any short-term financial or fiscal costs to the state. But the costs relative to the economic benefits of a second bridge may be slightly lower, and they will be much lower for the tenth potential bridge. The question of when any individual investment becomes unproductive relative to its fiscal and financial cost relies upon micro-level analyses of project finance and the local economies involved. For macroeconomic analysis, the usual metric is the growth of the volume of credit or investment relative to the growth of the underlying economy. China's credit-to-GDP ratio expanded from around 138 percent in 2008 to around 224 percent in 2016, and bank assets rose from 201 percent of GDP in 2008 to 310 percent in 2016, representing massive swelling of the financial system.[5] In comparison, for example, the United States only saw its credit-to-GDP ratio rise from around 138 percent in 2000 to 171 percent in 2007, just ahead of the global financial crisis.[6] The global economy had never seen anything like a credit expansion of one-third of global economic output in a single country in just eight years.

The seeds of China's current economic slowdown were sown during the post-crisis credit expansion that started in late 2008. The unprecedented scale of that credit growth multiplied the costs when the lending eventually stopped. But there were several other aspects of China's political and regulatory system that allowed the financial system to grow rapidly after the global financial crisis, while other economies were struggling to maintain lending growth at the same time.

Local governments drove the investment push. While some of China's post-crisis stimulus effort consisted of direct fiscal spending from Beijing, most of the actual implementation was driven by local governments. Localities and their officials have a high level of flexibility and control over economic decision-making within their jurisdictions. They also have political incentives to respond to Beijing's directives, and to maintain high levels of economic growth and employment. Faster growth and higher levels of production maintain tax revenues at higher levels, since most of China's taxes are collected based on levels of output, rather than incomes. This creates strong reasons for local officials to start large numbers of investment projects, and high levels of employment generally prevent protests and social instability. Throughout the period of "reform and opening," Beijing could use competition between local officials to maintain investment growth and drive overall economic growth. Immediately after the global financial crisis, Beijing had every reason to encourage local governments to invest heavily and therefore removed many of the macroprudential and regulatory constraints on lending that had been used to control inflation in the previous decade.

Local governments were also incentivized to set up new companies that could borrow with clean balance sheets to kickstart investment. These companies took several forms, but most were called "local government financing vehicles" (LGFVs). Usually, this involved creating a new corporate entity, which would be capitalized with land provided by the local government as equity. The newly created and capitalized company could then borrow from banks for projects using its equity as collateral or based on a guarantee of repayment for a project from the local government in the future. This was commonly labeled the "build–transfer" or "build–operate–transfer" model of infrastructure project financing, and it was widely deployed in China.

Placing local governments at the center of the post-crisis stimulus effort created significant later problems for Beijing when attempting to rein in localities and their banks. With so many infrastructure investment projects underway, halting financing across the board would leave numerous projects unfinished, along with significant fiscal costs to clean them up. Local governments could always argue that they needed more money to finish the projects, while simultaneously starting new projects and repeating the cycle. These developments also required Beijing to use much harsher limits on credit if they wanted to slow down local borrowing, which would have far higher economic costs. With multiple local government investment projects underway, it became far more difficult for Beijing to control the expansion of China's financial system.

Banks funded the expansion, instead of direct budgetary spending from Beijing. Following the global financial crisis, most countries attempted some form of counter-cyclical policy support, with some combination of fiscal spending and monetary easing. China's reliance upon banks rather than direct fiscal spending from Beijing was surprising in this context, given that China's fiscal conditions were generally considered healthier than those in other global economies at the time, measured via low fiscal deficits and low levels of central government debt relative to GDP. But direct fiscal spending in China typically relies upon government bond issuance, then transfers of funds to local governments and project implementation at the local level by state-owned enterprises (SOEs) or LGFVs. Even within the official budget, local governments end up spending around 80 to 90 percent of the money. And those processes were slower than simply encouraging banks to lend in larger volumes to fund exactly the same types of investment projects at the local level. Hence it made sense for Beijing to use banks to respond to the crisis, rather than fiscal spending.

Those incentives also encouraged local governments to develop and grow their own banks, and to force local SOEs to deposit funds in those banks. City, county, rural, and provincial commercial banks acted essentially as secondary fiscal institutions for local governments. Often, they were staffed by local officials themselves, or local finance officials would rotate between working at banks and the government or local SOEs. But this structure allowed local governments to expand their investment capacity beyond what tax revenues alone would have provided. Budgetary controls in China were usually strict after the central government had centralized control over official finances with the 1994 tax reforms, so it was difficult for local officials to reallocate funds from official budgets. But by directing companies to borrow from their own banks, financing for new investments became available. These local banks became some of China's fastest-growing financial institutions during the period after the global financial crisis.

Borrowers were mostly state-owned and had soft budget constraints. In the rest of the world, finding borrowers willing to take on new debt was far more difficult after the global financial crisis. Firms facing financial losses typically reduce output and investment and therefore are less interested in borrowing. In China, however, this was not a problem, as most borrowers in the country were not particularly concerned about their financial solvency. They were mostly enterprises owned by the central or local governments. They maintained financial records, particularly if they had listed some assets on equity markets to raise additional capital, but at their core they were tools of state policy and could be directed to borrow and invest on behalf of Beijing's policy objectives. Even if financial losses would result, these firms would likely be able to borrow more in the future, as insolvency was not a real risk.

The soft budget constraints at state-owned firms were one reason the financial system expanded so rapidly following the global financial crisis. Banks were happy to lend to institutions bearing government guarantees, as their loans could always be marked as performing. In the event they needed to make new loans to repay the old, the borrower would be willing to take on that debt. As a result, the banks were highly profitable and capable of expanding their balance sheets, enabling even more lending in the future. It was a virtuous cycle of credit expansion.

Regulators were reluctant to control credit growth. China's regulatory limits on credit were very light in the eight years following the global financial crisis, for several reasons. First and foremost, China's post-crisis stimulus effort needed to succeed in boosting the economy, which meant maintaining investment growth. Therefore, the risks of actively controlling credit in the years following the crisis were internally viewed as greater than the risks of an additional slowdown in investment, which would impact overall economic growth. Regulators were initially restrained in limiting credit. Then as China's economy became more dependent upon investment, the costs of any controls on credit were naturally higher, and the case for limiting credit became even more difficult to argue. Nothing was broken, so what was the case for fixing it?

Secondly, regulators were bureaucratically limited in responding to a local government-led credit expansion. Local officials usually outranked financial regulators within China's political structure, with a provincial or municipal Party secretary being far more influential than a ministry-level official leading the banking regulator. Officials from Beijing had little capacity to question the lending decisions made by local banks. If financial officials showed up at a local bank and instructed them to significantly limit lending, they would likely be ignored by the officials managing the bank. Regulators could use macroprudential limits and capital adequacy requirements across the entire banking system to control financial risk, and did so. Local banks' attempts to circumvent these macroprudential controls and maintain credit growth for political reasons became one of the driving factors behind the growth of China's informal or "shadow" banking system.

The rapid growth of China's financial system powered overall economic growth in China, but the reliance upon credit and investment also emerged as an obstacle to the structural reform of China's economy during the decade after the global financial crisis. As long as investment was still effective in powering a certain rate of economic expansion, there were incentives for political leaders to maintain the structure of the system that produced rapid economic growth. Within any political system, it is difficult to make the case for changing course while conditions are good. In China, this was especially hard because of the importance of economic growth and rising standards of living to the Communist Party's political legitimacy. Staying the course rather than rocking the boat was always the safer bet, given the potential political consequences of the economy slowing down, in the form of unemployment, defaults, and potential protests.

Therefore, if the financial system needed to expand at a rapid rate in order to maintain investment-led growth, then that became an acceptable tradeoff to Beijing: financial risk would rise to reduce political risks in the short term. Even if loans to government-led projects could not be repaid to state-owned banks, failing loans could be rolled over, and failing companies could continue operating and producing as a result. Following the global financial crisis, China's financial system became a shock absorber for the real economy and for China's political leadership, capable of pushing economic and political pain further into the future. But as credit growth eventually slowed, the financial system's capacity to absorb these shocks diminished, and the economic and political consequences of slowing economic growth started to emerge.

Government Credibility and Implicit Guarantees

Another factor contributing to the rapid growth of China's financial system was the widespread public consensus among Chinese citizens and investors surrounding the Chinese Communist Party's need to maintain political stability. Messages about the importance of stability were constant in Party statements, and officials quickly took action to stop protests, demonstrations, online dissent, or potential organization of political opposition. The fact that Beijing was quite comfortable substituting the political risk of companies going bankrupt with financial risks that could be contained within banks was readily apparent to Chinese citizens and investors in financial assets. As Charles Calomiris and Stephen Haber argue in their analyses of why banking crises reflect political choices rather than inevitable financial failures, "It is hard to stay in power when you tell the electorate that the banks lost their life savings and you're not going to do anything about it."[7] Even within an undemocratic, one-party political system, the same logic applies. Chinese investors generally assumed that because banks were state-owned, and the companies borrowing from banks were state-owned, that it was virtually impossible to envision one of these institutions failing. Therefore, the investment products that they offered were generally considered "safe," if not implicitly guaranteed by the state.

Put yourself in the position of a Chinese customer standing in line at a bank branch in 2012 or 2013. You're receiving around 3.5 percent interest on a one-year time deposit, offered by the bank at the official rate. But the bank branch also has signs in the lobby offering you higher rates for even shorter-term products, around 5 or 6 percent annualized returns for a three-month investment. There's a disclosure document, of course, but the bank salesperson is telling you that these products are basically risk-free, and none has ever defaulted before, which is true at this point in China's recent history. After all, your bank is offering this to you. Your friends and neighbors are all putting their money into the same types of products or investing in products from trust companies offering even higher rates. Under these circumstances, it's easy to see how one would view WMPs as generally as safe as deposits.

This widespread moral hazard – a process in which riskier behavior results because decision-makers assume risks will be borne by others – became a key enabler of the growth of China's financial system following the global financial crisis. It was easy for Chinese banks to make lending decisions without considering credit risks or being concerned that the borrower would potentially become insolvent. Moral hazard also naturally benefited entities that were explicitly state-owned relative to private firms. After all, why bother assessing whether a borrower could repay a 10-million-yuan loan, when you could make a 10-billion-yuan loan to a state-owned enterprise that was guaranteed, and earn 1,000 times the profit on the interest? These implicit guarantees distorted patterns of credit allocation throughout the Chinese financial system, directing credit to the inefficient state sector and away from more efficient private firms.[8] While the exact proportion of all new credit channeled to state-owned enterprises across China's economy is difficult to estimate given the constraints in the data, it is likely well over half of total lending in China's financial system. One study of a large sample of 300,000 individual business loans from over 1,500 branches of a single state-owned bank between 1997 and 2010 showed that 80 percent of all loans were made to state-owned firms, and that 30 percent of all loans were made to SOEs that had defaulted on loans in the past.[9] These proportions may have declined marginally in the 2010s, but the basic patterns of lending almost certainly continued.

The assumption of widespread implicit guarantees also provided counterintuitive incentives for investors. When there was sudden evidence of financial stress in China, investors would drive a "flight to risk" instead of a "flight to quality" or a search for safer assets. If banks offered higher rates on their WMPs or other investment products, investors usually flocked to buy them. After the interbank market crisis of June 2013, when short-term money market rates skyrocketed and provided opportunities for Alibaba's Yu'ebao to lend to banks at high rates, investors piled into similar WMPs from banks offering returns of 8 to 10 percent. Ordinarily, these high interest rates would send market signals that the products were risky, and conservative investors would therefore avoid them. But many Chinese investors snapped them up quickly, based on the assumption that the products were offered by banks and there was no possibility that the Chinese Communist Party would allow any of the state-owned banks to fail. Ironically, China did not have a specific deposit insurance system to protect depositors against bank failures for most of the period in which credit expanded the fastest, as the system was only introduced in 2015. Beijing did not need deposit insurance to convince investors that their money was safe – it was based on a belief in the Communist Party's demonstrated aversion to political instability and protests.

Perhaps the most prominent example of Beijing's predilection for limiting financial instability was the attempted bailout of the equity market after it crashed in 2015. Despite a weakening economy at the time and a correction in China's property market, China's stock market skyrocketed in late 2014 and early 2015, with the benchmark Shanghai Composite Index nearly tripling from a low of 2,075 points in July 2014 to a high of 5,166 points in early June 2015.[10] Banks began to offer higher returns on WMPs to investors, and the asset managers funded by the WMPs then indirectly funded margin financing for third-party investors buying stocks. This margin financing was estimated at around $230 billion at the time via official channels, and multiple times that level through informal lenders.[11] Of course, all such bubbles eventually pop, and the index dropped 29 percent from its peak by July 3, 2015. Against the recommendations of most of China's financial technocrats, Beijing started to take steps to support the equity market by buying stocks directly via state funds and lending indirectly to brokerages.[12] When this failed to stop the bleeding, the government took more extreme steps in early July, including refusing the execution of large sell orders. Eventually, the central bank indirectly lent as much as 2 trillion yuan ($315 billion) to buy shares in the market, but the broader Shanghai stock market index has still never regained the price levels last seen in July 2015. The state funds that bought shares are still likely nursing large losses on these investments. For individual investors, the entire experience only highlighted how the government would always respond to financial instability with a bailout and offer chances for risk-taking investors to exit at a profit. Taking aggressive financial risks made sense for these investors, as long as the government noticed you were doing so. The path from the equity market bailout to the 2018 protests in Beijing over defaulted P2P lending products was obvious.

The widespread assumption of implicit guarantees on most financial assets in China incentivized risky behavior throughout the financial system, and also helped the system to grow rapidly, particularly through "shadow" or informal channels. While this expansion of system-wide risk was unsurprising and may have appeared unsustainable by 2015 or 2016, it was far from clear that Beijing would change this pattern of behavior at the time. Structural reform of the financial system would require breaking state guarantees on large asset classes, and the true market-based pricing of credit. These reforms had been promised for years and yet still appeared distant. Ending these guarantees would involve the political leadership becoming less concerned about social instability. Virtually the entire financial system was state-owned, so if credit risks emerged, they would be the result of state decisions. The political bargain that investors had made was based on the assumption that the Chinese Communist Party was weak and avoided protests and demonstrations because it feared challenges to its rule, particularly after the political instability created by the Bo Xilai scandal and the leadership transition in 2012. Hence, nothing could default. That bargain changed under Xi Jinping, as will be discussed in the next chapter. If investors in riskier financial products suddenly thought that the Chinese leadership was not particularly concerned about isolated protests, and political stability could be obtained through other means, such as a more expansive surveillance state and greater centralization of power, then credit risk could emerge in financial markets very quickly. This was exactly what happened starting in 2018 with the protests over risky P2P lending products.

The Transformation of Finance and the Growth of Shadow Banking

One of the most important questions concerning China's rapid credit expansion was why it continued long after China's recovery from the global financial crisis was assured. Beijing was actually trying to tap the brakes on credit growth starting in 2011, when inflation emerged and interest rates started rising. The announcement of the Third Plenum reform agenda in 2013 promised further efforts toward rebalancing China's economy and reducing reliance upon investment. Credit growth continued nonetheless. Beijing's controls failed primarily because the financial system was transforming over the same timeframe, becoming far more dependent upon informal or unregulated forms of funding and lending – the shadow banking system.

"Shadow banking" is a term commonly used in many countries to describe unregulated or lightly regulated forms of finance, which usually occur outside of banks or official financial institutions. Often, activity is described as "shadow" because it is designed to avoid regulators' scrutiny or requirements. In the context of China's credit expansion, shadow banking was usually designed by banks to circumvent a few specific regulations: loan-to-deposit ratio requirements, loan quotas, caps on deposit rates, and capital adequacy requirements (CARs). Banks had incentives to avoid these regulations to either maximize profits by making more loans or avoid costs by reducing prudential requirements based on their lending levels.

There were many different forms of shadow banking activity in China in the 2010s, but most involved two types of financial innovations: the use of WMPs to raise money and the use of the "channel business" to hide loans outside of banks' official balance sheets, usually by placing them with third-party institutions such as trust companies, asset management companies, or brokerages. By issuing a WMP for a certain timeframe – three or six months, for example – rather than offering a deposit, banks could give customers higher interest rates and avoid the formal limits on deposit rates. Hence, banks could compete with one another to attract funding, outside of the caps imposed by the state system, and they could grow faster than regulators intended. The channel business essentially involved reclassifying the funds raised by WMPs as an "investment" or a "placement" with a third-party non-bank financial institution (NBFI). The bank would pay the NBFI a small fee to hold the loan off its formal balance sheet. This was still basically a loan, but because banks did not officially classify it as a loan, the bank would need to hold lower levels of capital and provisions against any potential losses. These assets would then receive lower capital risk weights in China's regulatory treatment, which allowed banks to expand lending faster and earn additional profits. These assets were variously called "investment receivables," "directional asset management plans," "trust beneficiary rights," and "interbank entrusted payments," but they were basically just loans from a bank to a company, routed through a third party. This process accelerated credit growth across the entire system.

The moral hazard within the financial system and the belief in implicit guarantees reinforced the growth of shadow banking, as most investors saw no meaningful distinctions between the risks associated with WMPs sold officially by banks and those offered by informal lenders. WMPs appeared just as solid as bank deposits to most investors, even though they offered higher interest rates. As discussed in the previous chapter, many Chinese officials saw the shadow banking system as an instrument of financial reform to break the power of the state-owned banks, even if it contributed to risks.

Between 2011 and 2016, the shadow banking system in China exploded, accounting for around one-third of all credit growth during that timeframe, or around $6 to 7 trillion in new, unregulated lending in only five years.[13] Beijing had little to no idea where all of this money was going. Most of this lending occurred via the channel business, with banks raising money via WMPs and channeling it through NBFIs. The fastest rates of credit growth during this time occurred within city and rural commercial banks, as local governments attempted to maintain lending to local infrastructure projects and ensure they were completed. But often these local banks engaged in riskier lending or financial speculation in other provinces, without connections to real economic activity in their own jurisdiction. One extreme example was the Bank of Jinzhou, located in a small city in northeastern Liaoning province and one of the most economically sluggish areas of China throughout the 2010s. The bank claimed 123.2 billion yuan in total assets in 2012. By the time it listed on the Hong Kong Stock Exchange in 2015, the bank's assets had almost tripled in only three years, rising to 361.7 billion yuan. Only 97.3 billion yuan of these assets were loans, or 26.9 percent of the total.[14] The rest were shadow banking assets in one form or another. The bank's assets doubled again between 2015 and 2017, despite the fact that the economy of Jinzhou and the entire province of Liaoning was stagnant throughout this timeframe.[15] A significant data revision revealed that there had been no nominal GDP growth at all in Liaoning province between 2012 and 2017, but that did not stop the Bank of Jinzhou from expanding its assets more than fivefold in those years.

Shadow banking transformed China's overall financial system in a very short time. Before 2012, China's financial system may have been large and highly inefficient, but it was generally stable. In fact, regulators valued that stability over financial efficiency. Banks generally took deposits from households at fixed rates. They could usually expect that more deposits would arrive via China's trade surpluses and capital inflows, so they did not need to compete for funding aggressively with other banks, as they had a growing base of new deposits. And generally, they made loans to state-owned enterprises. These loans may not have been the most efficient use of capital in China's financial system, but the system itself was mostly stable, and the proceeds of these loans were usually directed and monitored by authorities in Beijing.

In only five years, the growth of shadow banking created an entirely different financial system in China. By the end of 2016, the marginal source of banks' financing (their liabilities) was not a stable deposit held by Chinese households or corporates, but a WMP issued by a bank and purchased by either high-net-worth individuals, other banks, or corporates. These WMPs were typically one month to three months in duration, and the constant need to roll them over exposed banks to the possibility that they could face a rapid shortfall in funding, as had occurred in June 2013 during China's interbank market crisis. Banks' funding was suddenly short-term, while their loans were long-term. In addition, banks were facing far more volatile funding conditions because of the fluctuations in China's currency and international capital flows. Banks could not rely upon steady inflows of new funding and had to compete with other banks by offering higher interest rates on WMPs. That also required banks to seek out borrowers willing to pay those higher rates. That typically involved additional risk that those borrowers would default, and rising credit risk spread throughout the system.

By 2016, the marginal growth in banks' lending (their assets) was not to state-owned enterprises, but to third-party financial institutions such as trust companies, asset management companies, or brokerages. Those institutions were looking for additional yield wherever they could find it, including in speculative asset markets. Banks did not know where the money was actually being channeled, and neither did authorities in Beijing. Lending to these third-party institutions started to fuel financial bubbles – in real estate, in equity markets, and in commodity markets. At some points in April 2016, daily trading of Chinese commodity futures exceeded total annual import volumes of the physical commodities themselves, and rivaled trading volumes of the most frequently traded S&P 500 equity futures in the United States.[16] All of this was fed by money from WMPs being rechanneled from one asset market to another in a very short timeframe. As a result, Beijing now had very little visibility into where credit was actually going, and it was often channeled into destinations completely contrary to state priorities, such as the property market or equity or commodity market speculation. China was starting to lose control over its financial system, which had been an essential component of the Party's overall framework of political control.

This transformation was very similar to what took place in the US financial system ahead of the subprime mortgage crisis, as more US financial institutions started relying upon funding from the asset-backed commercial paper market and other non-deposit forms of financing, while channeling resources into special purpose vehicles (SPVs) that ended up collecting risky loans and becoming the repositories of the credit risks involved. At one point, I asked an official at an international financial institution what the difference was between SPVs and China's WMPs and he dryly replied that for WMPs, the contracts were written in Chinese – implying that otherwise there was no difference at all.

Beijing naturally took note of the similarities, concerned about the rise in systemic financial risks and funding risks for the banks, as well as the bubbles in several asset markets. This was the most significant inflection point in China's post-crisis credit boom, as systemic risks were clearly emerging. Starting in 2016, China's leaders launched an aggressive "deleveraging campaign" to try to control shadow banking activity once and for all.

China's Deleveraging Campaign and the End of Rapid Credit Growth

When the Chinese Communist Party intends to send a clear message to its own cadres about the changing priorities of Party leaders, the message is usually carried prominently in the *People's Daily*, the Party's most important newspaper. On May 9, 2016, when the paper carried an interview entitled "Asking About Big First Quarter Trends – An 'Authoritative Person' Discusses China's Economy," the messages from this "authoritative person" were clearly indicative of views from Party leaders.[17] The message was unmistakable: China's model of leverage-fueled economic growth needed to end, and quickly. "A tree cannot grow to the sky, and high leverage carries high risks. Mishandled, it will lead to a systemic financial crisis, causing an economic recession, and even lead the people's savings to fizzle out, which would be dangerous."[18] The responses to questions from this staged interview went on to position leverage as the key risk within China's financial system, contributing to pressures on the exchange rate as well as speculation in property markets and financial markets. The other key message was to caution officials against large credit-fueled stimulus efforts that China had deployed in the past, with the "authoritative person" arguing, "Big stimulus will only result in bubbles, which is a must-learn lesson."[19]

The "authoritative person" was widely believed to be Liu He, the close confidant of Xi Jinping, who at the time was the deputy head of the National Development and Reform Commission and the leader of the Central Leading Group for Financial and Economic Affairs, the most important center of economic and financial decision-making within the Party. The message from the Party's leading officials on May 9 created the political space for financial technocrats to start taking regulatory actions to rein in the growth of China's shadow banking system. China's leadership was increasingly worried about the parallels with the US subprime crisis and the potential for a systemic financial crisis.

The challenge for Chinese authorities was figuring out how to shut down the riskier elements of the financial system that had expanded so quickly, without damaging China's economy as a whole. After all, many borrowers depended upon shadow lenders for access to credit. The expansion of the financial system had incorporated new borrowers with new financial services, even if that came with additional credit risks. Limiting the shadow lenders also involved reversing that process, leaving these borrowers with nowhere to turn. The widespread implicit guarantee on assets created another problem: how could regulators encourage investors to distinguish between investment products that were risky and those that were safer, when all were perceived to be backed by the state? Chinese authorities would need to make difficult choices about whose claims were still considered guaranteed, and whose assets were suddenly at risk of default. Many analysts argued that China could ultimately solve these problems because China's government always had a high degree of control over its financial system, and any restructuring of debt simply involved transferring money from the state's proverbial "left pocket" to the "right pocket." The politics were far different, as the choices of whose pockets to raid and whose pockets to fill, all in the name of the state's objectives, were certain to alienate someone, namely those whose pockets were being picked. Those facing losses were likely to end up protesting either within the bureaucracy or on the streets, like the investors in the defaulted P2P lending products.

The "deleveraging campaign" was a term generally used to describe several different policies Beijing unveiled to limit the growth of the shadow banking system that started in late 2016 and built to a crescendo in late 2017 and early 2018. These regulatory measures were of three types: steps that gradually tightened monetary conditions in China, regulatory limits on specific shadow banking products and their accounting practices, and bureaucratic reorganization to facilitate greater control over informal financial institutions.

Tightening monetary policy and making it more expensive to borrow was the most straightforward step to limit leverage in theory, but perhaps the most difficult for Chinese authorities to execute in practice.

China's leaders had been concerned about the growth of shadow banking and WMPs within commercial banks for years. In June 2013, they had already attempted to squeeze shadow lenders and the banks that cooperated with them by suddenly limiting their access to liquidity. That experiment nearly brought the banking system to the point of crisis, with the short-term interest rates at which banks would lend to one another reaching 20 to 30 percent. When the PBOC relented and abandoned its effort to squeeze the system, investors understood that after this crisis, the central bank was unable to raise short-term interbank rates sharply and would have incentives to keep them stable. That perceived stability allowed borrowers to confidently add leverage and risk, even if they were investing in speculative products. After all, the PBOC had just demonstrated that the central bank did not have the capacity to squeeze the interbank money markets again. This failed experiment to control shadow banking in June 2013 actually ended up producing faster growth in informal finance.

To have a more decisive impact on shadow banking activity and raise the costs of these leveraged bets on speculative assets, the PBOC needed to guide money market rates higher, but also to make them more volatile over time. Over the course of more than a year from August 2016 to October 2017, the bank was able to raise average short-term borrowing costs in money markets (measured via the weighted average rates on overnight and seven-day repurchase agreements or "repos") by around 95 basis points, from around 2.1 percent to 3.05 percent.[20] The PBOC also introduced temporary volatility in interest rates, and this reduced the attractiveness of borrowing short-term funds to place longer-term bets in third-party asset managers investing in riskier asset markets.

Regulating shadow banking activity was difficult as well. The challenge was that some investment products needed to default to demonstrate to investors the risks involved, and regulators needed to decide which types of products (WMPs, peer-to-peer investment products, trust products, or others) should be at risk. However, because shadow banking products such as WMPs existed on the fringes of Beijing's regulatory visibility, no institution was explicitly responsible for oversight of these products. In addition, China's financial regulatory bodies were indirectly encouraging the growth of shadow banking within their respective industries to increase their own importance within the bureaucracy and, ironically, to further the goals of financial reform. It was logical, for example, for the insurance regulator to encourage insurance companies to use shadow banking products to grow their balance sheets, or for securities regulators to allow brokerages to cooperate with banks as long as these were seen as part of the reform of the financial system. Every regulator wanted their portion of the financial system to become more important within China's economy. But if banks responded to regulations on one form of financial innovation by shifting their cooperation to different institutions – transferring funds from trust companies to brokerages, for example – then there was no regulator with the power to monitor and penalize that activity.

To more effectively control shadow banking activity, leadership set up a new Financial Stability and Development Committee under the State Council in 2018, which technically oversaw all financial regulators, with Liu He at its head. This reorganization streamlined the process of establishing new regulations over the entire financial industry and reduced the probability of regulatory arbitrage. While there were several incremental changes in regulatory limits affecting banks and their cooperation with trust companies, asset management companies, and other third-party NBFIs, the most important rules for the deleveraging campaign were drafted in late 2017 and then finally implemented in late April 2018. These asset management rules were the first to take direct aim at WMPs as a funding source for banks, requiring them to match specific products with specific investments, and then to mark those investments to market prices, so that investors could clearly see when their investment products might be generating losses.[21] More importantly, with limited exceptions, the rules then prevented banks from guaranteeing their WMPs. As a result, investors started to see these products as risky, shifting out of WMPs and back into deposits within the banking system. The loans that these products had funded off banks' balance sheets and held at NBFIs then migrated back to banks' balance sheets. Banks then needed to provision additional capital against these loans. Because of the pressure this created on banks' financial conditions, the PBOC reversed course and started to take steps to reduce interbank interest rates for banks in 2018, undoing some of the monetary tightening steps that had been used to reduce leverage in China's money markets.

Overall, the deleveraging campaign significantly curtailed the activities of the shadow banking system in China. The more surprising element for

Chinese regulators was the fact that by doing so, there was a dramatic slowdown in overall credit growth, and therefore overall investment growth in China's economy. The shadow banking system had simply grown far larger than Beijing had ever anticipated, and controlling it had a significant impact on the entire financial system. Starting in 2017, credit growth was cut basically in half from its previous 2009–2016 pace, which had averaged 17.5 percent, and then it declined further in 2018 to only 6.8 percent. The deterioration in corporate credit conditions was even more pronounced, particularly within the private sector, with annual credit volumes to corporates dropping by around two-thirds, as households still borrowed aggressively via mortgage loans during this period. When roughly half of the borrowers in any economy are cut off from credit, they will reduce output, employment, and new investment. This was exactly what happened in China starting in 2018, and the slowdown in economic activity continued for several years as credit growth remained under pressure.

The significance of the deleveraging campaign was that it marked the end of China's unprecedented post-crisis credit expansion. After a period of financial innovation and deepening, China's banks became more conservative once again, with more of their liabilities structured as deposits, and more of their assets structured as loans. Beijing had reduced the risk of a short-term funding squeeze producing a systemic crisis, because banks were less dependent upon WMPs. This was one of Beijing's primary objectives when launching the campaign, and in that sense they were successful. But the unintended consequence of ending China's rapid credit expansion was to significantly slow economic growth. The shadow banking system was not just speculative froth that could be curtailed without generating risks, as there were real borrowers in the economy that had benefited from the expansion of shadow lending. The deleveraging campaign was one of the blunter measures that China was forced to use to rein in the unintended expansion of the shadow banking system.

The primary borrowers from shadow banks were property developers and LGFVs. Those industries had benefited the most from China's rapid credit expansion, leading the stimulus effort after the global financial crisis. Provinces that had relied heavily upon LGFVs for their own investment plans started to see credit slow precipitously. Regional patterns

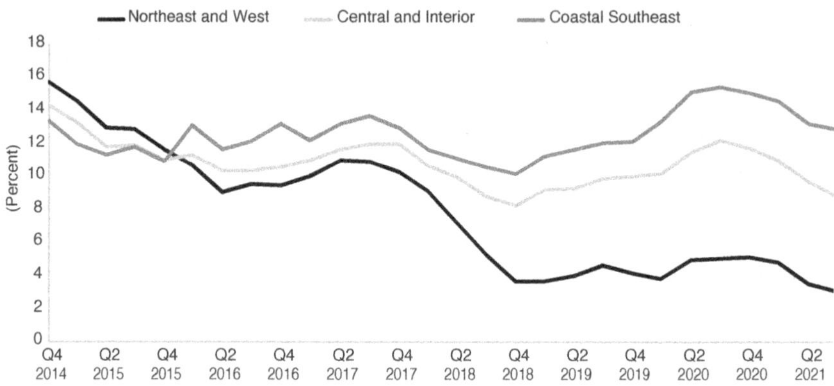

Figure 2.2 Estimated credit growth by region, 2014–2021. Data source: People's Bank of China.

were highly uneven, as northeastern and western provinces depended more upon LGFVs and saw their overall rates of credit growth collapse. Banks redirected credit toward borrowers perceived as safer in southern and eastern coastal regions, namely, the Yangtze and Pearl River Deltas. As a result, credit growth to northeastern and western provinces in China slowed sharply to an average of 3.7 percent by 2018, down from 15.7 percent in 2014. But for coastal and eastern provinces, credit growth held up, still rising at 10.6 percent in 2018, compared to 13.4 percent in 2014 (figure 2.2).

Local governments started to feel the squeeze of their past borrowing, suddenly finding their banks unable to continue extending new credit in the same volumes. By the end of 2018, China's financial system was reeling from all of the dramatic changes that had occurred, first from the shadow banking system's expansion, and then from its collapse. It was natural that there would be casualties, like the defaults faced by the protesting P2P investors in August of that year. But those credit risks quickly spread closer and closer to the core of the financial system.

The Spread of Financial Risks

By the end of 2018, with China's credit growth suddenly cut in half, rising numbers of borrowers from China's banks and shadow lenders found themselves unable to access financing and faced an acute credit crunch. For local governments and state-owned enterprises that operated infrastructure investments that were never designed to generate financial returns, the lack of credit required dramatic cutbacks in those investment plans. But local governments and SOEs still bore implicit guarantees, so even if banks could not extend them new loans, they were unlikely to amplify economic stress within these localities by actively calling in the loans. With less new funding available via WMPs, the non-bank lenders that had been holding these loans on behalf of banks through the channel business – trust companies, asset management companies, brokerages, and in some cases P2P lenders – suddenly faced acute liquidity shortages. If the borrowers on these loans defaulted, there were no returns for their investors, and no new money coming in to repay them.

As a result of these credit contractions, investors had to start considering the possibility that their investments may default, and this was the first sign of credit risk within many types of assets. There is no easy mechanism to break the widespread assumption that everything is guaranteed within a financial system. If regulators wanted to let an investment product or set of products default as a demonstration, it would likely be identified as a test, rather than an actual risk. The only way to create real risk perceptions in financial markets where they previously did not exist was to shock the system with defaults, risking political instability as investors faced significant losses for the first time.

Beijing may have been cautious about introducing credit risk into China's financial markets, but over time, Chinese authorities had little control over how quickly it spread. Once one set of assets that is perceived to be guaranteed suddenly becomes risky, it is natural for investors to start questioning what other government guarantees are worth. Credit risk and defaults on investors started on the periphery of China's financial system, within some of the riskiest investment products, namely, those funded by P2P lenders. Many of these were genuinely fly-by-night operations, offering investors double-digit returns to place money in products that were matched against high-interest loans to risky borrowers. There were several legitimate opportunities for informal lenders in China, given that private sector firms had always struggled to access the banking system. But the rapid expansion of these P2P products, from virtually nothing in 2014 to 1.3 trillion yuan in 2018, suggested far more exuberance than effective evaluation of credit risk.[22] Lenders exploded all over the country, inundating Chinese citizens with spam messages offering personal loans and high returns on investments. When these lenders were regulated more closely during the deleveraging campaign and then started to lose access to new financing, defaults became far more common. Ezubao, one of China's largest peer-to-peer lending platforms, collapsed suddenly in February 2016, in a sign of the turmoil to come.[23] The wave of defaults continued to build through 2018, before the protests that hit Beijing that August.[24] Cities started preventing new P2P lenders from registering their businesses within city limits, in order to avoid protesters in downtown areas. Beijing never had any intention of fully supporting P2P lenders and keeping them alive, as they offered little benefit to China's economy. But investors in the products offered by these lenders had assumed the opposite.

In 2019, credit risk began to spread to more conventional Chinese financial institutions. In May of that year, a Chinese bank suddenly defaulted for the first time in two decades. Baoshang Bank, based in Inner Mongolia, had become one of the largest lenders to China's NBFIs over the preceding years.[25] One of its primary shareholders was the Tomorrow Group, a private conglomerate owned by Xiao Jianhua, a financier who had been taken into custody by state security services in Hong Kong over the Chinese New Year holiday in 2017 as part of a corruption-related investigation.[26] The involvement of the Tomorrow Group in the bank may have explained why Beijing failed to offer Baoshang any help when it suddenly lost access to counterparty financing, but the bank's underlying credit losses likely came from its business with other shadow lenders. Very quickly, the public shock that an institution as large as a commercial bank could default overnight spread to other lenders that had similarly expanded quickly, were also partially owned by the Tomorrow Group, or had simply failed to submit their annual reports that year (as Baoshang's default followed a similar period of silence). The aforementioned Bank of Jinzhou was the next to need immediate assistance from the PBOC, and within a year, Hengfeng (Evergrowing) Bank, the Bank of Gansu, and the Bank of Harbin had all been restructured.[27] Regional commercial banks also started to merge, with stronger banks absorbing the losses of smaller and weaker banks.[28] Baoshang's default had started a slow-motion banking crisis.

Corporate bond defaults had started with a trickle in 2014, with the failure of one bond issued by Chaori Solar.[29] The wave of new credit risks started to build, with corporate bond defaults rising from 33.5 billion yuan in 2016 to 158.7 billion yuan in 2019.[30] Pricing risk in China's corporate bond market was difficult, because historically there were few defaults and many issuers were state-owned, so bond ratings were concentrated at the very high end of the scale. An estimated 95 percent of China's corporate bond issues were rated at AA or above, with the comparable figure in US bond markets around 6 percent.[31] But credit risks hit even highly rated bonds, issued by local government-backed companies. The collapse of Yongcheng Coal in November 2020 was a wakeup call for the bond market, as it resulted from local governments actively deciding to reallocate funds that bond investors had been promised to meet other local government obligations.[32] The rising risks within the corporate bond market made it even more difficult to operate investment portfolios that held these bonds, as new risks now lurked around every corner.

Trust companies were firms usually owned by local governments that offered investment products to high-net-worth individuals and generally lent to local governments and property developers at higher rates. They were governed by the banking regulator, as the industry had led China's last wave of financial distress in the late 1990s. The bankruptcy of firms such as the Guangdong International Trust and Investment Company (GITIC) was just one factor in the downgrade of China's sovereign outlook in 1999.[33] By the year 2020, trust companies ran into new difficulties, as loans to property developers started to default in larger numbers, leading to losses on their underlying investment products. Protests among even high-net-worth individuals started building in downtown Shanghai, with both Anxin Trust and Sichuan Trust defaulting on products they had offered in 2020.[34] The failure of the trust companies was the first sign that all was not well in China's property sector.

Deleveraging Hits the Property Sector

China's property developers were able to weather the first wave of the deleveraging campaign, but the strategies they used to maintain access to credit made the eventual popping of the bubble far more painful for

China's economy. Real estate developers all over the world are heavily dependent upon financing conditions and must carefully manage debt. When shadow financing channels contracted in China, property developers were some of the largest borrowers from the informal banking system, particularly from trust companies. Beijing's efforts to control the growth of the property sector had cut these firms off from traditional financing via banks and corporate bond issuance. Consequently, they turned to shadow lenders and offshore bond markets, where they were forced to pay higher interest rates than other borrowers. For many years, rising property prices meant that the margins on property development were so high that the companies were still profitable even at these higher interest rates, giving shadow lenders a steady stream of business.

The property market frenzy in China in the 2000s and 2010s was sustained by several beliefs widely held by the Chinese public and Chinese officials. First, China's economy was growing rapidly, and more people were becoming wealthy and capable of affording housing even at rising prices. Migration into China's major cities was accelerating during these decades. As a result, housing could be reasonably expected to rise in price for a long period of time in China's metropolises. In the 2000s, there was simply not enough new housing in most cities across the country. A long history of price appreciation made it difficult for most investors to envision a scenario in which prices would suddenly fall.

Second, the real estate industry employed millions of people, from construction workers to contractors to sales agents, which made it highly attractive to local governments, in addition to generating rising fiscal resources for localities from land sales. This created the public impression that local governments would simply never allow the housing market to fail and would prop it up when necessary. Housing was therefore considered by most Chinese citizens to be a much safer investment than stocks. The shells of apartment complexes, even without any furnishings, were the equivalent of gold bars not only for Chinese households, but also for local officials and for Chinese companies. As land values continued rising, Chinese companies often marked up their own buildings in order to show profitability and rising asset values, allowing them to borrow more from banks. Even more cynical Chinese citizens could look at the concentration of Chinese officials' personal wealth in the housing market and conclude that the sector was "too big to fail."

Third, decision-making by China's leadership was consensus-oriented until Xi Jinping started to change the processes of economic policy-making, as will be discussed in the following chapter. This created a strong impression among both Chinese policymakers and investors in the housing market that local governments would be able to moderate any restrictions on the housing sector, because they would have a seat at the table, and clearly needed the housing market to thrive in order to fulfill their own political mandates.

The housing market was the primary path to wealth for most of China's urban middle-class and upper-middle-class citizens. Without exaggeration, virtually everyone in China who had bought a house in Beijing, Shanghai, Hangzhou, Shenzhen, Guangzhou, or Nanjing before the global financial crisis in 2008 and had held onto it until 2020 was likely a US dollar millionaire or multi-millionaire on paper, simply based on the value of that home. Even after a dramatic correction in China's housing sector, prices in major Chinese cities are still far higher than those in other comparable global metropolises. Survey data concerning China's household financial conditions find extremely high rates of home ownership, almost always above 80 percent. Housing also likely represents the vast majority of households' net worth, between 60 and 80 percent depending upon the survey involved.[35]

In the last years of the property bubble, from 2017 to 2021, China's housing market transformed into a far more speculative beast, in part because of the response to the deleveraging campaign. China's working-age population was already declining by this point, and urbanization rates were slowing. Fewer people actually needed new housing, and there was no shortage of housing available. But the property market was still in full throttle, with new construction activity peaking only in 2021 (at 1.71 billion square meters annualized, or around 19 million new apartments per year), even as the plausible number of owner-occupiers was declining sharply because of China's demographic changes. Many Chinese bought an apartment after getting married, in order to raise a family. Marriages were declining already, peaking at 13.5 million in 2013 and dropping to only 7.6 million by 2021, an astonishing 44 percent drop in only eight years.[36] (Marriages have since declined even further, to only 6.1 million in 2024.)

The loss of shadow financing in 2017 and 2018 forced property developers into a conundrum: their underlying business was still profitable, as they could still sell houses at high prices, but the freeze in credit meant that they had lost the financial capacity to continue operations. They needed to come up with cash, quickly, to repay shadow lenders who were calling in loans and unable to extend new credit. The workaround that developers found was to expand their use of pre-construction sales to obtain financing and repay the shadow lenders with the sales proceeds. Homebuyers are often willing to purchase properties before final construction is complete. Typically in China at this time, a homebuyer would pay a 10 percent deposit to reserve a house and then add another 10 or 20 percent as a down payment while negotiating a mortgage loan. At the contract closing, the buyer would formally take out a mortgage loan for the remaining 70 or 80 percent and make the down payment to the developer. Sometimes developers would even help to arrange financing for the down payment with a friendly bank or informal lender. But importantly, the developer would immediately receive 100 percent of the purchase price for the house, well before construction began in earnest.

Usually, the proceeds used to complete construction are held in an escrow account by developers, in order to ensure final delivery to the buyers. What was different in the Chinese market was that the history of rising property prices allowed developers to charge homebuyers for new properties based on plans alone. Escrow requirements were seldom enforced strictly by local governments that depended upon property development. Homebuyers were happy to start paying mortgages immediately because the prices of the units would continue to rise even during construction (in some cases facilitating resale and profit even before the units were complete). To repay shadow lenders, developers rapidly accelerated their use of pre-construction sales of housing, raising revenue immediately from homebuyers and using those proceeds to repay the loans. Revenues from these pre-construction sales skyrocketed from 2014 to 2021, rising from 5 trillion yuan annually to 16.3 trillion yuan ($2.5 trillion) at the peak in June 2021, or an astonishing 14 percent of China's GDP.[37] Rather than being financed by shadow loans, developers were now financed by individual homebuyers taking out mortgages. But now they needed even more new buyers to build the apartments they had already sold.

The deleveraging campaign allowed these Ponzi-type financing structures to expand within the Chinese housing sector, in another round of unintended consequences. Pre-construction sales represented over 80 percent of all housing transactions in China in the late 2010s. China's housing market had become a form of financial engineering: developers printing notional pieces of paper denominated in land as promises to build, and homebuyers borrowing money to bet on the appreciation of those pieces of paper. China's household debt expanded by an astonishing $7.5 trillion between 2014 and 2021, larger in absolute terms than the expansion of US household borrowing before the subprime mortgage crisis.[38] Most of this borrowing in China was mortgage finance for housing purchases, with a rising proportion of them made for purely investment purposes, anticipating prices could only go higher. Developers needed to sell new houses based on new plans to have sufficient funds to complete the construction of the old houses they had just sold based on the previous round of plans.

Eventually, there are just not enough sales to keep this model going. The fundamental cause of the property market's decline starting in 2020 was the sheer imbalance between the pace of construction and the fundamental demand among owner-occupiers of housing (likely around 40 percent of the level of construction at the time). The rest of the demand was investors expecting that prices would continue rising. A series of events contributed to the property sector's sudden collapse, none individually decisive but cumulatively significant. First, regulations imposed in August 2020 had limited developers' channels for borrowing. Known as the "three red lines," the limits on leverage targeted any form of borrowing that developers could use, rather than specific types of loans from particular types of lenders such as trust companies.[39] The new rules were not concerned with the methods developers used to accumulate debt but simply limited how much debt they could accrue. This made it more difficult for developers to continue construction or buy land, as they needed larger proportions of their revenues to repay old debts. Second, the COVID-19 pandemic itself and associated lockdowns and restrictions on Chinese citizens' movement started to introduce new caution among homebuyers, particularly in 2022. The declines in consumer confidence caused by the lockdowns (which will be discussed in more detail in chapter 3) had a clear impact on nationwide property sales, adding to liquidity pressures on developers. Third, China's demographics were already changing, and there were fewer new entrants into the housing market every year. Without speculative demand for housing, and with many investors suddenly trying to sell their existing holdings, the Chinese housing market corrected very quickly.

China's housing market had become a form of financial engineering, with homebuyers and developers using different financial instruments to bet on rising land prices. And the collapse in China's housing market was also indicative of the broader change in risk perceptions within China's financial system. Suddenly, not only trust companies and small commercial banks but property developers could default. The housing market was always imbalanced, but by 2021, developers could no longer borrow from banks or shadow lenders, given rising risk perceptions among lenders and new government regulations limiting developers' debt. Developers such as Evergrande scrambled to raise money to keep construction underway, offering higher and higher returns to investors in their own investment products, and in some cases their own employees – the same people who would be protesting in the company's Shenzhen headquarters in September 2021. As liquidity for the sector suddenly vanished, it was harder to sell homes that were not yet complete. But these pre-construction sales made up the vast majority of China's housing market. The collapse in China's property market was a credit crunch, with homebuyers no longer willing to finance property developers.

Over the next three years, China's property market completely collapsed, with the decline amplified by the restrictions on movement during the COVID-19 pandemic in China in 2022. Housing construction declined by 69 percent from peak levels by the end of 2024, annual sales declined by 53 percent, and land purchases by the top 100 developers in the country collapsed by an astonishing 95 percent from 2020 levels.[40] Local governments tried to keep themselves alive by instructing their own companies to borrow money from banks to bid on their own land, in a form of financial round-tripping. One by one, property developers started defaulting on their debts, particularly the bonds issued in overseas markets. Estimates varied depending upon the classification of property firms, but at their peak, property developers had issued around $170 to 230 billion in offshore dollar-denominated debt. By the end of 2023, roughly 60 to 70 percent of those bonds were in default, according to both Bloomberg compilations of defaults and the firm CreditSights.[41]

The financial crisis among developers forced Chinese homeowners to rapidly consider entirely new risks. Their previously safe assets that constituted the core of their net worth might not even be delivered to them at all, and they may be left holding only pieces of paper. The property crisis then spread to individual mortgage loans, and then to local governments. In the summer of 2022, homebuyers who were concerned that they may not ever see their apartments delivered due to developers' financing problems started to take action, openly organizing on social media and declaring that they were suspending payments on their mortgages.[42] The threats may have been bluster, but they caused a new wave of concern in Beijing that the crisis among property developers would quickly spread to banks. Incremental policies were announced to allow developers to access financing simply to finish incomplete houses, but these were only modestly successful.

Local governments were among the hardest hit by the property crisis, as they depended upon selling land to developers as a key source of revenue. The shortfall in land sales forced them to cut back on new investments and on basic obligations such as providing social services, with several reports of civil servants facing late salary payments and reduced benefits.[43] LGFVs had long been heavily indebted, and now local governments were providing them with less support than ever. LGFVs started defaulting on some forms of debt, including corporate acceptances – short-term commercial obligations – and were likely defaulting on loans as well, forcing banks to roll them over.[44] But they still had not defaulted on publicly traded corporate bonds, providing China's financial markets with one new risk to worry about.

One by one, credit risk had spread across asset classes in China's financial system, from the riskier periphery of P2P lenders, to smaller banks, to corporate bonds, to trust companies, to property developers, and finally closer and closer to the core, namely, local governments themselves. With even commercial banks declaring bankruptcy and local state-owned firms defaulting on corporate bonds, the question that Chinese investors now had to ponder was where else government guarantees might falter. It still seems improbable that one of the Big Four banks or central SOEs might default, but the same assurance cannot apply to China's smaller banks. As moral hazard gave way to new credit risks, Chinese investors and depositors became more cautious and conservative, preferring bank deposits to WMPs. The financial system that had powered China's unprecedented credit expansion was now no longer able to provide the same volumes of credit growth and therefore could no longer insulate China's economy from the consequences of bankruptcies, defaults, and over a decade of unproductive lending.

The End of Investment-Led Economic Growth

The deleveraging campaign and its aftermath highlighted the extent of China's dependence upon credit growth in the 2010s. With less credit available, China's investment growth started to slow, and overall economic growth started to decline as well. China's current economic slowdown will continue because reviving investment-led growth at the same pace is not an option for Beijing. The financial system is unable to provide the same volumes of credit as in the past, and redirecting credit to more productive uses requires a restructuring or recapitalization of China's banking system that will by necessity slow investment sharply in the near term. The slowdown in credit to property developers and local governments has produced a structural, long-term decline in China's property and infrastructure investment. But China's economy still remains powered by investment even as it slows, as investment has represented a larger proportion of the economy than household consumption every year since 2004.[45]

The slowdown in property investment since the bubble burst has been dramatic. The 69 percent adjustment in annual property construction activity occurred in only three and a half years, while a comparable adjustment in Japan's property market took over fifteen years to materialize. That slowdown in construction impacted not only real estate developers, but their construction contractors, suppliers, the workers for those companies, and the local governments that sold them the land and generated tax revenue from their activities. The decline in property purchases hurt related consumer purchases of home appliances, automobiles, furniture, and decorating materials. There are several estimates of the aggregate upstream and downstream impact of the property sector on China's GDP before the collapse, with most concentrated between 20 and 30 percent.[46]

Local government infrastructure investment was another former bulwark of economic activity now under pressure. Investment was mostly financed by LGFVs, who could borrow and invest as if they were private companies but would execute project plans for local governments while remaining creditworthy because of implicit government guarantees, as if they were state-owned companies. As a result of these guarantees, LGFVs were often insensitive to borrowing costs, and accrued high-interest debt by borrowing from shadow lenders. While there is limited financial information about LGFVs, they are required to provide basic data when applying for new bond issues, including the rates of return on their assets and their total debt and borrowing costs. On average, by 2022, LGFVs were only reporting financial returns of 1 percent on their projects, and the real figure was likely much lower, while their average financing costs were 5.4 percent.[47] Under these conditions, as overall credit growth slowed, the years of financing infrastructure investment via LGFVs caused many to accumulate high levels of annual debt service. With less new credit coming in, the net result was that infrastructure investment started to slow, even when Beijing had intended for investment to accelerate and had issued more government bonds to fund investment.

The COVID-19 pandemic played a critical role in China's economic slowdown, but it primarily acted as an accelerant of some of the processes that were already underway by 2022, when the most severe restrictions were imposed. The most obvious effects of the pandemic and China's restrictions were the impacts on household consumption and services sector activity. Small service businesses, which are among China's most significant sources of employment, faced extreme difficulties operating under the pattern of restrictions from local governments. Consumption growth slowed, particularly in travel-related activity, and spending on restaurants, which declined by 6.3 percent in 2022.[48] Household deposits in the banking system rose by 17.8 trillion yuan, or around 15 percent of GDP, an indication of additional household savings rather than faster consumption.[49] Surveys of consumer confidence declined sharply in 2022 and have not yet recovered, reaching new record low levels in the summer of 2025 (figure 2.3).

By 2022, property investment and local government infrastructure investment were both slowing significantly. These sectors were the two largest drivers of China's investment activity. Given the weakness in credit availability following the deleveraging campaign, no other form of investment had emerged to replace them. Private sector investment

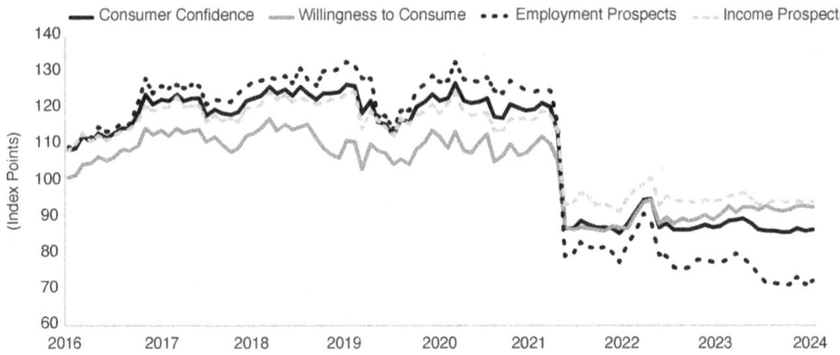

Figure 2.3 Measures of consumer confidence about employment, spending, incomes, 2016–2024.
Data source: People's Bank of China.

weakened during the pandemic as well, and slowing producer and consumer prices worked against a recovery in private investment. Slower employment and income growth from the lack of investment started to suppress household consumption. China's investment-led economic expansion had ended by 2022, as China's broader economy likely contracted that year, and it was unclear whether investment could return without a rebound in the property sector. But the decline in investment also started to amplify stress on other counter-cyclical policy tools that would be necessary to respond to the economic slowdown, particularly within China's fiscal system.

China's Local Fiscal Crisis

The slowdown in China's economy that had resulted from weaker investment activity started to create new pressures on China's tax revenues, particularly taxes raised by local governments. The decline in property construction in China between 2021 and 2024 severely impacted localities' capacity to sell land to developers, and the prices at which they could do so. Land sales revenues fell from 8.7 trillion yuan in 2021 to only 4.9 trillion yuan in 2024, a contraction equivalent to 3 percent of China's GDP.[50] The decline in land sales revenues directly impacted how much local governments could spend within their jurisdictions. As a result, even when Beijing had attempted to support the economy with more proactive fiscal policy in recent years, actual levels of government spending still slowed. Starting in 2021, China's total revenues and expenditures did not reach their targeted levels in the official budget for four consecutive years.

The pressure on local government revenues had far-reaching implications. For years, local governments had invested heavily and had accrued debts beyond the servicing capacity of local tax revenues, assuming that the good times would continue. Most budgetary responsibilities for local governments were fixed, and money could not be reallocated for different purposes. Land sales revenues offered an alternative for localities, with money they could use more flexibly and independently from Beijing's direct oversight. Hence the decline in land sales revenues started to produce new financial pressures on localities in multiple areas. As the crisis in local governments spread, there were even reports of entrepreneurs from other provinces and cities being randomly detained, with local governments alleging criminal charges against them in order to collect additional fees.[51]

The distribution of local government debt was uneven across China. Most of the heavily indebted provinces and cities were in China's southwest and the northeast, as they had relied upon LGFVs for infrastructure financing.[52] These provinces were also among the hardest hit by China's property sector slowdown, given the decline in populations in those areas and migration to more dynamic coastal provinces. As a result, many cities were forced to spend over 10 percent of their total fiscal revenues on annual debt service costs alone. This dramatically reduced their potential to continue financing infrastructure investment and initiating new projects. Based on Rhodium Group calculations of these cities' debt levels and average interest costs in 2022, roughly half of Chinese localities were paying more than 10 percent of their fiscal revenues as annual interest on existing debt.[53] Local governments were going bankrupt in order to repay Chinese banks. Banks were in turn making new loans to those same local governments to ensure that the financial pressure did not intensify. The cycle became impossible to escape, with the net result being slower infrastructure investment, and Beijing losing control of fiscal policy. Clearly, none of this was intended.

The broader problem that China faced was that the rest of its tax system was similarly dependent upon investment-led growth. China collected most of its taxes on industrial output, rather than household consumption. More of China's taxes are imposed on corporates than on individuals and households. This was the legacy of a manufacturing-led economy, but it also meant that when investment and output growth slowed, China could not collect taxes through other channels. The largest individual driver of China's tax revenues was value-added taxes, which were split between the local and central government. That split created strong incentives for local governments to centralize production within their jurisdictions, which led to expanding output in excess of underlying demand, along with local protectionism of industries. China has only collected around 8 percent of its tax revenue in individual income taxes over the past decade, or around 1.1 percent of GDP (an extremely low level compared to other major economies), and often struggled to obtain reporting of income taxes.[54] The Ministry of Finance did impose a domestic consumption tax on selected goods, namely alcohol, tobacco, and large purchases such as automobiles, but the coverage of the tax was limited. Many sole proprietorships or small service businesses that collected revenues via electronic payments effectively had no ongoing financial reporting or tax requirements at all.

The net result of this concentration in investment-based taxation is that China's tax revenues started to decline as investment-led growth slowed. Land sales had the most direct impact on local government infrastructure, but aggregate tax revenues declined as a share of China's economy, from 22 percent in 2015 to only 16 percent in 2024. The weakness in overall prices across the economy intensified the fiscal pressures in China as well, as taxes depended far more on China's nominal GDP growth rather than real growth. As producer prices fell into deflationary territory starting in 2022, nominal tax revenues also slowed. Officially China's fiscal deficits were in the range of 3 to 4 percent of GDP but including local government revenues and the shortfall in land sales, these deficits surged above 6 percent of GDP in 2020 and exceeded 7.7 percent of GDP in 2024 (figure 2.4).

Because so much debt had been accrued outside of official channels – by borrowing from the shadow banking system – Beijing had no clear idea how large the local debt burden had become, and no obvious way to find out. Numerous audits had been stymied by local obfuscation of the types of debt involved, as local officials tried to game the system to

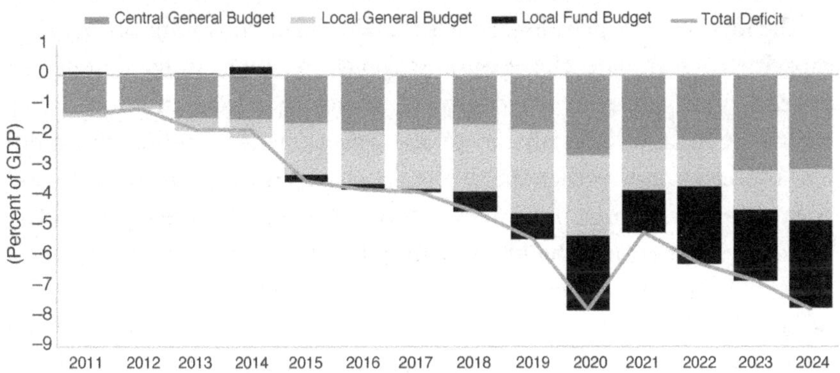

Figure 2.4 China's aggregate fiscal deficit, central and local governments, 2011–2024.

Data source: Ministry of Finance.

reclassify debt into forms preferred by Beijing, shifting out of LGFVs or holding debt in off-balance sheet channels. The central government was in a bind. Local governments were going to continue lying to them about debt levels. If Beijing promised to provide assistance to the localities, then the levels of debt that localities would say need to be refinanced would probably surge. If instead the central government pressured localities to reduce debt on their own, the likely result would be slower investment, a weaker economy, and ironically tighter fiscal policy as local governments scrambled to collect additional fees. Local debt was large enough to limit China's capacity to manage the economy, but Beijing could not effectively mount a response to the problem without localities potentially expanding the size of the debt burden that Beijing needed to fix.

The net result of this fiscal pressure was that Beijing lost control over one of its most effective policy tools for stabilizing China's economy as a whole. Most countries would ramp up government spending to stimulate additional demand to counter an economic slowdown. But China's budgetary projections no longer matched the reality of public finances, and both revenue and spending levels fell far below budgeted levels starting in 2020. Furthermore, local government finances continued deteriorating at a rapid rate, and by 2024 they required immediate assistance from Beijing, in the form of a 10-trillion-yuan swap of high-interest debt for lower-interest bonds.

The local government fiscal crisis remains a key constraint on Beijing's capacity to stimulate the economy today. As long as fiscal revenues depend upon investment-led growth rather than consumption-driven growth, China will be unable to use government spending to stimulate the economy further or resolve local government fiscal problems. A fundamental reorganization of China's tax system is likely necessary but does not appear to be forthcoming. Cosmetic responses to the most pressing local government fiscal problems leave unanswered the question of how infrastructure investment will be financed in the future, if not by LGFVs and from bank credit. The end of investment-led growth has severely constrained China's policy options in responding to its ongoing economic slowdown.

What Can Replace Investment-Led Growth?

While this chapter has discussed the end of China's unprecedented credit expansion as the most important cause of the slowdown in investment and the broader economy, it is certainly not the only cause. China's slowdown from an average of 9 percent annual GDP growth from 2000 to 2019 was always going to occur to some extent. A larger economy will naturally grow at slower rates. Eventually the marginal returns on investment will slow, as rapid growth becomes more difficult to maintain. China's demographic headwinds are well-known, as the working-age population has declined since around 2013, and the overall population peaked in 2022 and is likely to continue declining. There are only a few examples of major economies facing declining working-age populations over the past half-century, with Japan as the most prominent case, and economies with these demographic pressures have never grown at rates faster than 3 percent per year, at least five years after the working-age population peaked (so starting in 2018 in China's case). The external environment for China's growth was extraordinarily accommodative in the years following China's accession to the WTO, with exports growing by an astonishing 12.6 times between 2001 and 2021.[55] Those types of improvements were not going to be repeated indefinitely, particularly given rising political tensions between China and the rest of the world.

Economists often communicate this inevitable slowdown in terms of the "middle-income trap," which refers to a condition in which development stalls after GDP per capita reaches a certain level. After developing countries achieve faster economic growth from increasing investment or inputs, growth slows as countries fail to move up global value chains or absorb technologies to boost overall productivity, and as a result the economy never rises to higher-income levels. There were multiple causes of China's long-term economic slowdown, but the sharp adjustment in credit growth and the stress in China's financial system have amplified them, along with the resulting slowdown in investment.

With a declining population and slowing investment, economists have long known that China's future economic growth would depend upon rising productivity, usually represented in the economics literature as total factor productivity or TFP. The concept usually covers the total marginal growth in output produced by the available inputs of capital and labor in the economy, rather than growth in the inputs themselves. TFP usually includes factors such as technological improvements or changes in the structure of the economy, but conceptually it reflects the residual of economic growth that cannot be clearly explained by additional inputs. China's economy may feature some industries such as electric vehicles that use advanced, world-leading technologies, but as a whole, the economy has a very low rate of TFP growth because of the volume of inputs channeled into legacy industries and state-owned enterprises, and the inefficiency of capital allocation in the state-directed financial system. The IMF estimated China's TFP growth as averaging 0.7 percent over the past decade.[56] Others such as Harry X. Wu of the Conference Board China Center have placed it in zero or negative territory in some years.[57]

Productivity is central to the question of why China cannot maintain its current pace of economic expansion by simply adjusting its economy away from investment-led growth or finding an alternative model of growth. To do so, China would need to boost overall productivity to counter the slowdowns in the inputs of capital and labor in the economy. As the volume of these inputs slow, they would need to become much more productive to maintain the same growth rates in China's economy. At a bare minimum, this would require redirecting investment away from its currently less productive uses via local government infrastructure lending and toward more efficient private sector firms operating at technological frontiers. Then the redirected investment would need to find sources of domestic demand among China's household consumers, who would need to generate income growth commensurate with the expansion in output from the private sector.

There are two popular arguments in favor of China's potential to restructure its economy and maintain rapid economic growth into the future. First, China could redirect the economy toward household consumption-driven growth, providing a more sustainable base of economic expansion, even if the financial system cannot provide the same volume of future credit growth. Second, China could invest in advanced technologies that are more productive, revitalizing the efficiency of investment and maintaining growth across the entire economy. This is discussed in current Chinese government phrasing as releasing "new quality productive forces" in the economy.

Both ideas are instinctively appealing, and both have already been discussed for several years in China. There has been limited progress in redirecting China's economy toward consumption-led growth or toward more productive investment because either shift would slow the economy for some period of time even if Beijing did make difficult choices to recapitalize the financial system and transform the fiscal and tax system. As investment-led growth has slowed, Beijing has had no easy options to transition to a different economic model without paying for the high costs of ending the old system.

While consumption growth has surged along with the rest of the economy over the past two decades, household consumption remains extremely low as a proportion of China's economy relative to virtually all other economies in the OECD, at just 39.9 percent of GDP in 2024 (figure 2.5). Furthermore, since China joined the WTO in 2001, China's economy has become even more imbalanced toward investment and away from household consumption, a legacy of the rapid rate of investment growth and the expansion of the financial system.

The flip side of consumption remaining at low levels is that China's gross savings rates are extremely high, above 40 percent.[58] Those high savings rates help to fund investment at high levels. Adjusting the savings rate would therefore reduce growth from investment and produce additional consumption. While reducing the savings rate is possible, these changes are only likely to occur over the longer term, as they must be accomplished through long-term changes in tax policy. Most of China's

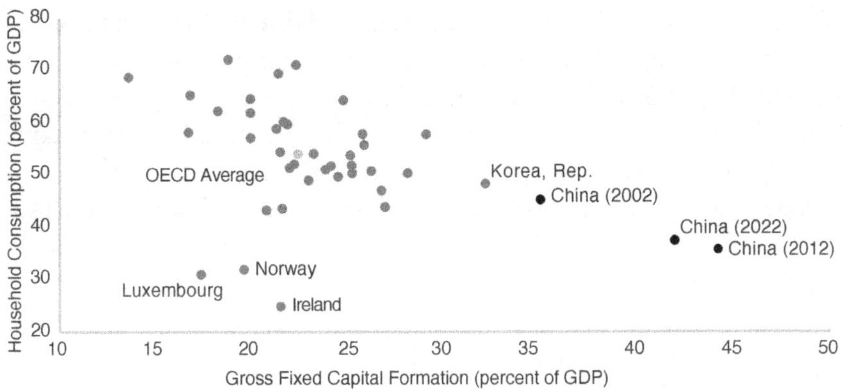

Figure 2.5 Proportions of investment and consumption in OECD countries, 2022, and China in 2002, 2012, and 2022.
Data source: International Monetary Fund.

high savings are concentrated in three areas: high-net-worth individuals (as is common in most economies), monopoly and oligopoly rents from state-owned enterprises, and private sector firms that tend to self-finance and operate independently of the banking system. While it is possible to envision changes – such as higher tax rates on the wealthy – that can alter these dynamics and reduce the savings rate, they are unlikely to shift the economy quickly.

There are generally four explanations for why China's household consumption remains low relative to the rest of the world. First, the share of household income in China's economy is much lower than in other economies, at around 61 percent of GDP.[59] As a result, even when China has seen rapid economic growth, households have not benefited to the same extent. This is typical in an export-led economy, as lower wages and other components of household income are often associated with the lower export costs necessary for global competitiveness.[60] Second, China's household income is very unevenly distributed, with household surveys typically indicating that 63 percent of savings are concentrated among the top 10 percent of households. As a result, even if household income growth improved, there would be only a minimal boost in overall consumer spending, given that the wealthy consume a smaller proportion of their incomes.[61] Third, China's level of household debt has expanded significantly along with the housing bubble, rising from

28 percent of GDP in 2011 to 62 percent of GDP in 2021, and from an estimated 66 percent of household income to 143 percent over the same timeframe.[62] Those levels of household debt have discouraged spending since the bubble burst, as households paid down debt rather than making additional purchases. Fourth, the more traditional explanation is that Chinese households engage in precautionary savings because of the limited availability of medical care and social services, particularly in China's rural areas. Improving the social safety net, therefore, might allow these consumers, particularly migrant workers, to become more adventurous and spend a larger proportion of their income.

Assessing all of these explanations, the importance of the household level of income relative to the size of the economy and the distribution of that income becomes clearer. Many countries have high levels of household debt and cyclical changes in indebtedness because of property market cycles. Precautionary savings is a problem in several countries as well, and China has made significant investments in the social safety net over the past two decades, particularly in the medical system. China's roughly 300 million migrant workers still save significant proportions of their incomes, but rural residents simply have lower income levels. Household savings still rose very sharply during the pandemic years and remain highly concentrated among wealthier households. Boosting household income growth overall is likely the fastest path to accelerating consumption growth.

However, any meaningful surge in household income growth to kickstart this process must ultimately come from the government, through changes in the fiscal system and modes of taxation and spending. This could include new dividends from SOEs to the government budget, transfer payments to individual households, or other adjustments in taxes that would directly boost incomes. China's tax system relies upon investment-led growth, so a rapid shift toward a consumption-led economy would quickly bankrupt the central government. Counteracting that pressure would require new taxes on domestic consumption and services-sector enterprises, which would likely slow consumption and the overall economy in the short term. But there is no other obvious source of income growth in China's households that would be sufficient to kickstart an acceleration of consumption growth outside of government-led transfers. These changes would require a fundamental restructuring of China's entire economy, altering the ways in which local governments incentivize investment and collect taxes. These are not easy choices for Beijing, nor can they be implemented quickly even if ideally designed. No current government official has ever worked within a different tax system.

The same constraints apply to China's ability to reorient the financial system toward more productive forms of investment in the future. State-owned financial systems do not redirect credit quickly. State-owned enterprises and local government companies have long depended upon ongoing flows of new credit to continue operating, since many of their investments have been quasi-fiscal in nature and not designed to generate financial returns sufficient to repay loans. In the absence of these new flows of credit every year, investment will collapse quickly, just as it did during the deleveraging campaign starting in 2018.

In addition, the industries that China is currently prioritizing as new drivers of growth – the "new three" sectors of electric vehicles, lithium-ion batteries, and solar panels – are simply far smaller in size than property or local government infrastructure. These are not the only potential opportunities for Beijing to improve efficiency within the financial sector by redirecting credit to more productive uses, but they currently appear as the highest priorities. Artificial intelligence and robotics will certainly receive additional government attention in the years ahead as well, but investment remains small relative to the size of the property sector or local government infrastructure. Total revenue in the entire auto industry reached only 10.6 trillion yuan or 7.8 percent of GDP in 2024, of which only a portion was the new electric vehicle industry.[63] Total investment in the solar industry was 2.5 trillion yuan in 2023.[64] In contrast, sales of new houses in the property sector, even after a dramatic collapse, still reached 8.5 trillion yuan in 2024, or 6.3 percent of GDP, without adding the economic impact of construction activity itself.[65] The total size of the "new three" industries is estimated at less than 10 percent of China's GDP, in contrast to the estimated 23 to 27 percent for the property sector at its peak and 14 percent for local government infrastructure investment. These industries are unlikely to become the dominant drivers of investment in China's economy in the next decade.

The banks themselves have different reasons to continue lending to the same state-owned borrowers, even if their customers cannot repay the loans. To cut these borrowers off requires writing down the previously extended loans, reducing bank profitability and the capacity to continue extending loans for new investments to other borrowers. China's banking system is extremely large, but not very profitable, with an average return on all assets of around 0.6 percent in recent years. To grow their balance sheets, banks must keep adding new capital. In a banking system as large as China's, with $60 trillion in assets as of the end of 2024, the only way that banks can continue adding capital is out of their own profits, which means they cannot recognize large volumes of non-performing loans. Actual levels of non-performing loans written off within the system have averaged less than 0.4 percent of assets over the last five years.[66] But the volume of actual bad lending every year is almost certainly much higher than this level. To keep loans to local government borrowers performing, banks need to keep rolling the same loans over and make new loans to the same borrowers. As overall credit growth declines, a larger proportion of loans are refinancing old debt, rather than being directed toward more efficient and productive borrowers.

The only way around this conundrum is to write off significant volumes of bad loans in order to clean the slate among commercial banks and make loans to new borrowers. But because this would consume significant proportions of the banking system's equity capital, large loan write-offs would also require an explicit recapitalization of the banks, which would likely involve direct funding from the state. China executed such a recapitalization following the Asian financial crisis from 1998 to 2003, when the banking system had only $1.5 trillion in assets, and the total costs of this bailout were still close to 50 percent of GDP.[67] Such a recapitalization today would be far more expensive in a $60 trillion banking system, and no such effort appears to be forthcoming. Beijing is adding dribs and drabs of new capital in order to maintain credit growth, such as a 500 billion yuan ($69 billion) addition to large banks' capital levels in early 2025, but there is no broader cleanup of older loans underway.[68] Individual banks can raise additional capital via selling stock or convertible bonds, but for the system as a whole, the past patterns of lending continue to limit the extent to which China can redirect capital to more productive uses in the future.

There is no obvious solution for Beijing to maintain economic growth at its targeted rates of around 5 percent per year now that investment-led growth has slowed significantly. Redirecting credit to more productive uses within the financial system requires some strategy to manage the legacy bad debt that was created from the investment boom following the global financial crisis. A large-scale recapitalization of the banking system that would permit this cleanup has not begun, and remains only a distant possibility. Boosting China's household consumption growth requires efforts to increase income growth, which in turn must involve transfers from the state and a likely restructuring of China's entire fiscal and taxation system. The slowdown in China's economy is difficult to reverse because the previous pace of growth was unsustainable in the absence of an unprecedented credit boom. And now that credit boom has ended. Beijing has some space for policies to improve the economy, but no easy ways to maintain previous rates of growth. Slower economic growth is here to stay.

China's post-crisis economic growth depended heavily upon the rapid expansion of China's financial system, which cannot be repeated. The future of China's economic growth depends upon whether China's financial system can be redirected to more productive uses. But Beijing's current approach to the financial sector is turning in a different direction. Since 2022, there has been an anti-corruption investigation running across the sector, and financial industry professionals have faced sudden pay cuts and pressure to surrender past wages and bonuses.[69] Financial regulators are under the same pressures, with investigations into over 500 officials, and some reports that salaries are being cut in half across the industry.[70] The political pressure seems to reflect a view in Beijing that the financial sector has grown too large and has profited at the expense of other sectors in the economy and Chinese society. This critique is fundamentally accurate, even if disciplinary investigations are unlikely to be an effective solution to inefficiency in lending. The financial sector grew rapidly over the past two decades, and this was ultimately subsidized by the state and implicit guarantees across the entire economy. Local governments unable to repay their debts were willing to borrow at high rates because they had no risk of defaulting. As a result, financial institutions booked large profits, which were necessary to fund the expansion of new lending to keep the entire economy growing at rapid rates.

Rather than making the financial sector more efficient in distributing credit within the economy, the anti-corruption campaign appears to target turning the financial sector back into an instrument of direct state control, operating as a type of state utility. Xi Jinping reportedly argued, "Serving the real economy is the duty of finance. [. . .] If finance is focused on self-circulation and self-expansion, it becomes water without source, a tree without roots, and a crisis will brew sooner or later."[71] A financial sector under investigation may slow credit growth to riskier companies and investments, but it is unlikely to generate significantly higher productivity growth for China's economy in the years ahead. Loan officers are far more likely to lend to "safe" state-owned enterprises rather than taking additional risks.

But the financial system can also no longer drive the same pace of credit growth to meet Beijing's long-term economic goals, which may leave China's leadership persistently disappointed in its performance in the future. The crackdown on the financial industry follows a broader pattern in Xi Jinping's third term as general secretary of the Communist Party, in which China's leadership suddenly attacked some of the most important and dynamic sectors in China's economy, raising questions about where economic growth fits within Beijing's priorities.

3

Policy Mistakes and Indecision

The day of the US presidential election in November 2020, the Shanghai Stock Exchange made a shock announcement: the initial public offering (IPO) of Ant Financial was being postponed. Ant Financial was the financial technology subsidiary of Alibaba, and its public share sale in Shanghai and on the Hong Kong Stock Exchange was set to be the world's largest of the year, at $34 billion.[1] Ten days beforehand, Alibaba's founder and chief executive officer, Jack Ma, had given a surprisingly combative speech at a major financial conference, criticizing China's regulation of financial technology firms. In the context of a long-running battle within China's regulatory agencies and political system concerning the power and influence of China's technology firms, Ma's speech appeared to tip the balance toward greater political control and regulation, leading to the abrupt cancellation of Ant's IPO only two days before its planned listing.

The postponement sent shock waves through global markets and immediately raised new questions about its implications for China's economic future. Ant Financial owned Alipay, one of China's two retail electronic payments platforms, and it was a pioneer in developing new technologies for China's consumer markets. Its parent company, Alibaba, had listed on the New York Stock Exchange in 2014, selling $25 billion in shares, the world's largest IPO at the time.[2] The companies had been prominent global examples of not only China's capacity for innovation, but the dynamism of China's consumer markets. The operating assumption for most financial investors at the time was that China would be actively promoting its champion firms in their attempt to expand their global influence and reach. To suddenly start regulating them and reining them in was an enormous shock.

This was clearly not a decision made based on a view of China's economic interests. While financial authorities were reasonably concerned about the firm's growth and the influence it had demonstrated in circumventing regulations while expanding its services, the bureaucracy was far from unified on the question of how to regulate Ant Financial. China's financial reformers were trying to break down the constraints imposed by the state-owned banking system, and innovative firms like Alibaba were part of that process. As Ma himself argued in the speech that likely triggered the IPO's cancellation: "There is no innovation in this world without risk."[3]

But the risk that Ant Financial had generated was probably more political than economic. The Chinese Communist Party under Xi Jinping appeared concerned about the growing power and political influence of Internet entrepreneurs like Ma, and their capacity to challenge the authority of the Party, as Ma had seemingly done with his speech in Shanghai. Immediately following the cancellation of the IPO, Ma made no public appearances at all for three months, before finally surfacing at a philanthropic event for one of his charities in January 2021, where he said nothing substantive about the cancellation of the IPO.[4] These were not the actions of an entrepreneur in a regulatory dispute, but the actions of the target of a top-down political campaign.

Over the following year, dozens of Internet entrepreneurs fell under greater regulatory scrutiny, with Chinese authorities responding to the example set by the cancellation of the Ant Financial public share offering. China's largest ride sharing service, Didi Chuxing, was suddenly subject to a cybersecurity review by Chinese regulators only days after its $4.4 billion IPO in New York in late June 2021.[5] Then in July, education and tutoring firms in China were suddenly banned from most of their commercial operations, essentially outlawing the businesses and wiping out billions of dollars in investments overnight. By the summer of 2021, it was clear that the priorities of China's leadership had changed. What remained unclear at the time was the relative importance of China's economic growth to Xi Jinping.

The COVID-19 pandemic created a different set of economic challenges for Beijing. After lockdowns and strict travel controls early in 2020 dramatically limited the domestic spread of the virus while it raged around the world, China's defenses against the virus started to break down when new variants emerged that were far more contagious. Outbreaks of the Delta variant flared in a few cities in late 2021, but it was the spread of the Omicron variant in early 2022 that caused a significant outbreak in China, with a large concentration in Shanghai. The resulting weeks-long lockdowns in that city and others were indicative of the unexpected constraints on Chinese policymaking, rather than its flexibility and adaptability. Faced with no good options to preserve China's propaganda line about fighting the virus more effectively than Western democracies, Xi Jinping held on to a system of strict controls on people's movement that failed to contain the spread of the disease in real time, even as the costs to China's economy and the Party's perceptions of competence rose rapidly. After some of the largest nationwide protests since the Tiananmen Square demonstrations in 1989, the controls were abandoned abruptly in late November 2022, while the consequences they had tried to prevent – a massive spread of the virus and a wave of deaths – unfolded quickly. Rather than the collective political leadership and decision-making of the Jiang Zemin and Hu Jintao eras, China's economic fate now seemed to be held in the balance by the choices of one man.

This chapter discusses the evolution of Chinese economic policymaking over the past decade, and how the centralization of power under Xi Jinping changed China's economic decision-making process and outcomes. The consequences of those changes have been both proactive policy mistakes that have set back China's private sector dynamism and weakened its economy, along with a passive and reactive approach to new threats to China's economy, including the flagging property sector, rising local government debt, and most dramatically, the consequences of limiting Chinese people's movement during the COVID-19 pandemic. Under Xi Jinping, a reactive Chinese leadership has become indecisive and lethargic in confronting China's most pressing economic problems, often choosing to delay decisions rather than face difficult choices.

The Legacy of Collective Leadership and Consensus-Driven Policymaking

Ever since the death of Mao Zedong, the Chinese Communist Party has described itself as a "collective" leadership, with one man as the "core" of that leadership. The "core" designation was applied to Mao Zedong, Deng Xiaoping, and Jiang Zemin, but not to Hu Jintao. In 2016, the same designation was applied to Xi Jinping, three years after he assumed the position of general secretary of the Chinese Communist Party. But the collective structure of China's leadership was meant to contain the potential for a personality cult similar to the one Mao had created during the Cultural Revolution in the 1960s, and to place limits on any one leader's influence within the Party.

For most of the 1990s and the 2000s, China's economic policymaking operated largely as a reflection of this collective leadership. The most important economic official was China's premier. The premier was always a member of China's Politburo Standing Committee but was also the leader of China's state institutions and the State Council, in contrast to Party institutions, led by the Communist Party's Politburo Standing Committee. For day-to-day decision-making concerning the economy, the State Council was usually considered the locus of activity. Zhu Rongji, who was premier from 1998 to early 2003, made difficult and painful decisions about restructuring the economy to facilitate China joining the World Trade Organization. Wen Jiabao was not considered as strong a personality and struggled to implement reforms given the need for consensus on the Politburo Standing Committee, but he was still the most significant decision-maker on economic policy during his tenure as premier from 2003 to 2013.

While China's policymaking process remains opaque, it usually follows certain steps within China's bureaucracy. In the years before the Xi era, economic policymaking typically featured a high degree of input from economic and financial technocrats. Often, the State Council would ask for input and consultations from economists at universities or government think tanks such as the Chinese Academy of Social Sciences. Campaigns for different policies would often play out openly in the media, sometimes with unsigned editorials in the *China Securities Journal* or the *Financial News* (a PBOC-managed newspaper). Policy proposals would generally be gathered at the offices of the Central Leading Group for Financial and Economic Affairs, which was an organization technically sitting between the Party and the state.[6] That office would revise proposals, seek additional input, and then provide options to the State Council. Policy formation would occur with some degree of compromise and consultation with experts. Policy decisions were usually made by the premier and the vice-premier in charge of economics and finance and were then approved by the Party leadership at the Politburo or Politburo Standing Committee level.

This structure of policymaking featured a high degree of compromise among institutions, and consequently produced gradual or incremental policy changes, rather than dramatic shifts. That gradualist method of policymaking empowered technocrats to adjust macroeconomic policy but also left structural changes to the economy or China's growth model off the table. Minxin Pei has described the constraints of this gradualist policymaking process as a "trapped transition" to a different growth model, and the problems that it generated were clear.[7] For example, when China adjusted its exchange rate away from a de facto peg to the US dollar in 2005, the move was so incremental that it invited additional capital inflows anticipating further currency appreciation. The adjustment was meant to provide the PBOC with more monetary policy autonomy and to set domestic interest rates without as much concern about the impact on the exchange rate. But the resulting inflows and expansion of the money supply then created new headaches for the PBOC to manage, including faster credit growth and inflationary pressures. Meanwhile, the central bank still needed to limit its interest rate adjustments even after the de facto peg to the dollar had ended, with the gradualist approach to exchange rate reform undermining one of the key rationales for the initial adjustment. Technocrats had influenced the policy, with most of the energy for the July 2005 reforms coming from the PBOC itself, but the results were mixed at best.

Consensus-driven economic policymaking generated very limited structural reforms to China's economy but also prevented larger policy mistakes and dramatic adjustments. Maintaining the perception of stability was always an important policy objective for China's leaders. With the State Council leading the formation of policy, more extreme options were generally winnowed out before the premier or Party decision-makers were involved. There was little role for freelancing by other bureaucrats or those not directly involved in economic policymaking, even if there was some degree of pushback against the final decisions being reached, should a significant economic policy choice reach the Politburo Standing Committee. As a result, China's export and investment-led growth model remained unchanged throughout the 2000s, as a consensus-driven process made it more difficult to push reforms through against bureaucratic resistance. This policymaking process generally mirrored the perceived structure of China's elite politics at the time, which involved a degree of balancing between different factions, in a structure that elite politics scholar Li Cheng called a "new bipartisanship."[8]

During Xi Jinping's first term as general secretary from 2013 to 2018, economic policymaking was still influenced by technocrats, but there were clear signs of a break from past practices, as Xi was far more directly involved in multiple decisions. China's most significant economic policy decisions of Xi's first term – squeezing the interbank market in June 2013, bailing out investors in the stock market after a dramatic decline, depreciating China's currency in August 2015, launching the deleveraging campaign in 2016 – were all done with technocratic input, but also involved some degree of opposition from key economic officials. Elite politics was changing more rapidly, influenced by a new anti-corruption campaign and a shift from a factional balance to a leadership comprised primarily of loyalists to Xi. While Xi had placed himself in charge of several institutions, including the Leading Small Group on Comprehensively Deepening Reform, there was no dramatic shift in decision-making processes throughout his first term. What was significant was that Xi was inserting himself into those processes in ways that had not been expected. As economist Barry Naughton argued in 2017, "It is quite unprecedented for a general secretary to dominate economic policymaking in this way in China. Even Deng Xiaoping never did."[9] When Xi's rule looked like it might extend beyond the two five-year terms customary for a Chinese leader, these changes in policymaking became far more important for China's economic future.

The End of Term Limits

The Third Plenum of the Eighteenth Party Congress in 2013 marked the announcement of a plan for significant structural reforms to China's economy, with pledges for a more "decisive" role for markets in allocating resources. But the Third Plenum of the Nineteenth Party Congress, five years later, marked an even more dramatic change in China's politics. In late February 2018, far earlier than a Third Plenum meeting would usually be held, China's leadership proposed changing the state constitution to remove the requirement that the president and vice-president "shall serve no more than two consecutive terms."[10] This was an earthquake in Chinese politics and upended the norms that had seen all Chinese leaders serve two five-year terms since the end of Deng Xiaoping's leadership. The removal of the term limits suggested Xi was planning to stay as China's leader beyond the end of his second term in 2022, which was exactly what took place, and potentially even beyond the end of a third term in 2027.

Following the death of Mao Zedong and the chaos of the Cultural Revolution, Deng Xiaoping had presided over a broader reorganization of Chinese politics focused on institutionalization of power in bureaucratic structures, rather than reliance upon factional alignments or the informal exercise of authority. This was typically characterized in Chinese as "separating the Party from the government" (*dang zheng fenkai*). Fixed terms for different positions, particularly for China's top leadership, were an important part of this process. Even after Jiang Zemin became general secretary in 1992, Deng had already set the stage for Hu Jintao to be promoted to his position after Jiang had served two terms. Xi's move to abolish term limits in 2018 risked upending the careful balance that had been struck in Chinese politics between a strong Party leadership and limits on any individual leader's authority, in order to avoid the miscalculations and campaign-style political movements of the Mao era.

The implications of the end of term limits for Xi's power were seen immediately, both within Chinese politics and overseas. Internally, all discussion of succession or the progress of the "fifth generation" of Chinese leaders after Xi ground to an immediate halt. One official associated with that generation and long discussed as a potential successor to Xi, Sun Zhengcai, was suddenly removed from his post in 2017 after being accused of a political plot against Xi, signifying that there was no plausible alternative to Xi remaining in his position.[11] Loyalty to Xi himself then became more important in Chinese politics than competence within a given issue area, as Xi was likely to retain authority for what remained of most officials' careers. Ideological conformity became more significant, as officials were tasked with reading "Xi Jinping Thought" during work hours and taking exams based on the lessons.[12]

Internationally, the move to end term limits was roundly criticized, as it put the nail in the coffin of the increasingly remote prospect that China might eventually evolve in the direction of Western market democracies. Moving intentionally toward one-man rule and the possibility of China having a "president for life" had no constituency in the democratic world.

In the 2000s and early 2010s, there were at least some arguments that Chinese politics was becoming more pluralistic and viewpoints within the Party were becoming more diverse, even if it remained a one-Party authoritarian system. There were at least plausible opinions that this diversity of views, in combination with a technocratic policymaking process, might produce more meaningful market reforms over time. Xi's decision to end term limits undercut all of these arguments and removed the foundation for continued engagement with China in several Western capitals.

The implications for economic policy were also readily apparent. Should Xi Jinping decide upon a certain course of action, there were now far fewer obstacles to those policy choices being enacted in China. The net result was a type of two-track decision-making process, in which more power became concentrated in the Party advisors around Xi Jinping himself, who might have their own ideas about economic policy changes, alongside the more traditional economic policymaking process under the State Council. What remains unclear to this day is the relative influence of these processes, and how they might intersect over contentious issues. The results of more centralized Chinese economic policymaking have been clearer, with more volatility and sudden reversals in policy decisions, less advance discussion of policy choices in Chinese media, and fewer attempts to seek consensus among Chinese leaders. Increasingly, in governing China's economy, only one man's view is important.

Changes in the Institutional Structures of Economic Decision-Making

Along with the end of term limits came more significant changes in the institutional structure of economic policymaking in China. Policymaking became a more top-down process, with fewer bottom-up attempts to use pilot programs, experiments, or trials of different initiatives before expanding them nationwide. Political analyst He Xingqiang describes Xi's concentration of power as occurring primarily through the creation and elevation of leading groups within the bureaucracy, and then Xi placing himself at the head of all of the relevant leading groups, transforming some of them into more formal "commissions."[13] These groups essentially undercut the authority of both the Politburo Standing

Committee on the Party side and the State Council on the state side. He summarizes, "The leadership of party central commissions in determining national political and economic agendas is the most distinctive feature of Xi's governance."[14] Within the Party itself, Xi started to change the rules of behavior of Party members, focused on increasing centralization of power and elevating loyalty to the Party center, and therefore to Xi personally.[15]

Perhaps most significantly for economic policy, Xi himself took the leadership of the Central Leading Group for Financial and Economic Affairs, even within his first term in 2013. Usually, this position would be held by the premier, rather than the general secretary. Xi then upgraded the group to a permanent commission in 2018, helping to solidify his authority over economic decision-making, and implicitly bypassing both the rest of the Politburo and the technocratic influence within the State Council. Still, in 2018, Liu He was the vice-premier in charge of economic and financial affairs and was viewed as an important voice on economic policy. As mentioned in the previous chapter, Liu spearheaded the consolidation of financial regulatory agencies into a single Financial Stability and Development Committee (FSDC) under the State Council.

By 2023, when Xi's third term began, he further expanded Party control over the economy and the financial industry in particular. Separating the Party from the government under Deng had been reversed and was shifting toward "replacing the government with the Party" (*yi dang dai zheng*). Two new Party organizations were created: the Central Finance Commission led by the Party to replace the FSDC, and the Central Financial Work Commission (CFWC), which Minxin Pei described as a type of "political commissar" for the financial sector.[16] The fact that the FSDC only lasted for five years suggested that the primary priority in any reorganization was not substantive or related to policy, but a structural change within the bureaucracy, to place Party officials more clearly in charge of the financial sector. The CFWC threatened political supervision of the financial sector, including the potential for anti-corruption investigations, and rising scrutiny over salary levels within the sector, by reclassifying financial technocrats as more ordinary civil servants. The implication of these changes was clear: the Party was now taking control over the direction of the financial sector in China, rather than the financial sector becoming more responsive to market conditions.

The combined effect of the end of Xi Jinping's term limits and the series of institutional changes he executed within the Party effectively ended the consensus-driven economic policymaking process in China and curtailed the influence of economic technocrats. Increasingly, government economists, advisors, and even central bank officials were on the outside looking into a policymaking process led by Xi and his hand-picked advisors on the leading groups and commissions. After Liu He's retirement in 2023, the Politburo itself featured few leaders with macroeconomic expertise. Those remaining, such as Vice-Premier He Lifeng, had their primary expertise in industrial policy and encouraging investment, relative to the complex challenges of China's financial sector. This centralization of authority set the stage for dramatic changes in China's economy starting in 2020 as the bureaucracy started to respond to Party leadership rather than the incremental steps proposed by the State Council. One central idea about the distribution of economic resources animated many of the changes.

Common Prosperity

Within a Leninist political system, repetition and endorsement of key phrases and slogans from the Party center become an important demonstration of loyalty and one's commitment to the correct course of action. A Party leader's endorsement of an idea or slogan is then multiplied throughout the system, with lower-level officials demonstrating that they understand the current political line and its implications. In the Fifth Plenum of the Nineteenth Party Congress in November 2020, China's leadership added the phrase "achieving more significant substantive progress toward the common prosperity of the people" by 2035, while also pledging "concrete promotion of common prosperity."[17] While the wording would likely appear to a normal observer as anodyne and commonplace, mixed within a series of other objectives mentioned in the communique, the phrase "common prosperity" evolved over the following year in 2021 to stand for a broad-based critique of China's development model, justifying a series of regulatory actions that severely disrupted the economy and devastated some of China's most important and prominent companies. Xi started using the phrase more commonly immediately following the Fifth Plenum communique, including the

Central Economic Work Conference statement in late 2020 and in his New Year's speech in 2021,[18] and Chinese officials reacted to the implications of these phrases to demonstrate their alignment with Party leadership, and with Xi Jinping personally. These types of disruptions would have been nearly unthinkable under Jiang Zemin or Hu Jintao, not because of those leaders' greater economic acumen, but because they operated within a policymaking process that would have likely moderated the impact of any individual slogan or political campaign on the economy and Chinese society.

In 2021, however, China's economic policymaking process was far more centralized than at any point over the previous decade. Therefore, when Xi Jinping made a widely publicized speech extolling the importance of common prosperity at the Central Leading Group for Financial and Economic Affairs in August of that year, cadres throughout the Chinese system listened. In the context of what became a dramatic crackdown on private sector firms, Xi's message in this speech took on heightened significance to global markets. The statement from the meeting emphasized the importance of balancing the goals of efficiency and fairness, increasing the numbers of China's middle class, raising the incomes of lower-income households, and controlling illegal sources of income, while adjusting high incomes. These types of statements about rebalancing incomes across Chinese society would also resonate in virtually any twenty-first-century liberal democracy. The key difference in circulating these ideas in China at this time was that the centralization of China's decision-making made the use of blunt policy instruments to remedy these economic imbalances far more plausible than in the past.

The year 2021 also marked the centennial anniversary of the founding of the Chinese Communist Party. Looking around at the nature of Chinese society under Communist Party rule, it would be rational for any observer to experience a high degree of cognitive dissonance about the nature of communism. Wrapped up within the concept of common prosperity were a series of critiques about the unbalanced nature of China's economic growth and its development model. While it is a common preconception among Western observers that China's leaders are capable of executing long-term economic plans on behalf of the Party, as this book has argued, the reality is that China's government is often adjusting to completely unintended consequences from its past decisions. There have also been powerful societal voices criticizing the Party's approach to economic governance. This was the case with the intellectual environment surrounding common prosperity, as critics of the influence of large services sector firms on China's economy had clearly found an audience within society and among Party leadership. Deng Xiaoping had argued that a few would "get rich first" in China's development. The need to encourage common prosperity implicitly rejected the benefits of that mode of development for China's future.

Furthermore, China's demographic situation appeared particularly bleak on the hundredth anniversary of the Party's establishment. China had just released census data in May 2021 that confirmed that birth rates were collapsing, despite the Party's attempts to relax the one-child policy back in 2016. In a rare about-face, Chinese authorities suddenly completely threw out the policy and reset the limits on family size to three children only a few weeks after the census data were published.[19] With China's population set to decline (which occurred officially for the first time in 2022), the pattern of property-led investment appeared to be on borrowed time, consumption-led growth appeared less plausible overall, and it was difficult to see how services-led growth built upon an American model would replace those previous drivers of growth.

Services sector firms such as the Internet platform companies were becoming increasingly powerful actors within Chinese society, and the billionaire entrepreneurs behind them started to build their own followings among the Chinese public, which could potentially pose a threat to the Party's own messaging. Jack Ma's speech in October 2020 criticizing financial regulation was clearly an unwanted message to Party officials, but Ma was not the only entrepreneur with an outsized platform at that point. In 2021, six of the ten richest people in China came from services sector firms, including Internet platform companies. Complaints about wealth inequality and the impossibility of keeping up in Chinese society were driving a different movement of younger Chinese to "lie flat" or pursue minimal employment given the limited possibilities available to them. While the Party exercised control over China's economy through the distribution of land and credit, services sector firms were a threat because they were light on assets and labor-intensive rather than capital-intensive.

An influential book by Zhang Xiaopu and Zhu Hongming of the staff of the Central Leading Group for Financial and Economic Affairs added to the criticism of China's growth model at that time. The foreword to the book was written by the prominent Chinese Academy of Social Sciences economist Li Yang, who used the space to highlight how China had always taken inspiration and lessons from foreign development models, including Hong Kong and Japan, before finally trying to emulate the US system. Li commented that, in China, there was more criticism of the American model of development, given its focus on the financial sector and large services sector firms, and more interest in German and Japanese patterns of development.[20] The argument that started to circulate in Chinese political circles was that it was far safer for China's political system and for the health of society to have thousands of entrepreneurs worth 200 million yuan than one Jack Ma worth 200 billion yuan.

The critiques of China's unbalanced development and rising wealth inequality were generally more coherent than any discussions of an alternative economic strategy at the time. As the demographic situation in China deteriorated, it was natural for China's leaders and different voices in society to question how long the current growth model could persist. But given the rising concentration of power under Xi Jinping, and the potential for sudden interventions into the economy unchecked by other forces, the discussion of the importance of common prosperity was a stunning development for global financial markets and foreign observers. China was not necessarily turning its back on the goal of maintaining economic growth, but was certainly willing to take steps to change its development path in ways that might sacrifice economic growth, by attacking some of the country's most dynamic and efficient private firms. And Beijing did so in ways that evoked the political campaigns of the 1960s in China, rather than the more anodyne regulatory and antitrust battles that played out in courtrooms in the Western world. "Common prosperity" was a slogan associated directly with Xi Jinping and his concentration of authority, and Party leaders and institutions demonstrated their alignment with Xi's vision through a series of actions that sent shockwaves across China and the world.

The Crackdown on China's Technology Firms

Following the suspension of Ant Financial's initial public offering in early November 2020, the firm found itself squarely in the crosshairs of

Chinese financial regulators intent on examining its business practices. What remained unclear at that point was whether the attack on Ant and its parent Alibaba was a specific response to the perceived transgressions of its founder Jack Ma, or the opening salvo in a broader regulatory crackdown against technology firms, or private firms in general. In late December 2020, Ant and Alibaba were formally subjected to an antitrust accusation from China's State Administration for Market Regulation (SAMR), which had just created new regulations concerning Internet platform companies.[21] One of the monopolistic practices that SAMR warned about was the tendency of Internet platforms such as Alibaba to require merchants on their platforms to sign exclusive deals to distribute products on only one platform.[22] In late December, the central bank asked Ant to separate its consumer credit data business from the rest of its operations, which the firm agreed to do by early February 2021.[23] The firm was restructured into a financial holding company with additional capital requirements and tighter regulatory supervision by April 2021, essentially ending the structure that had facilitated its rapid growth.[24] The firm is still held privately and has not made a public offering of shares since the November 2020 action by China's regulators. Alibaba itself eventually paid a $2.8 billion fine for monopolistic practices in March 2021.

Ant Financial was the first victim of China's crackdown against its technology firms, but it would not be the last. Many more firms were drawn into the regulatory dragnet over the following year. The typical accusations from Chinese regulators against the technology giants included monopolistic pricing or distortions of fair market competition. For others, like Didi Chuxing, new cybersecurity rules were invoked in order to establish a case for regulation. For delivery service Meituan, the accusation was unfair treatment of its delivery drivers and low wages.[25] Other firms would attempt to offset or mitigate the pressure by making "voluntary" contributions totaling tens of billions of yuan to Beijing's initiatives via funds explicitly earmarked for causes related to common prosperity.[26] But from the perspective of these firms and market participants, the crackdown had still been a significant policy surprise, and an event that no one could have realistically anticipated six months prior to it starting.

The reversal of regulatory treatment of China's technology giants raised fundamental questions about China's political prioritization of economic growth. After all, the firms that were being attacked were not only China's most dynamic private sector firms, but the face of Chinese industry to the rest of the world. For Beijing to suddenly attempt to sharply curtail their growth suggested that the leadership's priorities had shifted, and quickly. The attacks on these firms seemed to be entirely political in nature. Many entrepreneurs in charge of the firms disappeared from public view for months or resigned their official positions, acting as if they were the targets of a 1960s-style political campaign.[27] And that raised further questions about what other objectives Beijing now considered as high priority, if maintaining China's economic growth rate was no longer the most important goal. The property market was already starting to struggle in late 2020 and demographic headwinds were more apparent. If technological innovation was now considered too politically risky for Beijing, how would the leadership anticipate maintaining world-beating growth rates?

Throughout 2021, Chinese regulators took cues from the actions against Ant and Alibaba to initiate regulatory actions across China's Internet platform companies and other technology firms. In April, the crackdown broadened, as thirty-four separate technology firms were warned to end monopolistic and anti-competitive practices, with regulators claiming that the firms should "heed Alibaba's example."[28] In late April, SAMR suddenly imposed fines on ten firms for not disclosing acquisitions of smaller competitors.[29] Didi Chuxing and its overseas subsidiary Didi Global were subjected to reviews by a new player in Chinese regulation, the Cybersecurity Administration of China, who announced an investigation into the firm only days after their IPO in New York.[30] Soon, Tencent was under scrutiny as a series of editorials in state media outlets in August 2021 warned of the risks of online gaming, with one in the *Economic Information Daily* labeling games as "spiritual opium."[31]

The Party's efforts to use common prosperity as a cudgel against the political power of China's technology companies could best be understood in China's political context as a revival of campaign-style governance. Most common during the Maoist era, political campaigns involve the use of government propaganda organs and Leninist-style ideological conformity to direct Party and government efforts toward a single political objective. Party cadres and government agencies often try to outcompete one another to align with the ideological guidance from the Party center. A flurry of activity results quickly as the campaign progresses. In the Mao era, an extreme example was the campaign to root out the "four pestilences" ravaging Chinese agriculture. Chinese farmers stood on their roofs for hours to prevent sparrows from landing, while urban residents harassed them with pots and pans. When large numbers of sparrows died, insects ravaged crops around the country, contributing to famine. But this type of political energy cannot be sustained, and political campaigns all eventually end, not with an official repudiation of the effort, but simply because the Party moves on to some other objective.

Obviously, financial markets quickly appreciated the impact of this regulatory campaign against what had been some of China's most highly valued companies. The most significant uncertainties in markets were how long the crackdown would extend and what it would mean for the future of the sector. Under consensus-driven leadership, most investors could assume that eventually there would be some moderating elements involved in shaping policy choices and reining in the campaign. But under Xi's centralized authority, no one was sure, and investors were unlikely to be reassured unless they were convinced that Xi himself had changed his mind. In the end, the shares of China's tech firms lost over $1 trillion in market value as a result of the crackdowns.[32] There were reports that data-related firms would be prohibited from overseas stock offerings, and few have launched since the end of the regulatory campaign.[33]

The legacy of the crackdown against China's technology firms has been a significant setback for China's entrepreneurial culture and willingness to take risks. The rewards for taking such risks were devalued during the campaign, as fame and recognition for launching leading companies turned to public criticism and potential legal trouble. The crackdown also significantly reduced the attractiveness of Chinese markets to foreign investors and created significant concerns about China's growth overall. The slowdown in capital inflows into China's equity market caused overall stock market valuations to plummet, leading more foreign investors to consider the country "uninvestable" given the potential for dramatic regulatory changes. Xi Jinping and the Party leadership may still believe that the crackdown was politically necessary to sustain one-Party rule given the rising influence of the technology sector. But those political objectives also clearly took precedence over maintaining economic growth.

Education and Tutoring Firms Wiped Out

As draconian as the controls on China's technology sector became, these firms were still allowed to continue operating their businesses. China's education and tutoring firms were not provided that courtesy. In a dramatic announcement on July 24, 2021, Chinese regulators authorized by the State Council suddenly announced that firms in the online tutoring and education sector could no longer operate as for-profit enterprises, raise equity capital, or seek foreign investment.[34] In other words, all of the past investment into the sector over the past two decades, totaling between $100 and 120 billion, was essentially being wiped out with one stroke of administrative fiat. A separate commentary on the Ministry of Education website claimed that the sector had been "severely hijacked by capital."[35] Beijing had decided that these firms should no longer be allowed to raise capital or generate profits from after-school or weekend tutoring services that were aligned with the official curriculum. It was an extreme series of steps, with most of the publicly traded firms targeted by the new regulations losing more than half of their market valuations overnight. Government bonds and China's currency also came under pressure during the following week, reflecting the concerns of foreign investors about such steps.[36] Three days later, China dispatched financial technocrats from the China Securities Regulatory Commission (CSRC) to attempt to reassure foreign investors, to little avail.[37]

The political logic of the attack on education and tutoring firms was linked to the common prosperity agenda and China's newly announced declining birth rate. The competitive pressures to raise and educate children in China were generating rising costs as families felt they needed to spend more and more on online and after-school tutoring to get ahead. Some within the Party viewed this as inequitable and felt they needed to do something to make it easier to raise children in Chinese society, in order to boost a birth rate that was clearly under pressure. Hence reducing the incentives for companies to offer these tutoring sessions became a viable policy option. It is not difficult to see the linkages between these issues, but at the same time, virtually no one would have anticipated that the remedy would have been a nearly complete shutdown of the business prospects for the sector, announced with virtually no warning on a weekend in July.

Perhaps more than any other action during the regulatory crackdown, the measures targeting education and tutoring firms reflected the transformation and centralization of Chinese economic policymaking under Xi Jinping. Regulators were using the leading groups and commissions to advance policy ideas that would have ordinarily been eliminated or moderated during the policy formation process operating under the State Council. Campaign-style governance saw these measures advance quickly with little political resistance, as there was no significant political benefit to leaders appearing to contradict or oppose measures that were seen to be in line with the government's common prosperity agenda. As these measures moved rapidly through a revamped Chinese policymaking process, Chinese society and the rest of the world were shocked.

One of the ancillary consequences of the technology and education crackdowns was the impact on the labor market in China, particularly for recent college graduates. Both the technology giants and education and tutoring firms were large employers in China, and these were the types of jobs that were very attractive to recent college graduates in the country, with the potential for upward mobility. The attacks on these firms resulted in hiring freezes, layoffs, and salary cuts across both industries among white-collar professionals who generally lived in major cities.[38] Throughout the previous decade, China's birth rate had declined while college enrollments had surged. By 2025, over 12.2 million college graduates were expected, up from only 1.5 million in 2002.[39] This meant that a larger and larger proportion of new entrants into China's job market every year were college-educated, and looking for work suitable to that level of education. Faced with rising youth unemployment, China's statistical authorities took the unorthodox step of suspending the publication of data concerning youth joblessness in 2023.

This type of adjustment in China's labor market toward more college graduates requires a change in the structure of the economy itself. But that rebalancing away from investment-led growth and toward a more dynamic labor-intensive services-led consumer economy had barely occurred over the past decade. Now, with the crackdown on Internet platforms and education and tutoring firms, even the limited progress that firms in some labor-intensive industries had made was being actively rolled back. Importantly, these regulatory crackdowns were occurring at the same time as China's property sector was starting to weaken, with several signs of distress at major developers brewing. China's new planned drivers of growth – advanced manufacturing prowess in strategic industries such as electric vehicles – are similarly capital-intensive industries, with few potential job opportunities for China's millions of college graduates. The crackdown on technology giants and education and tutoring firms only made restructuring China's economy to align with its new labor force even more arduous.

The broader implication of the regulatory crackdowns that started with Ant Financial was that they placed additional hurdles to China achieving faster productivity growth in the future. There was no plausible argument that China could meaningfully boost its productivity growth from the currently low levels of 0 to 1 percent per year by continuing to allow state-directed credit to fund investment-led growth. Chinese leaders, including Xi, had already agreed that the previous model had reached a dead end in the 2013 Third Plenum reform blueprint. The economy's future depended upon a labor-intensive, services-oriented private sector that would more efficiently deploy capital. And it depended upon the financial system prioritizing credit to those more productive firms. The regulatory crackdowns had raised new questions about the role of private firms in China overall, as those that had risen quickly had just as rapidly been slapped down. Beijing would eventually ease the crackdown, as all political campaigns end, but the impact on entrepreneurial risk-taking behavior would persist.[40]

Even more dramatically, China's economy had shifted from a place where it was difficult for any investor to imagine losing money because of the pervasiveness of state guarantees to a world in which billions of yuan of investment could be wiped out overnight at the stroke of a bureaucrat's pen, because that bureaucrat thought that they were acting consistently with Xi Jinping's policy direction. This was an entirely new level of political and economic risk under a more centralized decision-making structure. But nothing would rival the economic impact of the policy most closely aligned with Xi Jinping and indicative of the centralization of power in China: the zero-COVID controls on people's movements.

The Economic Catastrophe of Zero-COVID

Easily forgotten in the tumultuous years of the pandemic was that, after the initial lockdowns and attempts to control the COVID-19 virus in 2020, China's worst year for controls on people's movements was actually in 2022, immediately after the regulatory crackdowns on technology firms had started to ease. The Delta variant of the virus challenged China's defenses, which included regular testing for all citizens, the use of a government-provided health app for access to virtually all public facilities, periodic lockdowns and restrictions on movement, and two- or three-week quarantine periods for inbound travelers. Outbreaks still flared up in Chinese cities from time to time throughout the latter half of 2021 but usually stayed under control. Chinese vaccination programs had progressed, and while Chinese vaccines generally appeared less effective in controlling the spread of the virus than the mRNA vaccines elsewhere in the world, they still provided the population with a degree of protection against worst-case outcomes. The impact of COVID restrictions on macroeconomic conditions in 2021 was far more limited relative to the other regulatory actions that China was taking, as well as the emerging financial pressure on property developers.

In 2022, the year started with a degree of optimism about a potential economic recovery in China. The Omicron variant of COVID-19 had other ideas. Far more transmissible, Omicron overwhelmed China's defenses, which were still more extensive than those in virtually any other country not pursuing a complete quarantine and isolation (such as North Korea). And in an unfortunate turn of events for China's leaders, the most significant outbreak emerged in China's most important economic center, Shanghai. By March 2022, there were reports of close to 20,000 cases per day emerging in Shanghai alone.[41] These events forced China's leaders into stark choices. China's defenses were likely to break down should these trends continue, meaning a nationwide spread of the virus that might kill millions of people. This would undermine China's public claims that the Party's centralized rule had controlled the spread of the virus more effectively than Western democratic systems. But doubling down on China's existing control measures was no guarantee of success given Omicron's transmissibility, even while the controls were undoubtedly becoming more difficult to enforce. Eventually the virus would spread, and the controls could not last forever. But despite these drawbacks, the decision was taken to tighten controls in Shanghai and surrounding cities, implementing a complete and total lockdown of all 25 million residents of Shanghai.[42]

The costs of this decision started accumulating immediately, as the distortions in citizens' regular lives that were necessary to sustain this lockdown began multiplying. The inability to access food or groceries meant that online delivery apps were jammed with orders and quickly ran out of stock. Entire armies of enforcers of the controls were necessary, with residents labeling them *dabai* or "big whites" because of their white hazmat suits. Abuses by these officials started to multiply as the lockdowns continued, with cruelty toward the elderly and pets among the accusations.[43] Supplies of food and other materials ran low as truck drivers avoided the city, concerned about arbitrary quarantines.[44] Tragically, there were numerous deaths that occurred as people were locked in their homes, unable to access medical care or sufficient food.[45]

Economically, the effects of the lockdowns in Shanghai and other major cities in China were catastrophic. Logistically, truck traffic was dramatically impacted across the country, with some measures of freight suggesting a nationwide decline of around 40 percent, based on Gaode and Baidu mobility data.[46] Sales of properties declined by 39 percent in year-on-year terms in April 2022, auto sales dropped by 48 percent, headline retail sales fell by 11 percent, and overall industrial output – a traditionally smooth data series – dropped by 3 percent.[47] Alibaba's online sales via its platforms on Taobao and Tmall declined by over 25 percent in year-on-year terms during the month of April.[48] These were not minor adjustments to the economy. They represented significant contractions in activity. China could control the spread of COVID-19, despite the difficulties in doing so. But Beijing could not grow the economy at the same time. Those dramatic and binary choices posed a new test for Xi Jinping's centralized policymaking.

Societally, the Shanghai lockdowns were an enormous shock. For years, China's middle and upper classes living in major cities were largely comfortable with the political bargain that the Party had struck, given the rapid improvements in their quality of life over the previous two decades. Most homeowners in major cities had become US dollar millionaires by the 2020s, based simply on the rise in property prices. Political campaigns and crackdowns in places like Xinjiang occurred in China, but not in the financial capital. But with the zero-COVID lockdowns, now the rich and the poor were locked in their homes, all together. For many middle-class Chinese, the lockdowns provided a lesson that no one was safe from the Party's political campaigns.

The controls affected Hong Kong as well, with the Hong Kong leadership eager to emulate Beijing's measures in order to eventually justify a reopening of the border between Hong Kong and the mainland, to permit more travel. As Omicron spread rapidly through Hong Kong in February and March 2022 and quarantines and political repression became far more frequent, hospitals were completely overwhelmed and an exodus of tens of thousands of residents took place, with the official Census and Statistics Department figures showing a net outflow of 95,000 people from June 2021 to June 2022, and a total decline in population of 121,500, equivalent to almost 2 percent of Hong Kong's population.[49]

The lockdowns of Shanghai and other cities were unsustainable from both an economic and political perspective. They started to ease in May, and the lockdown formally ended on June 1.[50] The seasonal pattern of the virus (spreading more rapidly in cold weather than warm) also seemed to provide some temporary relief. Chinese authorities declared victory over the outbreak, with the *People's Daily* talking about the "great achievements" in defending Shanghai from the virus.[51] But the broad measures that Beijing was using to control the outbreak had not changed. If and when the virus returned, it was entirely possible that lockdowns would resume as well. China appeared to be fighting an unwinnable war. There were clear models for how to relax quarantines and defenses against the virus over time, with Singapore's example prominent in the region: high levels of vaccinations, extensive public health education, and then gradual relaxations of controls. But throughout the summer, there seemed to be no preparation at all for how to relax the zero-COVID policies. The rest of the world was opening up following the pandemic. China and Hong Kong still had lengthy inbound quarantines and extensive travel restrictions.

As the summer turned to fall, Xi Jinping personally defended zero-COVID policies in a July Politburo statement, arguing, "We should put the people and human life above all else, work to prevent both inbound cases and domestic resurgences and uphold a dynamic zero-COVID policy. Immediate responses and strict measures should be adopted once an epidemic outbreak occurs, so as to ensure resolute and effective control wherever necessary. No let-up is allowed in relevant efforts."[52] Quickly, those measures were necessary again, as the virus returned in Chengdu, requiring another extensive lockdown of the city.[53] The economic consequences of more extensive lockdowns were not far behind.

The key question that emerged over the fall of 2022 was why Xi Jinping did not change course, even after hearing extensive public complaints and seeing the clear economic consequences of his policy choices. While it is impossible to know for certain what motivated Xi's thinking, the upcoming Twentieth Party Congress likely loomed large, as Xi had been preparing for a historic third term as general secretary, and to install even more of his allies in key positions. Admitting a policy mistake such as the pursuit of zero-COVID may have been seen as damaging these political efforts, despite the costs to the economy and society. When the final lineup of the new Politburo Standing Committee was announced in late October 2022, China's stock market sold off extensively and the currency remained under pressure. For Xi to be able to centralize power more thoroughly even following the economic consequences of zero-COVID was seen as a profoundly negative signal for the future of China's economy.

The end of zero-COVID in China has been well-documented. Following the deaths of several people in Xinjiang in a fire while under lockdown, there was a new wave of nationwide protests in late November 2022, with people around the country holding up blank A4-sized pieces of paper, seen as safer than attaching slogans to their discontent. In the wake of measures that were failing to control the spread of the virus that had sparked some of China's largest protests since the Tiananmen Square demonstrations in 1989, China suddenly abandoned all of its controls on the virus in a matter of days in early December 2022. The virus spread quickly across the country, and with no preparation, hospitals and other facilities were overwhelmed.[54] Independent scientific estimates suggest that around 1.4 million people likely died from the virus between December 2022 and February 2023.[55] These were exactly the consequences that zero-COVID had meant to forestall, but they happened anyway.

The lack of a plan for gradually paring back controls was indicative of the centralized nature of policymaking under Xi. To prepare a plan to end Xi's signature zero-COVID policies would have been seen as disloyal and contrary to the objectives of the Party center. Hence, the plan could only be developed once Xi had decided to end the initiative. And only the protests and the failure of the controls to stop the virus forced that decision in late November 2022. Many of the eventual consequences would have been avoidable under different public guidance, which would have provided time for additional vaccinations, for preparing hospitals, and for accumulating sufficient drugs and treatments, or for relaxing controls incrementally. A more consensus-driven or technocratic leadership might have developed additional contingency plans to exit from China's stringent controls. But a centralized leadership directed by Xi Jinping did not, as no one would have credibly believed that a shift was underway until Xi himself signaled a change. The experience of zero-COVID revealed how the concentration of political power in China had limited the flexibility of the system to correct itself as economic conditions changed.

The overall economy in 2022 officially posted 3 percent growth in real GDP. But as the next chapter will detail, this official result was difficult to understand for anyone monitoring conditions in China at the time, and the dramatic adjustments in economic activity that had occurred under lockdowns. Even within China's official data, new housing starts declined by 40 percent, cement output declined by 11 percent, land sales dropped by 53 percent, and refinery output for petroleum products fell by 3.4 percent for the full year.[56] It was difficult to see how any part of the investment portion of China's economy grew at all in 2022 in this context. While the official GDP data suggested continued growth in investment by 1.5 percentage points of GDP, unofficial data from industry-specific sources pointed to larger declines. Asphalt capacity utilization rates fell by 22 percent, unsaturated polyester resin (UPR, used in construction activity and pipes) capacity utilization rates fell by 38 percent, and the average working hours for Komatsu construction equipment fell by 14 percent.[57] In terms of household consumption, official retail sales fell by 0.2 percent, Alibaba's online sales dropped by 6.5 percent, and Chinese households placed a whopping 17.8 trillion yuan in bank deposits (around 15 percent of GDP), rather than spending those funds. The costs of China's zero-COVID policies were astronomical in economic terms and continue to impact sentiment among consumers and entrepreneurs in China to this day.

Indecision, Incrementalism, and Industry-Specific Crackdowns Return

As China relaxed its COVID-related controls on people's movement and economic activities in early 2023, it was natural to assume that the economy would rebound quickly. In other developed economies, once restrictions were lifted and the spread of the virus ebbed, there was a surge in spending to satisfy pent-up consumer demand. This did not take place in China in 2023 for several reasons. Primarily, China's economy was still under pressure from the weakening property sector, and fiscal policy was becoming less efficient in driving infrastructure investment because of rising local government debt levels. But unlike Western consumer-focused economies, Beijing had not provided additional transfers to households during the pandemic to boost incomes. So while Chinese households were eager to return to regular life and spend more, they were also nursing lower incomes and looking at weaker employment prospects. Consumer confidence measures remained low throughout 2023 and beyond.

In particular, Beijing had done very little to support the property sector, which remained China's most important industry. Land sales had declined by over 50 percent in 2022, which meant that developers were certain to have a weaker pipeline of new construction in 2023, unless Beijing intervened dramatically to support the sector. Officially, China's government targeted 5 percent GDP growth for the full year. But if the property sector continued contracting, it was difficult to see what other source of investment could offset that decline. By the summer of 2023, it had become apparent that the post-pandemic recovery was already sputtering, and China's Politburo made a subtle change in approach to the property sector, expressing concern about the imbalance between supply and demand in the market.[58]

Yet even after this change in tone, few concrete policy measures emerged to support property developers, and the sector continued to drag on the overall economy. New housing starts declined by 20 percent for the full year, marking a dramatic three-year adjustment that had shrunk the industry by more than half. Indicators of construction activity such as cement output continued declining in 2023, and retail sales of decoration and construction materials were down by almost 8 percent year-on-year.[59]

Consumer demand was anemic as well, even as it started to recover from the pandemic. Headline retail sales growth was only 7.2 percent for the full year, roughly in line with per capita household income growth of 6.3 percent.[60] At the start of 2023, financial markets had anticipated a strong bounce in Chinese consumption and were actually worried about China contributing to global inflationary pressures. By the end of the year, China's consumer price growth was only 0.2 percent and had been below zero for most of the year. Individual income tax revenues by the Ministry of Finance actually declined 1 percent for the year, indicating very limited growth in overall household income (and likely some tax evasion as well).[61] Rising confidence was not enough, and Beijing had provided little reason for consumers to become more confident. The consumer economy and services sector businesses were recovering from the pandemic, but only slowly.

On the fiscal policy side, China's options appeared more constrained than ever. Local government debt had been rising significantly throughout the years of the pandemic. It was apparent that even though more government bonds were issued each year, the actual payoff for China in terms of infrastructure investment was diminishing. Fiscal resources were also declining because of the weakness in investment-led growth, which reduced tax revenues. Even if Beijing's intention was to maintain investment-led growth in the years ahead, there needed to be a restructuring of the tax system both to reduce the burden of existing local government debt and to provide alternative financing channels for local government infrastructure projects. But a five-year financial reform conference, the National Financial Work Conference, came and went in October 2023 with no formal plans to manage China's local government debt burden. Instead, an unpublished document, Circular 35, was reported in Chinese media as offering debt relief for localities in "risky" regions of the country, along with promises to control debt within those same provinces.[62] Nothing was done to address the underlying imbalances in central–local revenue sharing and inefficiencies in investment that had created rising local government debts.

The continued slowdown in property and infrastructure investment extended China's deflationary pressures as well, particularly in producer prices. Without downstream demand from property and infrastructure construction, multiple heavy industries created industrial capacity far in excess of China's domestic needs. The net result has been falling prices within these industries, and efforts by these firms to export excess production abroad, at lower prices. China's producer prices fell outright in 2023 and 2024, a trend that continued in 2025.

Overall, China's leadership appears highly reactive and reluctant to confront China's most pressing economic problems, including slowing productivity growth, persistently weak domestic demand, deflationary pressures, weaker household consumption, and ongoing capital outflows. These issues are all byproducts of an end to China's broken growth model that depended upon a continued expansion of credit and investment. The question that now confronts analysts of China's economy is to what extent Xi Jinping acknowledges the problems in the economy, or whether he is no longer concerned with China's economic growth rate.

Following the Asian financial crisis, China's premier Zhu Rongji launched a series of dramatic adjustments to China's bureaucratic organization to make it more resilient against financial crisis, while also restructuring domestic industries to make them more compatible with requirements to join the World Trade Organization. The costs were significant in domestic employment and fiscal resources, but the decisive actions that Zhu initiated in coordination with China's economic and financial technocrats helped to catalyze both domestic and overseas confidence in China's long-term economic plans. This in turn enabled a wave of inbound investment in China and produced rapid rates of economic growth throughout the 2000s.

China's economy now needs similar structural solutions to even more pressing long-running problems that have resulted from the end of the credit-fueled investment-led growth model. But Zhu Rongji is no longer in charge, and the leadership under Xi Jinping continues to offer only incremental steps – interest rate cuts, swaps of local government debt, and salary adjustments for civil servants – that do not address the underlying constraints on Chinese growth. In his masterful analysis of Soviet debates over economic reform in the 1960s, Yakov Feygin argues that after a series of failed reforms, Soviet officials under Brezhnev made decisions that effectively *chose* economic stagnation or revealed a preference for stagnation relative to the alternatives, given the existential political costs to the Soviet state of continuing with reforms.[63] China's leaders under Xi Jinping may not be consciously or actively choosing economic stagnation at present. But in the absence of more proactive structural reforms to deal with the inefficiency of the financial system and fiscal policy tools, continued economic stagnation will be the result.

The centralization of economic policymaking under Xi Jinping created conditions in which China's bureaucracy was prone to aggressive policy moves dictated from the top leadership, rather than more incremental and tested moves that emerged from economic and financial technocrats. China's economy was already slowing because of the exhaustion of credit growth and a weakening property sector. But under these conditions, Xi Jinping's campaigns against China's technology firms, education and tutoring firms, and the enforcement of zero-COVID restrictions on people's movement amplified the economic pressure. In addition, these moves created new obstacles to recovery, damaging confidence in the private sector, among entrepreneurs, and among China's households and recent university graduates. Course correction in a centralized system requires Xi Jinping himself to lead the process, reversing or overturning some of his own past decisions, and hence it becomes more difficult to envision. Incremental adjustments or reactive moves are easier to understand in this political context, but they will merely extend the life of a fiscal and financial system that cannot produce the same rates of economic growth as in the past.

4

A Contested Story of China's Economic Future

By the autumn of 2024, China's leadership had become far more concerned about the direction of China's economy and was starting to take action. Xi Jinping visited far western Gansu province in early September and reportedly became alarmed about the extent of the economic slowdown and the debt pressures on local governments, telling officials there to "strive to fulfill economic and social development goals" for the year.[1] On September 23, 2024, the central bank, the banking regulator, and the securities regulator held a highly unusual joint press conference announcing cuts to interest rates and the amount of cash banks needed to hold in reserve at the central bank, along with new tools involving hundreds of billions of yuan to support China's equity market. Other ministries held their own press conferences in the following weeks to pledge policy support. In a sign of the level of concern for a system regulated by a strict party-guided calendar, the Politburo held an unusual economic meeting in October, and then in their regular December meeting statement, they pledged "extraordinary" measures to support the economy, while changing the formal monetary policy stance to "appropriately easing" for the first time since the global financial crisis.[2] Additional policy support included a 10-trillion-yuan ($1.3 trillion) swap of local government debt for lower-interest government bonds and an extremely rare retroactive salary hike for civil servants in late December 2024.[3] This followed the expansion of subsidy programs where consumers could trade in home appliances and automobiles for new products, amidst slowing consumption and auto sales. This was a strong flurry of economic stimulus late in 2024.

But looking at China's official economic data, the panic among China's leadership that year seemed extremely odd. After all, the National Bureau of Statistics (NBS) reported that real GDP growth in 2024 had been perfectly in line with the government's targeted level of 5 percent, following 5.2 percent growth in 2023. This raised two possibilities: either China's leaders were dramatically misjudging economic conditions in late 2024, or China's official GDP data were simply inaccurate.

China's economic data and how they are presented and analyzed are important because they inform two entirely different and conflicting views of China's economic future. Beijing's official narrative of China's future emphasizes that the economy remains on a glide path toward slower growth, but that China will continue to produce world-leading growth rates that are consistent with a "great rejuvenation" of China's prospects and will eventually power China to global economic primacy, overtaking the United States as the world's largest economy. In this narrative, China can manage the problems of the older growth model, phase out lower-productivity lending and activity, and mitigate the effects of structural imbalances. How? Advanced manufacturing, artificial intelligence, robotics, green technologies, and other innovations will help to deliver the necessary productivity growth to escape the middle-income trap.

In Beijing's preferred narrative, China's economic growth slowed from around 10 percent per year in the 2000s to 7 percent per year in the 2010s and will likely remain around 5 percent per year in the 2020s. The COVID-19 pandemic and related controls on people's movement provided temporary disruptions, but China's economy has generally returned to its pre-pandemic glide path. Moreover, China's demonstrated track record of state control over critical levers of its economy provides confidence that Chinese authorities are not only aware of the critical economic headwinds but still have the capacity to manage them.

There are also several alternative views of China's economic future, which are still informed directly by China's official economic data and financial reporting. These narratives, such as the argument of this book outlined in chapter 2, focus on the costs generated by China's past patterns of economic growth, relative to the potential from new growth drivers. And because those costs are much higher than what has been acknowledged, China's economic slowdown is structural in nature, with the economy likely to decline in size and influence relative to the rest of the world. The data that highlight China's structural constraints are still official data, published by China's financial authorities, in addition to series produced by China's statistics bureau. But they require looking beyond headline real GDP growth, and usually China's fixed asset investment growth statistics as well. In this narrative, the decline of nominal GDP growth is far more significant than the stability in real GDP growth, as China has missed its implicit nominal GDP growth targets by wide margins in recent years. Nominal growth and not real growth is necessary for China to manage its growing debt problems and to maintain corporate profitability. Declining producer prices and weakening consumer price growth point to the inefficiencies of an economy structured around unproductive investment relative to domestic demand. More capacity and output without enough demand to absorb it continues to produce lower and lower prices, and the need to find markets abroad for excess production. Those same pressures reduce incentives for new investment by private firms. The constraints of the inefficient and state-directed financial system will prevent a redirection of credit flows toward more productive firms and new growth drivers.

These are two starkly conflicting views of China's economic future. Beijing has clear political incentives to propagate its official narrative relative to the alternatives predicting China's structural economic decline. In the Central Economic Work Conference statement in 2023, Beijing pledged to "strengthen economic propaganda and public opinion guidance and sound a bright view of the Chinese economy."[4] The official economic narrative serves both internal and external political purposes for the Communist Party. Internally, it reinforces support among both the public and Party cadres that the Party's governance can continue to deliver improving standards of living, a brighter economic future, and national glory. Stability in growth rates also points to the Party's capabilities in economic management. Externally, the message of China's inexorable rise is an anchoring tenet of China's diplomacy, encouraging economic engagement with China among developing countries, while strengthening China's negotiating positions in international institutions and justifying Beijing's claims for a larger role and a more powerful voice. In this context, the ways in which China's economic data are presented publicly and the choices of which data series to highlight have become significant political priorities for Beijing. If something is truly wrong with the Chinese economy, Beijing has clear incentives to minimize those perceptions, both at home and overseas.

This chapter will explain why global views of China's economy remain highly contested, despite the recent collapse in China's property sector and rapidly widening trade imbalances pointing to weaker domestic demand. At its core, the debate over China's economic future is a battle over the credibility of Beijing's political narrative of China's inexorable economic rise. This chapter argues:

- There are clear problems with China's official economic data as reported over the past decade, but particularly within the years 2022 to 2024. At times over the past decade, China's economic growth rates were far too stable to be credible, but at present, they are far too high to be credible.
- While China's headline economic data are highly problematic, there is no objective or comprehensive alternative set of indicators that can clearly contest the official data series. As a result, discussions of the past and future of China's economy become competitions of narratives, anchored by different selections of data.
- Beijing has strong political incentives to maintain its own preferred narrative, emphasizing China's ongoing economic dynamism, the benefits of the Party's governance, and the Party's capacity to control and manage any structural problems.
- China also has an interest in obscuring certain data series that contradict its narrative, to prevent alternative views of China's actual economic performance from gaining salience.
- Beijing's primary tools to promote its economic narrative are its own internal and external propaganda apparatus, along with the "authority bias" of international institutions to accept official economic data in good faith.
- China's effort to reach unrealistically high economic growth targets will ultimately fail or the commitment to these goals will reverse. Beijing's objectives are likely being dictated by political imperatives tied to strategic competition between the United States and China.

The Case Against (Some) Chinese Economic Data

Disputes about China's economic data have existed for years. The famed China scholar Lucian Pye claimed that, in 1974, he asked Deng Xiaoping personally about China's population level, and Deng replied that the data were unknown within the Party, because local officials reporting these levels made deliberate errors in conflicting directions, with some thinking that higher totals would result in additional subsidies, and others thinking that they may be forced to pay additional taxes to Beijing. Pye claimed, "So according to Deng it was best not to take any government statistics seriously" and that the Party set policy with a certain degree of guesswork involved.[5] In 1995, Zhang Sai of the National Bureau of Statistics warned about "false and deceptive reporting" of statistics, creating widespread discussion of a "wind of falsification and embellishment" of official data.[6] In the 1990s, even during the years of China's economic reform, the NBS would often implausibly publish GDP data the day before the quarter or year covered by the data had ended.[7] More recently, in 2001 Thomas Rawski raised realistic concerns about the extent of China's economic slowdown during the Asian financial crisis, pointing out the disconnect between China's electricity output and official economic growth rates.[8]

In early 2009, the global economy was reeling from the effects of the financial crisis sparked by defaults in US subprime mortgages. China was similarly feeling the effects of the crisis via weaker exports but had pledged a world-leading economic stimulus package in response, and China's leaders were still officially targeting an extremely high economic growth rate, at 8 percent real GDP growth for the year. Premier Wen Jiabao had defended the aggressive target as necessary to maintain confidence in China's economy.[9] At a lunch that spring, I asked an official who had previously worked in an economic staff role for the Party's Central Committee why the growth target needed to be so strong, at 8 percent. My argument to him was that even if China's potential growth rate at the time was as high as 8 to 9 percent, China had just come from a dramatic surge in economic growth to 14 percent in 2007. Given there was weaker global demand the year following the financial crisis and China remained an export-led economy, shouldn't the leadership target something more conservative, like 5 to 6 percent? After all, the world would still view China's recovery as powering the world out of recession via policy-led stimulus, and a lower growth rate might prevent the rapid credit expansion and excess investment that might fuel financial bubbles down the line (as eventually occurred). The official nodded to me, and said, "I completely agree with you. But if we publish 5 percent, everyone will think it is actually zero."[10] Throughout my fourteen years living in

Beijing and over two decades speaking with Chinese officials about the economy, not a single one would defend the official GDP growth rates in private conversation. Some argued that they were roughly accurate, in a similar fashion to Deng Xiaoping's guidance to Lucian Pye, but probably still involved a certain degree of "smoothing."

China produces thousands of macroeconomic data series. Not all are published by the NBS directly. Some come from financial regulators, the central bank, the Ministry of Finance, or other ministries. Over the past two decades, the NBS has made significant changes to its methodologies in calculating key economic indicators, introduced new economic data series, and retired others. Moreover, the NBS has made meaningful improvements in its methods and brought them more in line with international standards. In 1993, the NBS moved away from the Soviet Material Production System (MPS) toward the usage of the internationally standard System of National Accounts (SNA) in calculating GDP.[11] In 2004, China started conducting a quinquennial national economic census, in line with most international practices. China also pledged to comply with the IMF's Special Data Dissemination Standard (SDDS) starting in October 2015.[12] There are still very meaningful gaps between the data series that China produces and those that are available in developed economies, particularly in terms of the actual levels of key statistics such as industrial value-added, which corresponds closely with China's GDP statistics. Even as those gaps remain, it is simply inaccurate to claim that the official *methods* of China's statistical agencies are far outside of global norms and practices.

With those important caveats, the *results* that emerge from China's statistical authorities raise clear questions about whether those official methods are actually used consistently at the NBS. The case against the accuracy of China's official statistics is clearest and most convincing when analyzing the highest-profile economic indicators, particularly GDP and GDP growth. But there are also concerns about fixed asset investment, industrial value-added, and retail sales, which are the monthly NBS data series most commonly used by economic analysts to assess the short-term direction of China's economy.

For China's real GDP growth, there are two trends that are difficult to reconcile with the vast majority of the economic data series that China produces, as well as Beijing's policy signals. The first anomaly is the

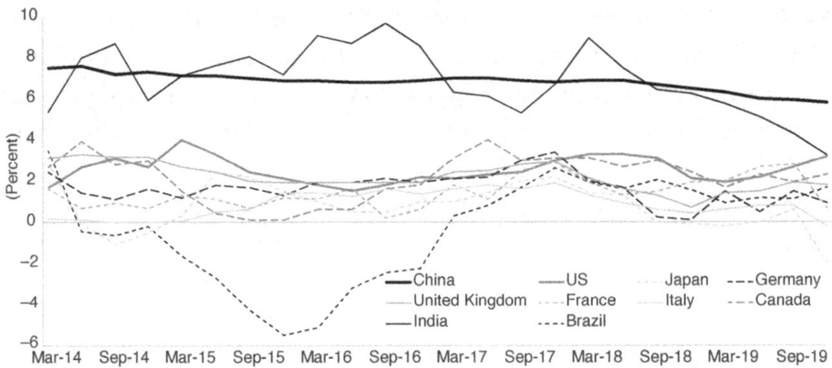

Figure 4.1 Reported quarterly GDP growth, top 10 global economies, 2014–2019.

Data source: World Bank.

extraordinary stability of China's headline real GDP growth rates from 2014 to 2019. Real year-on-year GDP growth over the twenty-four quarters during those six years never varied outside of a range from 5.8 percent to 7.4 percent. That is an extraordinarily narrow corridor for an emerging economy, particularly one that relies so heavily upon exports, and therefore upon parts of the global economy where Chinese policy has little influence. Emerging market economies typically show *higher* levels of volatility in growth rates relative to more developed economies, particularly those economies that rely upon exports. Looking back through all GDP growth rates for the twenty largest economies in the world over a period longer than thirty years, there is no other country that showed the same stability in headline GDP growth rates over a six-year interval relative to what China posted in its official data from 2014 to 2019.

In comparison to other countries, this pattern of stability is remarkable. Once you understand the dramatic actual changes in China's economic performance during the same timeframe, this degree of stability in GDP growth is incredible in the literal sense. In 2014, the property market experienced a severe correction, as the shadow banking system was curtailed and construction growth slowed, impacting global commodity prices significantly. In commodity markets, the term "supercycle" referred largely to China's extraordinary demand during the late 2000s and then its collapse in the mid-2010s. Iron ore prices, for example, a key component of steel for the Chinese property sector, fell from close to

$140 per ton in early 2014 to below $40 per ton in only two years.[13] In 2015, China experienced a dramatic stock market boom and bust, and a shock depreciation of the currency in August, touching off significant capital outflows from China and fears of China exporting deflationary pressures. The central bank cut interest rates and banks' reserve requirements several times in response. In 2016, China fought deflationary pressures and excess capacity in the steel industry in particular, consolidating firms within the industry and reducing output, while the property market recovered and supported rising producer prices and a cyclical recovery. In 2017, in the course of China's deleveraging campaign, the central bank guided short-term interest rates higher to squeeze leveraged positions taken by non-bank financial institutions. By 2018, the impact of the deleveraging campaign had significantly slowed credit and industrial output, forcing China to reduce interest rates to manage the consequences of slowing credit growth. These were all dramatic changes in domestic economic conditions, in both directions, but they produced virtually no impact on China's official headline GDP growth rates at all (figure 4.1).

Chinese officials also spoke about the economy's significant changes at official press conferences, discussing economic conditions in 2014 and 2018 in very different terms. Tracking all of the terms to discuss the economy used by Chinese officials during these official NBS press availabilities, the use of negatively toned words and phrases and positively toned phrases varies considerably, peaking at over forty instances of negative phrases in 2014 and 2015 and then reaching over thirty once again in 2018 and early 2019. In 2016 and 2017, by comparison, the use of any negatively toned words and phrases in NBS press conferences dropped to fewer than ten instances.[14]

In addition, simple averages of the seasonally adjusted growth rates of the 103 industrial output series that the NBS reports for individual products suggest significant changes in China's industrial activities over these six years, with growth rates from positive 11 percent (in early 2017) to negative 7 percent (in late 2018) over this interval.[15] All of this evidence suggests that there was a regular business cycle operating in China during those six years from 2014 to 2019, with considerable changes in overall industrial output, even though the headline GDP data revealed almost no changes at all.

The second major anomaly occurred starting in 2022, when China's extensive zero-COVID restrictions were imposed on large proportions of the population at some point during the year. Despite the draconian restrictions on everyday economic activity and the impact on the services sector in particular, China still officially reported real GDP growth of 3 percent in 2022, with growth in both consumption and investment activity. For China, this was officially a weak result for overall economic growth, but it was far too optimistic given that year included the worst moments for China's all-important property sector, with new housing starts falling by 40 percent, making any overall improvement in investment growth highly improbable.

The more accurate description of China's economy in 2022 was an outright decline in growth or a recession. Many of China's official data concerning individual industries in the economy point to the same conclusion in 2022:

- China's new property construction activity fell by 40 percent for the year, and then a further 20 percent in 2023. Sales of land declined by 53 percent in 2022. Data covering national land sales were subsequently discontinued.
- Cement production dropped by 11 percent, while steel output fell by 2 percent.
- Independently reported data on the average hours worked on construction equipment from the Japanese firm Komatsu showed a 14 percent decline in implied construction activity nationwide.
- China's official NBS household survey showed that per capita consumption fell by 0.2 percent overall and by 1.7 percent in urban areas.
- Official retail sales growth, the most commonly used high-frequency indicator of household consumption, fell by 0.2 percent.
- Alibaba's online sales via Taobao and Tmall, its primary e-commerce platforms, fell by 6.5 percent for the year, and these online sales alone were around 17 percent of total retail sales in China.
- Households continued paying down mortgage loans and saving money, rather than spending more, as household deposits rose by 17 percent, with new deposits totaling 15 percent of GDP.
- Official consumer confidence surveys hit all-time lows in 2022, with only limited recoveries since that time.

Obviously, this is only a small selection of economic indicators in 2022. But if the actual output of critical industrial materials such as steel and cement fell as official indicators of consumption also declined, it raises pertinent questions about what parts of the economy were actually growing at all during the year.

The discrepancies continued in 2023. Following the end of COVID restrictions early that year, most analysts had expected a strong bounce in the economy. Yet because China had provided no direct stimulus to households during the pandemic restrictions, there was only a tiny surge in pent-up consumer spending after controls were lifted. The NBS tried to flatter early-year data on household consumption by changing the data for the previous year, making 2023 growth rates look stronger. The property market continued its adjustment, and overall investment growth slowed, with nothing else large enough to offset the impact of slowing property construction. By the summer, Chinese officials were contemplating an unprecedented mid-year budget revision in order to provide additional fiscal support for the economy, and eventually delivered it in October.

Yet, for the full year in 2023, official GDP growth powered ahead by 5.2 percent, in line with targets set at the beginning of the year. The same performance occurred in 2024, even as credit growth dropped to all-time lows and Chinese authorities pledged "extraordinary" support for the economy, while the central bank launched its own quantitative easing (QE) programs to purchase government bonds, matching those of major economies following the global financial crisis. None of these policy measures made any sense if China was actually meeting or exceeding its targeted economic growth rates.

There are far more detailed analyses of China's macroeconomic statistics available in the academic literature, and there are some notable defenses of the data as well.[16] Wei Chen and co-authors noted in 2019 the increasing disconnect between local output statistics and the national aggregate GDP calculations, pointing out the incentives for local government distortions of the data.[17] William Barcelona and co-authors argued in 2022 that China's GDP data had become far too smooth to explain China's clear impact on global economic conditions.[18] Scott Kennedy and Maya Mei conducted an extensive review of the multiple critiques of China's GDP data, and argued for a more expansive approach to analyzing China's economy, stretching beyond the official data, given its limitations and the widespread concerns about smoothing of growth rates.[19] John Fernald and co-authors used import data from third countries to highlight changes in China's cyclical activity and found that while many of China's economic indicators do track cyclical changes, GDP generally does not (although by 2019 they noted it was starting to improve).[20]

But since the slowdown in China's economy in 2022 and the collapse of China's property sector, there has been far weaker official defense of the data and far more direct criticism. The property sector was China's most important industry, representing around 23 to 27 percent of China's GDP during its peak years.[21] As overall new construction activity has fallen by 69 percent from June 2021 to the end of 2024, it is difficult to argue that this could occur while the contribution of investment to China's GDP and real GDP growth every year remained almost unchanged from levels before the property sector's correction. If China's most important industry collapsed, this should be apparent within China's macroeconomic data, particularly concerning investment.

Economist Gao Shanwen was reportedly reprimanded by Chinese authorities in December 2024 when he argued publicly on a trip to Washington that economic growth was likely around 3 percentage points below official levels from 2022 to 2024.[22] At this point, global policymakers, investors, companies, and even Chinese officials themselves knew that there was something fundamentally wrong with China's headline economic data and growth rates. *The Washington Post* titled an editorial on January 26, 2025, "China Says its Economy Grew 5 Percent Last Year. It Probably Didn't."[23] *The Wall Street Journal* also conducted an extensive review of China's 2023 economic data, entitling an article in March 2024, "Why You Shouldn't Trust China's Growth Data."[24] The inaccuracies in China's economic data raise important questions, notably concerning how much slower China's economy has performed relative to the official figures. But the critique of the official data alone is unsatisfying, particularly in the absence of a defensible and comprehensive set of economic indicators.

China's Postmodern Economics

Despite clear problems with China's economic data, the narrative of China's inexorable economic rise has considerable staying power in global policy circles and financial markets. The problem with criticizing China's economic data, and real GDP data in particular, is that there is no independent secondary measure of China's economic performance that can serve as a readily available and credible alternative to the macroeconomic data published by the NBS. But the absence of a clear alternative dataset has also generated a cottage industry of secondary indicators of Chinese activity, underlining the high demand for a different view into China's economy. This insight is widely understood in popular culture as well. A subplot in one episode of the show *Billions* involves hedge fund traders arguing over whether China was deliberately manipulating satellite photos of a microchip factory in order to change Western perceptions of the company's growth.[25] Industry experts can produce alternative metrics of China's economic output in particular industries. Certain industrial output series such as steel, cement, or electricity output can be used as alternative proxies for overall economic activity, while measures such as rail freight volumes take logistical activity as a proxy for the economy. Famously, former premier Li Keqiang argued in a conversation with an American diplomat that he preferred to use credit growth, rail freight, and electricity output in order to assess economic activity, rather than the official GDP series, and these indicators have been dubbed the "Li Keqiang Index."[26] Other alternative methods include monitoring nighttime electric light usage at factories via satellite photographs in order to estimate total industrial activity, and in some cases these produce stronger indications of growth than the official data.[27] Measuring online receipts at certain groups of restaurants or online sales even among large platform companies such as Alibaba can provide some insight into the behavior of Chinese consumers.

All of these alternative measures have their own limitations, and they cannot be easily combined into a measure of the economy as a whole. Even if one had nearly perfect industry-level data coverage of most of China's industrial and consumer activity, such a measure of China's GDP would still fall short of the immense amount of data needed to assemble the sets of tables required by internationally standard SNA accounting. There remain few substitutes for the survey-based measures of output, investment, and sales that the NBS conducts nationwide, and there are few ways to replicate China's economic census process. As a result, any alternative measure of China's GDP will always be contrasted with the official NBS data and will generally appear unsatisfying. No alternative measure can eventually be proven "correct" when it produces a growth rate different from China's official statistics, as no one else has a secondary, objective measure of China's overall economic output. The closest to validation of alternative measures of economic growth like Gao Shanwen's estimates would be for the official data series to eventually be revised in line with those estimates. But in the current political climate in China, that is highly improbable.

Moreover, there is no clear evidence that there is a "second set of books" or an internally held series of macroeconomic data that China's leaders use to guide economic policy choices. The effort involved in the NBS's calculation and presentation of the headline economic data is considerable and not easily replicated. It is plausible that China's leadership has access to different types of economic survey data or different data series that are not released publicly, such as those concerning rural income levels, urban unemployment, or consumer confidence. But when it comes to the official GDP, fixed asset investment, retail sales, and industrial value-added data series, China's leaders are almost certainly using the same data series as those available to the public in order to make policy decisions. The results of GDP data are either manipulated or smoothed, but it is also difficult to identify the precise moment in the custodial chain of data at which the NBS conducts the smoothing or manipulation. Secondary data series only available internally are not likely to be the source of discrepancies in official GDP growth rates.

This discussion also raises the broader question of why alternative measures of economic activity would aim to replicate GDP growth specifically, rather than any other economic indicator. British economist Charles Goodhart is often credited with a withering critique of political manipulation of economic data, arguing that once an economic indicator becomes a political target, its utility as a measure of economic activity will decline. Goodhart argued, "Any observed statistical regularity will tend to collapse once pressure is placed upon it for control purposes."[28] GDP was a measure constructed by the United States and Britain to measure economic output during wartime and the capacity of an economy to sustain a war. It is a measure of a particular set of economic variables, heavily focused on industrial output, and the capacity of statistical authorities to measure changes in those variables. China may be erring in calculating its GDP, but it is clearly selecting GDP growth as a political target. At the same time, GDP itself may also be an outdated measure of a modern economy. Compromises are always made in selecting units of measurement in order to make appropriate cross-country comparisons, which is one reason that GDP became so widely used when the SNA system was established as an international standard.[29] But there are clearly legitimate concerns about the usage of a single set of economic metrics to gauge both a heavily services-oriented economy such as the United States and a heavily industrial and manufacturing-focused economy such as China.

The critique of China's economic data quickly leads down the path of an almost "postmodern" economics, with reference to the philosophical movement in which the position of the observer of any text or fact is highly salient in the presentation of that text or argument. In this framework, independent knowledge of reality cannot exist without considering its source or its presentation. For China's economy, an official set of economic data that is losing credibility and the absence of a credible alternative dataset explain the emergence of the competing economic narratives of China's economic future described earlier in this chapter. How one views both China's economic past and therefore the implications for Beijing's future choices depends upon the credibility of the narrative being chosen and the source presenting that narrative.

In the case of the current divergence between Beijing's preferred interpretation of its economic trajectory and the alternative view that a structural slowdown is underway, the credibility of the official narrative becomes vitally important for assessing an appropriate policy response. If Chinese authorities actually believe their own portrayal of the economy's performance, then presumably very little needs to be done to maintain economic growth in the years ahead. This would suggest that the actions Beijing has taken over the past year – cuts to interest rates and banks' required reserves, restructuring local government debt, a mid-year budget adjustment, new subsidy programs for consumers, retroactive pay hikes for civil servants, quantitative easing by China's central bank – were not necessary to stabilize the economy. But because Beijing has actually done all of these things and reacted as if the economy is facing a meaningful correction, their actions make the narrative of China's broader economic slowdown more credible in comparison, even if the official economic data do not support it.

Most importantly, as China's official economic data have become less credible, observers have had to search for an alternative explanation or theory of what is actually happening in China's economy, and not just a better set of economic indicators. A credit and financial system-focused explanation coherently links the slowdown in China's economy to weakness in the property sector and local government infrastructure investment, which are in turn linked to the end of China's unprecedented credit expansion after the global financial crisis. The credibility of these competing narratives depends upon the explanations behind them. It is less credible for Beijing to argue that newer growth drivers will replace the property sector and local government infrastructure spending, when those new growth drivers are much smaller as a proportion of the economy than the old ones. Beijing needs the world to believe its official data, but also the logic behind it and the explanations for economic growth.

It is impossible to know how Xi Jinping himself interprets the accuracy of China's economic data but judging from the years of Chinese officials' skepticism of GDP growth rates, China's leaders probably know that their data are overstating economic growth but are probably unsure of the extent of that overstatement, similar to how Deng Xiaoping reportedly viewed China's population statistics. Policy support for the economy since late 2023 seems to indicate that officials are aware of weak investment activity and consumer spending since the property sector's collapse and are increasingly concerned about building deflationary pressure. Occasionally, these facts leap out at China's leaders, as they seemingly did on Xi Jinping's inspection tour in Gansu province in September 2024. The leadership now seems to be taking significant actions to at least mitigate the effects of a structural slowdown in China's economy. But acknowledging this economic weakness publicly is an entirely different matter.

The Political Drivers of China's Economic Narrative

The most important question raised by potential Chinese data quality issues is why China would systematically manipulate the reporting of its economic data, given that this would clearly complicate economic policy-making and produce poorer decisions. The extent of China's data quality problem is still debatable, but the underlying causes of its data quality issues are easier to understand. The Chinese Communist Party sees a high and stable rate of published economic growth in China as consistent with their political interests, both inside and outside China. Ever since the death of Mao, delivering improving economic performance has been considered one of the most important sources of the Party's legitimacy. The stability of China's economic growth rates demonstrates the stability provided by the Party's rule, while high rates of economic growth reinforce China's growing international economic clout, allow China's leadership to point to rising standards of living for Chinese citizens, and raise confidence in larger objectives such as China's "great rejuvenation." Communist Party rule is meant to imply a high degree of perceived stability, even if it comes at the expense of economic efficiency.

Nor is China the only country to face the same political incentives. In an extensive cross-country analysis of reported politically motivated data manipulations, Roberto Aragao and Lukas Linsi argued that there are several reasons for national statistical authorities to manipulate economic data for political purposes, and different methods they can use to do so.[30] These statistical manipulations have been alleged in controversies over Greece's fiscal data or Argentina's inflation. What appears different about China's political incentives is the close linkage between economic performance and the Chinese Communist Party's political legitimacy. In 2015, India engaged in a widespread data reclassification and revision of its methodology that resulted in significant adjustments to the level of GDP and past GDP growth rates. Discussion was heated in technocratic circles, with several accusations that the government was manipulating the data for political purposes.[31] But the political legitimacy of the Indian government probably does not rest upon the differences between GDP data before and after revisions, while an alternative interpretation of China's economic trajectory would suggest that many of China's long-term political objectives are in jeopardy.[32]

There are multiple audiences for the message of China's inexorable economic rise. For foreign companies, the narrative of China's improving long-term economic prospects has anchored billions of dollars of foreign investment into China over the past three decades, despite the difficulties of operating in China's markets. Joe Studwell's *The China Dream* highlighted how the prospect of the world's largest population eventually becoming consumers with comparable levels of spending power to those in the West inspired hundreds of multinational businesses to enter the Chinese market and endure losses for years in the hopes of eventually gaining sufficient market share.[33] Companies were willing to take risks in China that they would not take in other markets simply because of China itself, and because their competitors were doing so. Nobel-winning economist Robert Schiller has explained how these types of persistent economic narratives alone can move markets, change investment patterns, and help investors and companies to organize incoming data.[34] At present, Beijing is threatened by the developing economic narrative of "decoupling" or "de-risking" from China, as the popularity of the narrative itself can aggravate China's economic problems. The discussion of rising risks from sourcing products within China can independently shape corporate decisions to seek market opportunities elsewhere or move investment into different countries to pursue alternatives to China within global supply chains.

In communicating China's inexorable economic rise to foreign governments, the Party seeks to improve China's external economic influence, the willingness of other countries to engage with China and receive inbound investments, and to improve China's position within international organizations and in negotiations. Far better to negotiate a good deal with Beijing now than to wait when the country is even more powerful and capable. If China's economy was likely to slow over the following decade, developing countries might think twice about accepting investments from Chinese firms that may struggle to implement them.

Beijing also benefits internally by communicating that China is producing rapid economic growth rates. For the domestic economy, Chinese investors and entrepreneurs are more likely to deploy capital in an economy with positive long-term prospects. Chinese citizens are more likely to spend more money now if they believe that living standards and incomes will continue to improve in the future. The idea that Chinese incomes would continue rising was one of the anchoring assumptions behind China's two-decade property market boom. In a domestic political context, stronger economic growth rates reinforce internal loyalty to the Communist Party. When the official with whom I spoke in 2009 about China's economic statistics said that "everyone" would know that a published growth rate of 5 percent was probably closer to zero, he was not referring to foreigners but to officials within the Party-state, and the problems that might result if cadres became more concerned about China's weakening economic trajectory. A Party that is achieving its economic objectives and capable of deploying more resources will have an easier time maintaining loyalty among its members.

As a result of this, the Party is also highly responsive to alternative perspectives on China's economy. Reprimanding Gao Shanwen for his public criticism of the GDP growth rates fits a larger pattern over the past several years of criticizing Chinese economists who question the official data. When economist Hong Hao started to discuss the catastrophic effects of COVID-19 restrictions on China's economy and foreign investment in China's stock market in 2022, his social media accounts were suspended.[35] When onshore market analysts started discussing China's building deflationary pressures and the resulting slowdown in economic growth in 2023, Chinese authorities instructed economists not to discuss these trends publicly or on social media.[36] Prominent economics analyst Wu Xiaobo was censored for having "hyped up the unemployment rate" in 2023.[37] Usually this pressure is directly focused on any skepticism of China's headline economic growth rates themselves, since these are among the most prominent claims in media. As a result, a type of coded language about the economy has developed in WeChat rooms among traders and investors, with euphemistic terms for some of China's most pressing problems. Notably, censorship of negative views about the economy online increased markedly in late 2023, even when headline data were reporting that China was meeting its economic growth targets.[38]

Chinese authorities also take aim at "theories" of China's economic decline and use state media and similar channels to criticize these approaches. Minxin Pei argues that there has been a state media campaign to criticize the "theory of peak China" since March 2024, after Xi Jinping made a speech criticizing the concept directly.[39] These campaigns usually feature accusations against Western proponents of these theories for "ulterior motives," and usually frame the criticism in terms of strategic competition between China and the United States.

The usage of these state media channels reinforces the point that even as Chinese leaders and economists openly discuss the importance of rebalancing the economy and shifting toward "higher quality" growth rather than focusing on the quantity of growth, it is still vitally important to the Party that China is seen as rising economically. The pace of GDP growth still matters to Beijing. The narrative of China's inexorable economic rise benefits the Communist Party both within domestic politics and in its external economic and political relationships. Critics of China's official data are silenced domestically, and China's problematic official economic data still receive prominent placement in state media. Debating and defending the quality of its economic data is one part of China's approach. But Beijing has also simply stopped publishing economic indicators it finds unhelpful to its preferred vision.

Thickening the Fog

China continues to publish thousands of economic data series every year from multiple ministries and institutions. Revisions are common, and new series are launched while old ones are discontinued. In this context, it may seem odd to suggest that China is deliberately obscuring its economic data in the service of a particular narrative. Any changes that China actually makes to official data reporting would usually be portrayed as part of an ongoing process to improve the accuracy and frequency of economic indicators. But there is also a growing body of evidence to suggest that Beijing intends to obscure alternative indicators of growth, leaving only the official data series as authoritative. This extends even to influence over lower-level economic data series that only economists and professional analysts would use. The *Financial Times* conducted a preliminary analysis of all official data series published on the government statistical service via the China Economic Information Center (CEIC), including those published by municipal or provincial authorities, and found a dramatic decline in the sheer number of data series published during the Xi era, with the total falling by more than half.[40]

These changes to data reporting can generally be categorized into four types. First, the straightforward removal or suspension of specific data series, which usually follows their publication in international media. Second, revisions in the calculation methods of existing data series – either announced or unannounced – that are usually designed to change political perceptions of the series. Third, revisions to data in previous years intended to flatter the headline growth rates of current-year indicators in year-on-year terms. And finally, new restrictions on the cross-border transfers of certain economic data series, or of their publication for foreign audiences. All of these have combined to make the data published by China less accessible to external analysts, leaving the majority of the remaining series pointing toward Beijing's official narrative of the economy.

In recent years, several economic data series have simply been discontinued. Usually this would follow some unflattering headlines anchored around certain data points. The prime example in recent years was China's youth unemployment rate, which was regularly showing jobless rates above 20 percent throughout the pandemic and the post-pandemic recovery. Even though there were notable problems with the series itself – it tended to focus on SOEs and undercount employment within the private sector – and those could have been explained publicly, China simply discontinued the publication of the series in August 2023, sparking broader concerns about data transparency.[41] Similarly, amidst the stock market's difficulties in 2024, China suddenly stopped publishing daily volumes of foreign trading in Chinese markets and Chinese trading in Hong Kong markets via the official Stock Connect program (while still reporting some of the monthly totals after the fact).[42] This was thought to be done to obscure the level of capital outflows from China at the time. During the height of China's property market correction, the government stopped publishing national data concerning land sales.[43]

When data are used to assemble alternative indicators and those indicators are released publicly, the result can often be the discontinuation of individual series. One regional economist for a major investment bank once told me that every time his team used a different set of indicators in their alternative proxy for China's economic activity, one or more of the indicators they used was suspended a month or two later. Suspensions can also occur for reasons that are only tangentially related to macroeconomic performance. China stopped reporting certain data on renewable energy generation in the summer of 2024 after it had posted declines.[44] Similarly, China's major state-owned power plants stopped releasing data on daily coal usage in 2020.[45] The removals of these series were generally thought to mitigate inconvenient headlines related to China's efforts to meet energy efficiency and carbon emissions targets.

The second type of data adjustment is a revision in calculation methodology that is usually designed to change the perception or implications of the data series. This has been done with some of China's credit aggregates in recent years, with the total social financing (TSF) or "aggregate financing to the real economy" (AFRE) statistics revised several times between 2018 and 2019, usually to include new components. The net effect of these revisions was to boost headline credit growth at the time of China's deleveraging campaign, which was severely restricting overall credit growth in the country. Other series such as China's monetary aggregates have been recently reclassified as well, with the M1 measure, which had been declining in recent years, suddenly revised to include household demand deposits in December 2024.[46] The revision can be seen as aligned with international practice, but no explanation was given as to the timing of the move, despite ongoing declines in M1 growth, which suggested weaker corporate demand for credit, particularly in the private sector.

In addition, Chinese statistical authorities often make unannounced changes in data from previous years, presumably in order to flatter current year-on-year growth rates.[47] In the first quarter of 2023, for example, Chinese authorities reported a remarkably strong rate of GDP growth for a quarter in which the COVID pandemic was still raging through China, at 4.5 percent year-on-year and 2.2 percent in quarter-on-quarter terms. However, most of the outperformance of China's economy was related to revising down the level of GDP in the first quarter of the previous year and revising up quarter-on-quarter growth in the last quarter of 2022 from zero to 0.6 percent. The latter revision seemed particularly improbable given that this was one of the worst periods of COVID-related lockdowns, along with nationwide protests against these controls, and it was highly unlikely that the economy had expanded at all on a sequential basis.

Similar revisions to China's retail sales statistics took place in the first quarter of 2023. China officially reported a strong rate of consumption growth at 10.6 percent in year-on-year terms. But China's March sequential growth rate was extremely low, at only 0.15 percent. A closer analysis of the data revealed that the outperformance of China's headline consumption data was the result of revisions to the previous year's month-on-month growth rates, which were then adjusted twice more in 2023.[48] However, almost no analysts commented on these revisions or their impact on the corresponding headline figures, as they were unannounced. Another statistical quirk that can produce unexpected data revisions are changes in the samples of different data series. For example, year-on-year growth rates in industrial profits should be calculated based on roughly the same sample of firms from one year to the next. But in China's system, a firm that falls below a certain threshold of revenue no longer qualifies for the sample. As a result, changes in year-on-year growth rates are often not measuring data in a like-for-like fashion. In reality, this can produce errors in both directions.

The last category of data management has been the restriction of certain data series from leaving China's borders or only offering them to domestic rather than foreign researchers. As data have become a more significant focus of China's national security, these changes may be expected. At the same time, the restrictions on data series are highly unusual. WIND, the Chinese financial information services provider, reduced its offshore customers' access to particular data series in 2023.[49] Similarly, some of China's academic databases, such as China National Knowledge Infrastructure (CNKI), started restricting access to foreign researchers in 2022.[50]

All of these changes make objective analysis of China's economy far more difficult for external observers, and the absence of credible alternative indicators complicates the task for analysts crafting a competing narrative of China's economic trends. While data revisions are extremely common throughout the economics profession, China appears to be engaging in practices that deliberately obscure unwelcome economic indicators or data series. But these persistent data revisions and omissions similarly weaken the credibility of the official narrative of China's inexorable rise.

"Authority Bias" and China's External Messaging

There are legitimate reasons to question the accuracy of China's economic data, but the same types of arguments can be made against many countries' statistical agencies. Beijing uses the implied legitimacy that comes from the official status of its economic statistics as a critical source of support for its external messaging concerning the economy. For international financial institutions such as the World Bank and the International Monetary Fund, raising questions about the quality of a country's economic data that still conforms to certain acceptable reporting standards (such as the SDDS) would likely open up a political Pandora's box, concerning which national statistical agencies are credible and qualified and which ones are not. Still, this presumption alone does not mean that the IMF accepts every country's data as equally credible, as the Fund formally censured Argentina for its data reporting practices in 2013.[51]

Underlying the implicit acceptance of macroeconomic data is an assumption that global policymakers want reliable economic data in order to make better decisions in managing the economy. Falsifying the data per se would likely be contrary to that objective, even if errors are inevitable. As a result, there is a strong presumption across the economics profession – and in international financial institutions in particular – that economic data as published by national statistical agencies are generally reported in good faith, with an eye toward international best practices. At the same time, the IMF also occasionally acknowledges the problems with China's data, commenting in the 2016 Article IV annual report on China, "While data are broadly adequate for surveillance, they are only barely so, and are not commensurate with China's systemic importance."[52] The Fund repeated this warning in several additional reports in the following years.

The implicit credibility associated with official economic data can best be described as an "authority bias" toward national statistical authorities. This bias reduces the need for Beijing to explain or justify its statistical methods and places a greater burden on critics of the official data. As a result, the official forecasts of China's annual GDP growth that are produced by international organizations such as the IMF, the World Bank, or the Organization for Economic Co-operation and Development (OECD) often anticipate the results that China will officially report, rather than representing their own independent assessments of China's actual economic performance. Or more precisely, the economic forecasts of these institutions are typically clustered around China's officially reported growth rates, because there is little history of China deviating from their targeted growth rates. Furthermore, the data that must be used to estimate potential growth in China in the future depend upon the smoothed data reporting in the past, creating a bias against forecasting abrupt slowdowns in growth. In turn, Chinese officials then cite these international institutions' forecasts as evidence of China's economic resilience and then push the same institutions to raise their growth forecasts for China in the future. Every year's Article IV report in China also features a memorandum from China's Executive Director to the IMF. The statement from Zhang Zhengxin in the 2022 report is indicative of Beijing's consistent priority to boost China's GDP forecasts, stating, "Comparing China's annual growth rate of 6 to 7 percent before COVID-19 with staff's projection of 5.1 percent in 2024 and around 4 percent afterward, we don't think the projected slowdown is reasonable."[53]

Reading the IMF's annual Article IV reports for China in sequence is an exercise in sustained cognitive dissonance. Throughout the past decade, Fund economists have dutifully and persuasively argued for China's need to reform its economy, given the overextension of credit, the growth of local government debt, declining returns from investment-led growth, and low levels of total factor productivity growth. These headwinds are consistently described as reducing China's medium-term economic growth rates in the future, unless reforms are initiated. But year after year, the expected slowdown never arrives, even as the need for reform persists. Some explanation is offered in the following year's report for how China maintained economic growth close to the official targeted rates, despite the inefficiencies in the system that the Fund staff had already identified. The IMF economists are accurately diagnosing the problems in China's economy year after year, but the official economic data barely adjust when these problems materialize. The economic slowdown is always over the horizon in the IMF's official projections, but somehow China muddles through and maintains strong official growth rates without structural reform.

These problems of herding toward consensus estimates exist among private sector economists as well. Picture yourself as an economist at a major investment bank operating in Hong Kong. You are responsible for producing a GDP growth forecast for China's economy next year, and you understand that China's economic data have distinct problems. But you also know that Beijing will likely continue reporting its official GDP growth rates within a very narrow range around the official target. Therefore, there is little benefit to publishing a forecast of China's GDP growth far below the targeted level, even if you independently think the economy will weaken significantly, because there is a very low probability that you will ever be validated by Beijing's official data. Even worse, you may lose access to officials in Beijing or face criticism from the market-facing divisions within your own bank. No dealmaker generating millions of dollars in fees wants to lose potential business because you are putting your hand up in the economics department of the bank and displaying some intellectual independence. An out-of-consensus forecast that is likely to be outside China's officially published growth rates is just an invitation to be ignored within the bank, or at worst, dismissed altogether.

Furthermore, Chinese officials are highly critical of alternative measures of China's economic performance. Usually, indirect pressure on analysts would center upon public skepticism of GDP statistics, similar to what happened to Gao Shanwen. However, there is also pushback from Beijing even concerning less important statistics than GDP. Starting in 2010, the IMF published a different view of China's fiscal deficit, using an "augmented" measure that included an estimate of the indirect borrowing by LGFVs. The logic was that these LGFVs were not actually corporations but were government-backed and guaranteed pass-through vehicles for local infrastructure projects. Therefore, their borrowing should presumably be included within calculations of the government deficit. In the "authorities' views" section of the IMF's Article IV annual report on China's economic conditions, China would often criticize these augmented measures, arguing that LGFVs could actually generate cash flows to repay the debts they had incurred, and therefore they should not be included within government obligations.[54] For staff at international financial institutions, any public challenge to China's official data would likely escalate into a diplomatic issue, where Chinese signoffs and cooperation were necessary for the international institution both to operate in China and to publish reports on consultations with Chinese officials. If the purpose of the institution was to try to advance policy changes to make global economic growth more sustainable and insulated from financial shocks, it made little sense to publicly criticize China's headline economic data.

Similarly, for most of the 2010s, many foreign governments had no real interest in trying to question China's high economic growth rates, as the agenda for most governments was focused on incentivizing China's market opening and structural reform. As a result, these messages from the United States and other Western governments were focused on convincing Chinese officials that they had the necessary economic strength to implement reforms and that the costs of those reforms were manageable. Focusing on China's economic weakness or the volatility of the economy might slow the internal political momentum for reform. There was little interest in expending the political energy to engage in a broader public debate about the accuracy of China's growth rates.

Beijing has a clear political interest in maintaining the perception of China's inevitable economic rise, and uses its state media apparatus, informal influence over Chinese economists, and direct and indirect pressure on international financial institutions in order to maintain its preferred narrative. But most of the acceptance of Beijing's narrative occurs passively, because of the authority bias implied within officially published data and the lack of credible alternative data. This explains why even highly informed observers and analysts of China have been slow to accept China's economic decline as structural. But the problem Beijing faces is that China cannot rely upon this authority bias indefinitely. Eventually the gap between economic reality and China's narrative becomes too wide, and the credibility of China's official narrative weakens. The question then becomes why Beijing persists in publicly holding onto economic objectives it cannot achieve.

Why Persist? Strategic Competition and Economic Growth

Despite all of the evidence of policy support for the economy that indicates China's leadership is aware of the severity of China's economic challenges, Beijing remains committed to targeting high rates of economic growth in the future. Officially, China holds onto a goal contained within

Xi Jinping's "Vision 2035" of doubling China's GDP between 2020 and 2035, which implies at least 4.7 percent growth per year. Even though Beijing set a target for a larger fiscal deficit in 2025, China left the official GDP growth target for 2025 unchanged for another year, at "around 5 percent." It is nigh on certain that China will eventually publish a 2025 GDP growth rate close to that targeted level. As of this writing, the official growth rate of real GDP for the first half of the year was 5.3 percent. The growth targets have their own internal bureaucratic logic as an anchoring mechanism for the expectations of local officials. Too sharp an adjustment would communicate a lower priority on maintaining economic growth. But the broader question is why China is willing to risk its economic narrative becoming far less credible in the future, and why Beijing is willing to expend considerable resources to shape the narrative of China's economic future over the next decade.

This question can be addressed as a counterfactual: Why is targeting 2 or 3 percent economic growth simply not acceptable for China's leadership? A lower growth rate would reflect the leadership accepting economic gravity and the constraints created by their previous choices, notably the overhang of bad debt within the financial system and the debt levels of local governments. China could persist with overly optimistic growth rates for ideological reasons: Xi Jinping simply believes that China must continue growing at rapid rates in order to achieve the "great rejuvenation" of the nation. It could be an analytical objection, in that leadership does not believe that China's potential growth rate has slowed, so that it sees no benefit in targeting slower growth. But this argument is difficult to square with Beijing's recent policy actions to shore up the economy. The more probable explanation is grounded in strategic competition with the United States, as China's leaders could feel that a lower growth rate would cost them influence amidst rising global competition. Alternatively, they may want to demonstrate China's economic resilience during the trade war. Strategic competition is likely the most credible rationale, but there may also be ideological elements that are driving Xi Jinping's thinking about targeting high rates of economic growth.

Independent of the political benefits that the Party accrues from projecting high and stable rates of economic growth, China has sent a different propaganda message over the past decade, particularly during the Xi Jinping era. This message has revolved around the concept of "great changes unseen in a century" that have created a global environment in which "the East is rising and the West is declining."[55] These arguments focus on the political polarization and disunity in Western democracies, combined with China's world-beating economic growth and rising political influence in recent years.[56] A more multipolar world with greater economic vitality in developing economies is a world shifting toward China's interests relative to the post-World War II order anchored by American power. Economic power in this context also extends beyond simple GDP to the control of global manufacturing and advanced technologies. In this context, Xi Jinping personally has staked out a particular vision of China's economic future, which is completely incompatible with a structural economic slowdown in China.

Beijing has expended considerable effort in the propagation of its preferred narrative of a rising China working for the betterment of the developing world. Samantha Custer and her colleagues at AidData define Beijing's efforts in narrative competition as a "strategic imperative" for China.[57] They argue that Beijing uses the narrative of its own prosperity to encourage other countries to sell raw materials and resources to China based on belief in its long-term reliability as a market. The political benefits of an active propaganda strategy include winning support from developing countries in international institutions and projecting strength in its diplomatic outreach relative to the United States.[58] Custer highlights the extensive reach of Chinese state media throughout the developing world as a critical enabler of this influence. These efforts are not likely to be modified based on an abrupt change in economic momentum in China itself.

It is difficult to ascertain to what extent the logic of strategic competition between China and the United States, or the belief that "the East is rising and the West is declining," is driving China's day-to-day economic decision-making. Certainly, China's concerns about losing access to critical technology imports have created worries about economic self-sufficiency, as defined in China's "dual circulation" policy detailed in 2020. It is more likely that concerns about strategic competition constrain Xi Jinping's political options in messaging China's longer-term economic trajectory or in backing away from policies with which he is identified, as was the case with zero-COVID restrictions in 2022. These political pressures can generate resistance to targeting lower economic growth rates in any particular year, because any dramatic adjustment in the economic growth target would send a signal that overall conditions in China's economy have changed fundamentally.

Most governments want their economies to grow at rapid rates. But China also needs a strong global belief in its economic prospects in order to push back against US economic statecraft tools such as export controls and financial sanctions. Ultimately, banks and companies comply with US rules to limit exports of advanced technologies to China and other countries because they value access to the US marketplace, primarily because of the strength of the US economy. Economic sanctions are powerful tools of statecraft that can cut off companies' and banks' access to the US dollar clearing system, but they largely work based on the behavior of banks themselves.[59] Those banks make their own assessments about the importance of managing the risk of losing access to the US dollar financial system, which is currently essential to any private financial institution.

In order to counter the effects of these tools and circumvent sanctions and export controls, China needs trading partners who see the long-term benefits of dealing with China relative to the potential long-term costs of losing access to the US market. In this context, maintaining a narrative that China is continuing to rise in global economic power and influence becomes vitally important to convincing other countries to accept your currency as payment for goods, develop trade linkages that grow relative to those with the United States, and conduct business with your banks *even if* the United States chooses to target them with sanctions. The obvious example here is the China–Russia economic relationship, after Russia was sanctioned following its invasion of Ukraine. Russia had no choice but to expand its trade with China, having had several of its financial institutions cut off from the US dollar system. But for other countries with only modest linkages to China's financial system and limited trade relationships, their perceptions of China's political power and influence play an important role in whether they will ever assist China in circumventing American sanctions and export controls. If China's economy is declining structurally, it will become far more difficult to encourage other countries to take the risk of being sanctioned or restricted by the United States simply to help Beijing maintain some degree of independence from US economic sanctions and technological controls.

As a result, all else being equal, the United States benefits in its usage of economic sanctions, export controls, and other statecraft tools from the relative attraction of US consumer markets compared to China's, and the relative growth of those markets. At the same time, the narrative of China's structural economic decline is not particularly popular within US foreign policy circles. Even a significant decline in China's economy will not diminish the currrent military threat China poses or the industrial and technological competitiveness of Chinese industries, which may also contribute to the country's military strength. Successful experiments in artificial intelligence, such as DeepSeek's surprise developments in January 2025, only reinforce the view that strategic competition with China stems far beyond strict GDP comparisons for the United States. This generates a highly contested view of China's economic future even within Washington, where all of the uncertainties about China's actual economic performance rise to the surface very quickly.

But China needs the narrative of its inexorable economic rise and expends considerable resources to propagate and defend its preferred narrative. Beijing's need for its version of China's economic story is revealed via a different counterfactual: Were Beijing to acknowledge China's economic weakness, it is probable that there would ironically be *less* political momentum toward erecting trade barriers and export controls around the world against China's economic influence. China would actually have an easier time reducing trade tensions and maintaining exports if Beijing acknowledged the country's structural slowdown. The fact that China cannot abandon this narrative of rapid economic growth – and the political incentives behind it – highlights how intrinsically linked the Party's political interests and China's unprecedented financial system expansion have been over the past decade. But the financial system can no longer serve as the shock absorber for China's political system and cannot continue expanding at a rate sufficient to power investment-led growth. China continues to cling to unrealistic economic objectives. But at present Beijing is spending far more time and energy simply trying to muddy international perceptions of China's economy and create a different vision of the next decade of China's prospects.

5

What a Prolonged Economic Slowdown Means for China

What a difference five years makes. It's still a rare event when Xi Jinping publicly reverses a policy stance with which he is closely identified, but the scene in February 2025 marked a surprising turnaround for China's preeminent leader. Xi sat at one end of a long conference table in the Great Hall of the People, while around the rest of the table were seventeen of China's most prominent entrepreneurs, including Jack Ma of Alibaba, whose intemperate speech in October 2020 had catalyzed some of the surprise regulatory crackdowns against China's technology firms that had destroyed hundreds of billions of dollars in market value in short order. But this was a different day in the late winter of 2025. Now that Beijing was struggling to revive its economy, old enemies had become new allies. The private entrepreneurs involved were more than grateful to take their seats around the table with Xi for a vote of public confidence in their status, which touched off a brief round of market optimism that China would be able to drive additional private sector investment and stabilize an economic recovery.

The meeting with private entrepreneurs highlighted an important aspect of Beijing's own views of its economic slowdown. Chinese officials often describe the problem with China's economy as a lack of confidence among critical segments of society, from entrepreneurs to young people. Reverse the decline in confidence, this argument follows, and the economy will recover. There is a similar line of reasoning in China blaming problems in the economy on local governments' inattention to the implementation of central government policies, rather than the lack of local government capacity to simultaneously manage debt and produce economic growth. The constraints of China's financial system and its current limits in funding additional investment may not be convenient problems for Beijing to highlight in their own diagnosis of China's slowing economy. It is far easier to cite problems in private sector confidence; at least you can claim to be doing something about those.

The extent to which China's economic slowdown has been internalized among ordinary Chinese people remains unclear, but China's official narrative of steady and stable growth appears to be falling upon deaf ears both inside and outside of China. For many of China's youth, who have known only rapid economic growth and China rising in power and influence throughout their lives, the disconnect between the vibrant past and the stagnant present looms especially large. Chinese social media users often need to use euphemisms and analogies to engage in discussion without running foul of an extensive censorship apparatus. But in recent years, the euphemism often used to discuss China's economic stagnation in online discussions has been to describe the current era as the "garbage time of history" in reference to societies confronting an inevitable decline. Commentaries have cited both the experience of the Soviet Union and the late Qing dynasty, implicitly criticizing China's political and economic trajectory.[1]

One of the targets of Chinese official propaganda has been the movement among Chinese youth interested in "lying flat" (*tangping*), usually associated with a passive or withdrawn approach to pursuing a career or economic success. Young people increasingly choose to "lie flat" because of the perceived impossibility of keeping up within Chinese society, given weak employment prospects and wide disparities in incomes and wealth.[2] The movement itself is often viewed as an implicit rebuke of the push for development by China's leadership. Another increasingly common movement among Chinese youth is declaring their own intentions to "let it rot" (*bailan*), meaning a general withdrawal from society and minimizing effort.[3] Other Chinese youth describe themselves as "rat people," in that they only scurry to the front door to receive delivered food and are reluctant to harbor larger ambitions.[4]

It is of course impossible to know how widespread these sentiments are among China's youth or within society as a whole, but it is notable that these online phenomena have emerged in only the past few years, since the COVID pandemic and the adjustment in China's property sector. The slow pace of structural reform in China's economy has hit China's younger generations particularly hard. A rising proportion of new entrants to the job market every year are college graduates, but China's economy has not restructured around the high-wage jobs for highly skilled and educated workers that those graduates are seeking.

Some of the highest-salaried jobs available to graduates were in the technology companies and online tutoring and education platforms that became targets of Beijing's political crackdowns in the name of "common prosperity."

Why is Beijing Out of Easy Options?

This book has argued that China's economic slowdown has resulted from the overextension of China's financial system, and the resulting decay of Beijing's counter-cyclical policy tools. The obvious response to this argument that probably occurs to most readers is that China's leaders certainly know China's economy far more deeply than the author does, and therefore they are already contemplating a significant policy response to the current economic slowdown. And if that response is not forthcoming, China's leaders probably have good reasons for that restraint, in pursuit of some other strategic objective. This begs the question why China's leadership has failed to stabilize the economy in recent years, if China's government still has considerable influence over its economy and operates based on long-term strategic plans.

The answer proposed in this book is that neither the unprecedented credit boom nor the resulting bust was part of a long-term plan, and Beijing has now lost control over its primary policy tools for directing China's economy: the financial system and fiscal policy. The investment-led growth model is broken, and so are China's tools to respond to its demise. This is not to say that Beijing has no options whatsoever to change its economic fate, but they are not the same conditions that China has faced since the global financial crisis, and different levers over the economy will be necessary. The financial system can no longer serve as the shock absorber for China's economy and the political consequences of slowing growth, because credit can no longer expand at the same rates as in the past.

What can Beijing still do, despite these constraints? China can still provide incremental counter-cyclical policy support for investment, consumption, and exports. It is often forgotten that after Japan's equity and real estate bubbles burst in the early 1990s, it was still one of the world's fastest-growing economies in 1995 and 1996, even as its financial crisis intensified. It is possible that China's economy can still recover cyclically from time to time, even at lower growth rates than in the past.

Even if credit growth has reached all-time lows, Beijing can also ease regulatory constraints on banks and reduce interest rates to boost credit growth by a few percentage points over a year or two. But restoring credit back to the pace seen before the deleveraging campaign, at 13–15 percent, is now impossible without a wholesale restructuring of the banking system and a dramatic reduction in bad loans on banks' balance sheets. The previous pace of credit growth involved rapid growth within the shadow banking system, which is now far smaller, beset by new regulations and the emergence of new credit risks.

Beijing can also provide short-term subsidies to boost national sales of automobiles, home appliances, and other durable goods, as they have done since 2024. They can propose one-off transfer payments to certain types of households, provide annual allowances for families with young children, or boost pay for civil servants. All of these measures can temporarily generate more consumer spending. But the ultimate test is whether Beijing can generate longer-term growth in household income that would be commensurate with China's targeted economic growth rates of around 5 percent. China's household consumption has already surged at extremely rapid rates over the past two decades, even as investment growth has risen even faster. Under conditions of slowing investment growth and employment resulting from that investment activity, the only way for China's consumption activity to surge would be via transfers of wealth from the state to households. But China's fiscal resources are diminishing over time, because the fiscal system is linked to investment activity. To create more sustainable growth in household incomes, the fiscal system must be fundamentally changed, from a system that primarily taxes investment to one that taxes mostly consumption and income, and provides additional transfer payments to households, particularly those at lower income levels.

The Ministry of Finance can issue new government bonds and direct that the proceeds are spent on new investment projects, including bridges, roads, railways, and other construction projects that will temporarily boost demand, provide employment, and additional wages. But this type of investment activity has already been occurring extensively for several years. The test of any investment is whether it eventually pays for itself by boosting overall economic growth through rising consumption (and additional private sector investment) over time. Without that corresponding rise in consumption activity, additional investment will simply add to government debt levels. Heavily indebted local governments implement these investment projects through their own LGFVs, but are more likely to use the proceeds to manage their existing debt burdens than to initiate new construction, so that process is also less efficient. The "last mile" of fiscal policy transmission remains highly inefficient, because local government companies with high debt burdens struggle to repay banks. A temporary boost in investment is always a possibility, but a sustained improvement in investment is not possible if funded by the banking system, given structurally declining flows of new credit. Fiscal deficits in China are already substantial, sitting at 7.7 percent of GDP in 2024. These deficits can rise by a few percentage points, but the marginal benefit of such an expansion to the economy will remain limited. Additional fiscal investment will not be sustainable without a shift in how China's tax system operates.

China can also continue to support growth through exports, at least temporarily. This is the fear of most of the world at present. Even though China's economy is slowing, China has incentives to maintain output and employment within its industrial base, while reducing prices and exporting abroad what cannot be sold domestically. Beijing can both permit depreciation of the currency to improve export growth or adjust export tax rebates of value-added taxes to explicitly subsidize export industries. All of these measures are likely to be considered at some point in response to the US tariffs imposed in early 2025. None of these measures resolve the problem of inadequate domestic demand in China, of course, but they can provide a palliative effect on Chinese industry and support the export manufacturing sector in the short term. Over time, however, China will face growing resistance from most of its trading partners in continuing to expand exports, when China is already the largest exporter in the world. Every year in which exports continue to power China's economy is a year in which trade restrictions on those exports become more probable.

These are just a few of China's short-term options to boost the economy. But they are all far short of the structural reforms Beijing needs to initiate to boost growth over the long term. All of the necessary structural changes are costly to growth in the short term, and usually they would entail significant political changes in China, by impacting employment or the influence of key political constituencies over the economy. As mentioned previously, reallocating China's investment via the financial system involves a significant recapitalization of the banking system, starting fresh after writing off old loans, and paying the fiscal costs of that misdirected lending. A pivot toward consumption-led growth requires redirecting the fiscal system toward boosting household incomes, while also raising taxes on China's households and consumers. There are no easy choices for Beijing, or they would have likely already been made. The costs of decisions in China's past limit the choices Beijing can make to preserve the country's economic future.

Investment in Advanced Technologies Solves Little

In response to this prolonged slowdown, Beijing's stated strategy is to push ahead with aggressive investments in advanced technologies, including advanced manufacturing, green technologies, artificial intelligence, and robotics. But this proposed adjustment to "new quality productive forces" still involves capital-intensive industries that are focused on maximizing China's manufacturing prowess and efficiency for the purpose of expanding global export market share. Even if Beijing succeeds beyond its wildest expectations in boosting industrial productivity, it remains unclear how Chinese consumers or workers will benefit without dramatic changes to China's taxation and fiscal systems. For China's youth, it remains unclear where Beijing's industrial policy ambitions will create new jobs. For China's leaders, even massive success at their chosen path of boosting industrial productivity via investments in artificial intelligence and robotics will not produce the strength in household consumption necessary to sustain China's future GDP growth. Nor will it reduce the problem of China's continued reliance upon exports, and China's potential vulnerability to tariffs and trade defenses from other countries. The goods and services that may be produced more efficiently by China's new technology firms will still need to be mostly sold abroad. If Beijing has a plan to address its structural economic slowdown, it is certainly a closely guarded secret. China's current economic strategy requires reducing reliance upon the rest of the world for manufacturing, while becoming even more reliant upon the rest of the world for economic growth.

Intellectual bubbles usually take longer to burst than financial or credit bubbles. But sentiments strong enough to drive movements toward "lying flat" and "letting it rot" are unlikely to suddenly disappear after a few quarters of stronger economic growth, or a modest cyclical recovery, or even nationalist rallying cries around competition with the United States, which have become more common in 2025. These sentiments reflect longer-standing changes in China's economic fortunes that have developed a degree of societal resonance over the past several years. The pervasive belief that China's economy will continue growing is already under pressure within Chinese society. But it remains uncertain exactly how those popular sentiments will evolve in the years ahead. Less controversial is the fact that China's structural economic slowdown will continue.

This chapter outlines the probable consequences of slowing economic growth for China, while the following chapter discusses the implications for the rest of the world. For China's leaders, the slowdown in the economy severely limits and narrows their policy choices. Options are increasingly stark. On the one hand, Beijing can always take limited steps to forestall the potential for economic crisis today, or this week or the next. But the reforms necessary to reduce risks over the longer term and establish a foundation for more sustainable growth increasingly implicate core questions of the Party's legitimacy and levers of control over the economy and society. There are always good reasons readily available not to take more fundamental restructuring steps, and instead to use short-term palliative measures to mitigate the most immediately pressing political and economic damage. Being proactive is dangerous today, while being reactive minimizes risks today at the cost of greater risks tomorrow. Being reactive is always the easier choice, and it is the choice that Beijing has made so far.

Predictions are always difficult, particularly concerning economic trends. This chapter takes the existing trend lines in a number of sectors in China's economy, as well as the policy dilemmas currently facing China's leadership, and extends them for around the next five years to 2030. This analysis is based on the assumptions outlined above, that there will not be a fundamental restructuring of China's financial or fiscal systems in the years ahead. The implications of China's long-term economic decline will be revealed in the following areas:

- China's property sector will remain a long-term headache for leaders in Beijing, as the value of most households' most important asset will remain under pressure. Given the historical importance of the property sector for China's development, no other industry will replace the sector in terms of total size within the economy.
- Infrastructure investment will continue to decline over time, given the long-term pressures on China's fiscal system and declining fiscal revenues. Until Beijing changes the fiscal system to tax household consumption in greater volumes, the slowdown in overall investment will limit China's long-term fiscal capacity to respond to cyclical weakness.
- Deflationary pressures in China's economy will persist as investment growth slows, the population ages further, and the overhang of weaker demand from property and infrastructure construction weighs on demand from upstream heavy industrial sectors. Deflationary pressures in a heavily indebted economy will only exacerbate the longer-term difficulties Beijing is facing in encouraging private sector investment and reducing local government debt.
- Social pressures from weakening employment prospects and declining household net worth will intensify in the years ahead, particularly if the government appears lethargic in addressing longer-term economic problems. The appetite for investment among entrepreneurs and the private sector will remain suppressed as this social malaise continues.
- China's economy will remain heavily dependent upon export-oriented manufacturing and, therefore, will become even more vulnerable to global restrictions on China's exports.

The most important policy choice China's leaders will be forced to consider concerns the difficult question of whose debts should be repaid and whose will face default, with all of the associated implications for China's future economic development. These are intensely political questions, and they help to explain why fundamental reforms are so difficult. While China's fiscal and financial systems are decaying, the process of decay generates no immediate pressures or crises for Beijing. Ironically, China's system is most vulnerable to systemic crisis when reform becomes a realistic possibility, because government guarantees are then quickly reconsidered among lenders and investors. This dilemma – ongoing decay is debilitating but reform is acutely dangerous – highlights the limited but stark economic policy choices currently available to Beijing.

China's Property Market Remains a Headache

While this book has focused on the decline in China's property market extensively, it is difficult to properly contextualize the importance of China's property sector in the development of China's economy over the past two decades. The liberalization of the sector in the late 1990s was accompanied by a massive and unusual subsidy to China's households, who were able to purchase housing from state-owned enterprises at far below market prices. Over the next decade, China's middle-class population grew quickly, along with their demand for housing, particularly in larger cities. Prices skyrocketed in major cities, with per square meter housing costs in Beijing and Shanghai eventually rising by as much as ten to fifteen times their levels in the early 2000s. With price appreciation in these ranges, the most important bottleneck for growth became access to land, which was controlled by local governments. Some developers chose not to develop the land at all, as they could benefit from rapid price appreciation by just leaving the property undeveloped. In the 2000s, there were several large plots of land in the central business districts of Beijing that remained vacant for years before they were eventually developed, likely exchanging hands among property developers several times at consistently rising prices. One of the capital's bookstores, the Bookworm in Sanlitun, used to take photos of visiting authors posed in the vacant, dystopian, unconstructed urban landscape located right in the middle of a highly developed commercial area of the city.

The property sector had represented around one-quarter of China's economic output, including its effect on upstream and downstream industries.[5] Removing it as a source of growth within China's economy naturally raises the question of what will take its place as a driver of investment. But importantly, the property sector also represented several million Chinese households' path to wealth through the appreciation in the value of their houses. Leaders in Beijing will be pressured to offer

Chinese citizens an alternative path to wealth and prosperity or another reason to continue investing in China's future rather than seeking opportunities outside the country. But it is difficult to see what can deliver the same scale of broad-based gains that the bubble in China's property sector had delivered in the 2000s and 2010s.

Beijing is still managing the problem of developers who are now unable to finish houses that they had promised to buyers. Astonishingly, the problems in delivery have not produced additional protests or unrest, in part because many of the aggrieved were investors looking for higher returns, rather than first-time homeowners. Housing market activity has now largely shifted to the secondary market in most cities, where people can clearly see what they are buying.

The future of China's housing market is likely to be bifurcated. In interior cities in central China and in western and northern provinces, where there are outflows of workers and citizens, there will be little new housing built at all. Local governments will likely take over unfinished projects from failing developers. Eventually the large volumes of completed but unoccupied housing will be written off by developers or repurposed by local governments. But no new people are coming to these cities, and birth rates across the country continue declining. In coastal cities, however, people are still moving in. Very little new housing has been built over the past three to four years as developers have faced severe financial pressure. New migrants are buying into the secondary market, allowing existing homeowners to upgrade to larger houses offered in the primary market. Overall, the housing market can stabilize, only at a much lower level of activity than what occurred in the late 2010s. Most likely, the housing sector across China will stabilize at levels of construction and sales around 35 to 45 percent of its previous peak.[6] It can even contribute to cyclical growth in the economy on occasion. But housing and construction activity overall are never likely to be structural drivers of investment growth in China again.

For Chinese households, the impact of the declining housing market is far less certain. Headline statistics suggest that housing prices have not fallen significantly, by less than 20 percent in many cities. This seems improbably low, but many households are still sitting on large paper gains on their initial housing purchases, while the markets in which those houses are priced have become far less liquid. Most homeowners probably do not know what their house would sell for in any given month. Importantly, however, most can no longer expect that price appreciation will resume in the future, even if prices fall at a slower pace. Investors and speculators will continue to place more of their holdings on the market, keeping prices under pressure. The "wealth effect" of rising asset prices describes a phenomenon in which expectations of continued wealth accumulation help to drive household consumption. The opposite can also be true, with declining asset values leading households to pull back on spending. Such a decline in property values is unprecedented in China but may be having an impact on the widespread phenomenon of "downgrading" consumption, with households buying cheaper versions of the same goods or services. Those conditions are likely to continue over the next decade, given the extent of overbuilding that occurred in the late 2010s.

Fiscal Policy is Impaired, Slowing Infrastructure Investment

The decline in China's property sector has implicated several industries, particularly those in construction and heavy industrial sectors, but in financial terms, local governments have been directly in the line of fire. Local governments perform most of the direct spending by the Chinese government as a whole: 88 percent of both general obligation spending and "fund" spending – a secondary fiscal budget – in 2024.[7] The central government can set tax collection methods, but the majority of actual implementation of fiscal policy takes place at the subnational level, through direct local government spending and through quasi-fiscal local government borrowing through state-owned enterprises and LGFVs. Hence, the health of the "last mile" of fiscal policy – where money is actually spent and projects are executed by local governments – becomes the most important determinant of its overall effectiveness in supporting the economy.

The problem Beijing is facing at present is that this "last mile" is clogged with debt, which was the result of the last decade of quasi-fiscal investment that was never really expected to generate financial returns to repay lenders. Most of China's infrastructure investment was intended as public goods to improve the overall efficiency of the economy. Highways can always charge tolls, and hydroelectric dams generate power that can be sold to downstream users, but these financing cash flows were never the most important considerations in local government decisions to approve the projects themselves or in banks' decisions to lend to them. For local governments trying to manage these projects while also maintaining a flow of new investment within their jurisdictions, the important factors are not the underlying returns of the projects, but how much new fiscal revenue and borrowing they can access every year. As long as that pool expands, it is relatively straightforward for localities to keep funding new projects and using new borrowing to cover the interest expenses on old borrowing. Most local government expenditures are carefully controlled within budgeted outlays, so the discretion that local officials have to direct spending comes from their capacity to borrow from banks and to sell land to property developers. The pace of credit growth and fiscal revenue growth from land sales are important determinants of the pace of investment.

But when the property sector's collapse suddenly delivers a shock to fiscal revenues to the tune of almost 4 trillion yuan in annualized terms, or 3 percent of GDP, then a rising proportion of local resources will be used to repay and manage solely the interest on existing debt, while launching new investments becomes more and more difficult. The fiscal problems for localities are even more acute given that the land sales revenues that collapsed were the discretionary funds under their direct control. These pressures explain the dramatic decline in infrastructure investment growth since 2020, and the deterioration of China's fiscal capacity. Analysts often cite the low level of Chinese central government debt to GDP, at only 25 percent as of the end of 2024, as evidence of Beijing's capacity to add more borrowing and spend its way out of a slowdown in China's economy.[8] Missing in that analysis is the fact that almost all Chinese spending occurs at the local level, and to change that process, the entire fiscal system in China needs to be restructured. Including debt accrued by localities and their financing vehicles, total government debt in China is closer to 145 to 150 percent of GDP, or around six times the level accrued by the central government alone.[9] More borrowing by the central or local governments can certainly continue, but the question remains whether or not it will be efficient or effective in maintaining economic momentum, given the debt constraints that impair the "last mile" of China's fiscal spending. The slowdown in overall credit growth directly impacts Beijing's capacity to implement its fiscal policy objectives at the local government level.

Local governments were truly in dire fiscal straits in 2023 and 2024, with multiple stories proliferating in China related to cutbacks of social services, unpaid wages, and even demands that local officials pay back their salaries and bonuses from previous years.[10] Zero-COVID policies were largely enforced by local governments, without receiving transfers from the central government to compensate, and costs reportedly reached as high as 352 billion yuan in 2022 alone, or around 2 percent of total fiscal revenues.[11] Protests and demonstrations kicked off in several cities over suspended services and payments by local governments. In Wuhan and Dalian, there were extensive protests in early 2023 over cuts to medical benefits.[12] Some cities such as Shangqiu warned of suspended bus services before a public backlash, and municipal workers in large cities such as Zhengzhou, the capital of Henan province, reported facing payment delays for wages.[13] Even zoos were cutting back animal feed and wages to local employees, as a public appeal from the Endangered Species Fund, a Chinese conservation group, called for contributions for a zoo in Wafangdian in Liaoning province after local government funding appeared to have been cut off.[14]

Local governments started collecting additional "fees" and finding other sources of income to compensate for falling tax revenues. Those non-tax revenues surged by 25 percent in 2024. Usually this was done via arbitrary fines on small businesses, but there were also credible reports that entrepreneurs were being extorted for funds or back taxes, even in provinces or cities where they had no operations at all.[15] An investigation by the *Financial Times* in late 2024 found eighty detentions of senior executives in listed companies, and there were probably several more among unlisted firms. Most of this activity is likely linked to the problems in local government finances, as these types of detentions were extremely rare in the past. In another example, *Jiemian News* reported that a higher than usual number of truck drivers in the city of Anyang in Henan province were fined repeatedly at local weigh stations, with many drivers suspicious that these were just pretexts to collect additional fines.[16] The common thread to all of these unexpected fines and fees seemed to be their sudden imposition as land sales revenues declined and the economy weakened starting in 2022. At one point in June

2024, the State Taxation Administration in Beijing was forced to issue a statement claiming that there was *not* a nationwide effort to claim back taxes over the past two decades underway, in order to refute claims by local governments that they were entitled to pressure businesses to obtain these taxes.[17]

Beijing faces several difficult choices ahead as it confronts a clogged fiscal system. Local government investment is still an important driver of China's economy, roughly equivalent in importance to the downsized property sector including its upstream and downstream impacts, at around 14 to 15 percent of GDP.[18] Changing the financing mechanisms for local governments overnight would cause that portion of investment to contract very quickly. But relying upon the existing funding channels would only cause a continued slowdown in infrastructure investment. The existing stock of local government debt – around the size of China's GDP – needs to be restructured in order to keep debt levels from growing. But that would involve banks being forced to acknowledge that loans are not going to be repaid, or to accept lower interest rates on those loans to LGFVs, reducing bank profitability and their capacity to continue lending to fund new investment in the economy.

In addition, local governments need an entirely new source of financing for investment that is more sustainable and will not continue to add to local government debt levels. This could be through direct bond issuance to localities, or indirect borrowing via policy banks such as the China Development Bank, at lower interest rates. But these bond issues would likely involve a decline in overall credit available to local governments, and therefore weaker investment. The key question for Beijing is what role China's leaders expect local government infrastructure investment to play in the future of China's economic growth. This local investment will definitely slow, along with growth in China's economy as a whole, but the extent of that slowdown remains unclear.

The broader fiscal challenge facing Beijing, of course, is that China's entire tax base depends more upon investment-led growth than consumption-led growth. Even though China officially posted 5 percent real GDP growth in 2024 and 4.2 percent nominal GDP growth, tax revenues declined by 3.4 percent for the full year (another sign that actual economic growth was far weaker than official levels), and only the sharp 25 percent rise in non-tax revenues prevented an even larger decline. The

2025 full-year budget only anticipates a 0.1 percent rise in overall fiscal revenue, even if China's economy meets its growth target of "around 5 percent." In the first half of 2025, overall fiscal revenues declined, and these trends will likely continue in the years ahead absent a fundamental restructuring of China's fiscal system, including how revenues are raised and how fiscal resources are distributed.

Should current trends continue, local government infrastructure spending will decline gradually, and measures such as the late 2024 decision to swap 10 trillion yuan of high-interest local debt for lower-interest bonds are likely to be repeated or extended. A Chinese government with weaker tax revenues will need to make tradeoffs between its ironclad fiscal obligations, like local pensions and salary payments, and more discretionary objectives such as spending on military modernization, industrial policy objectives, and technological innovation. Beijing can delay these tradeoffs with additional deficit spending and government bond issuance but cannot postpone them indefinitely without changing the tax system entirely. In the meantime, Beijing will increasingly need to use "special" or "extraordinary" types of bond issues in order to circumvent existing channels for government spending, which are less and less efficient in generating growth because of the debt constraints in the "last mile" of spending.

The fiscal strains in China's economy will show up first far outside of Beijing and Shanghai, in the basic operations of local governments and their inability to carry out their official obligations and provide social services. China's fiscal constraints mean that Beijing's ambitions in spending and investment will remain limited by declining levels of revenue collection and borrowing.

Deflation and Growing Debt Pressures

Chinese officials have studied Japan's economic history carefully. They have done so to try to avoid falling into an extended period of deflation, which has limited Japan's economic growth since the early 1990s. Deflationary pressures are brutal for a highly indebted economy, as debt levels and interest rates keep rising in real terms if prices fall and are expected to continue falling. Most importantly, when deflationary expectations become entrenched, it is very difficult to dislodge them, which ends up reducing implied rates of return on corporate investment. In Japan, demographic pressures combined with the end of a historic real estate bubble and a strong currency to reduce investment growth over time, extending deflationary pressures in the economy for years. Only through extensive fiscal stimulus was Japan able to place a floor under economic activity in the late 1990s and early 2000s. This option is probably unavailable in China, as discussed previously. Even then, Japan's deflation persisted throughout the 2000s and 2010s, improving only following the COVID-19 pandemic.

After Japan's real estate bubble burst, the country experienced what economist Richard Koo first called a "balance sheet recession," in which companies nursing high levels of debt on their balance sheets were reluctant to borrow in order to invest further, and instead used operating cash flows to pay down debt.[19] The net result was weaker investment in the economy as a whole, requiring the government to step in and generate demand via fiscal spending. Furthermore, monetary policy was ineffective in generating credit demand, as the key constraint for companies was the level of debt on their balance sheets: even interest rates at zero were not encouraging investment.

China's economic situation is fundamentally different from Japan's, but Japan's experience is still likely the most closely analogous to China's in recent history. The adjustment in China's economy that is currently taking place more closely resembles Japan's long-term economic slowdown than an acute or severe crisis. China's problem is slightly different to Japan's balance sheet recession dynamics in that fiscal policy levers are now constrained, and the companies that need to pay down debt in China are typically local firms that are not generating sufficient operating cash flows, rather than Japan's larger corporate conglomerates. A restructuring of debt would be a more significant boost to China's outlook than a simple handoff from monetary policy to fiscal policy.

Japan did face its own slow-motion banking crisis that migrated from non-bank financial institutions (the *jusen* housing loan companies) in the mid-1990s to major banks in 1996 and 1997. After the failures of Sanyo Securities, Hokkaido Takushoku Bank, and Yamaichi Securities, credit risks spread throughout Japan's financial system and forced authorities to provide direct liquidity assistance to the defaulting institutions.[20] The Governor of the Bank of Japan and the Minister of Finance even issued a statement in November 1997 reaffirming the government's guarantee of all bank deposits to mitigate further liquidity pressures on financial institutions.[21] The result of Japan's financial crisis was an acute slowdown in credit growth, much more severe than what has happened in China so far. But there were no major panics or bank runs in Japan from depositors similar to other financial crises. The result was a more gradual slowdown in the economy and the "zombification" of the banking system. Japanese banks were essentially insolvent because they had high levels of non-performing assets on their books, but these assets were not marked down or recognized as non-performing. The result was a banking system that could not extend large volumes of new credit, but was also under no immediate liquidity pressure, so it could continue operating. These conditions are very similar to those prevalent in the Chinese banking system today.

The impact of changing demographic conditions in Japan also offers warning signs for China. There are very few major economies that have faced shrinking working-age populations and declining populations overall. Japan's working-age population peaked in the mid-1990s and its broader population started dropping in 2010, around a decade before China's.[22] But given rapidly declining birth rates, the contraction in China's working-age population may prove more severe than Japan's over the next two decades. In addition, given the historically strong relationship between savings rates and investment activity, declines in China's overall savings rate as the population ages are similarly expected to weaken investment growth in China, as occurred in Japan.

The most important factor driving China's deflationary pressures is the persistent imbalance within the domestic economy between investment activity and consumer demand. As credit growth has slowed and contracted the property sector and local government infrastructure investment, these imbalances have widened, forcing China's excess production in heavy industrial sectors abroad via lower-priced exports. Currently, China is facing deflationary pressures in producer prices and close to zero growth in consumer prices. The adjustment can best be described as "disinflation" rather than outright deflation. Xi Jinping himself reportedly questioned the significance of falling prices when consulted on China's emerging deflation threat in the fall of 2024, questioning why consumers were not more pleased that prices were down.[23]

But deflation is an important threat to China's economic future precisely because corporate investment is likely to slow if prices continue declining, and debt burdens are likely to rise in real terms. Not only are the two critical drivers of investment – property and local government infrastructure spending – under pressure, but overall credit growth that could fuel private sector investment is also weakening. For years, China's upstream heavy industries producing steel, cement, and other raw materials and intermediate goods used in construction had benefited from the downstream demand of China's investment activity, particularly in the property sector. In the absence of that demand, output in these industries has slowed. If output continues at close to the current pace even as investment growth and downstream demand slow further, the likely result will be even lower producer prices.

China's official producer price index has been declining in year-on-year terms since October 2022 and has remained negative more often than positive over the last fifteen years. As a result, if China seeks to avoid Japan's fate, nominal GDP growth at current prices is the more important measure of economic performance. Nominal GDP growth measures the revenues, corporate earnings, cash flows, and tax payments that are necessary to repay debt and fund future investment. Falling prices imply that nominal GDP growth will be slower than real GDP growth. If China's nominal GDP growth was 4 percent, for example, it would be far healthier for the economy to post 2 percent real GDP growth and 2 percent inflation (adding up to 4 percent nominal growth), rather than 5 percent real GDP growth and deflation of around 1 percent, which is close to what China officially published in 2024 (actual growth was likely slower, as previously discussed). The latter scenario would suggest far weaker economic prospects ahead, particularly if deflationary pressures extend for several years, as they already have in China.

The same pressures impact China's consumers, even if they are not quite as acute. Slowing corporate revenues because of declining prices also weaken job and wage growth. Retail sales growth in China has averaged only 3.1 percent since 2020, compared to 12.6 percent from 2010 to 2019. Income growth per capita has slowed to 4.9 percent since 2020, compared to 9.2 percent over the previous decade.[24] Most of this slowdown in consumption can be linked to the change in consumer credit conditions since the deleveraging campaign. The crackdown on shadow banking activity reduced riskier lending but also impacted low-income households' access to credit. While there are multiple influences on consumer prices, ever since the deleveraging campaign, core consumer price index (CPI) growth has remained in a very narrow range below 1.5 percent while trending lower. Consumer spending growth has similarly slowed along with household income growth since 2021. Even though headline consumer price growth has remained barely positive for most of the past three years, some Chinese researchers from the economic think tank China Finance 40 argued that if China's housing costs within the CPI were calculated in line with international standard practices, China's real inflation rate would have been negative from 2022 to 2024.[25]

As mentioned previously, China's Internet censors have prevented economic commentators from discussing deflationary pressure openly, after deflation became an indirect way to debate China's slowing economy and the problems with official data in public. And it remains unclear how persistent China's current deflationary pressures will become. But the danger looming over China's economy is that deflation becomes a self-reinforcing phenomenon, in which expectations of falling prices reduce incentives for future investment, which then further reduces domestic demand and credit demand, leading to additional declines in prices. Tariffs that reduce demand for China's exports will also add to deflationary pressures within China's domestic economy.

In a highly indebted economy such as China's, deflation becomes especially dangerous because the capacity to service a high level of debt deteriorates quickly. Ever since 2012, the estimated aggregate interest burden on all debt extended in China has exceeded nominal GDP growth every year, even using very conservative estimates to calculate overall interest costs. In 2024, for example, aggregate interest on credit in China was estimated at around 14 trillion yuan, while nominal GDP growth was only 5 trillion yuan for the year. In other words, China's debt problem continues growing at faster rates than Beijing's capacity to manage it. Interest rates in China have come down over the past decade, making even a high level of total debt more serviceable. But if deflationary pressures take hold, nominal GDP growth will continue to slow and real interest rates for companies and local governments will rise, even if real GDP growth remains in the current range (figure 5.1). As a result, a larger number of borrowers will default on their debt.

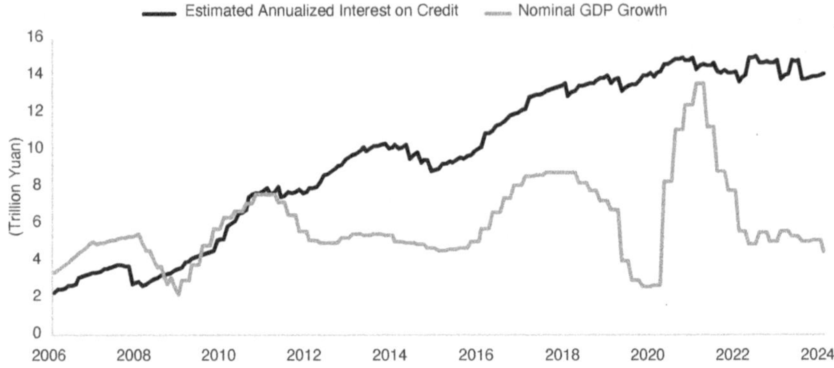

Figure 5.1 Estimated interest on credit vs. annual nominal GDP growth, 2006–2024.

Data source: People's Bank of China, Rhodium Group estimates.

To counter deflationary pressures, structural solutions are necessary: increasing household incomes to boost consumption, as well as redirecting credit away from state-owned enterprises and sectors associated with investment-led growth. Encouraging additional credit to sectors facing excess capacity will only increase the supply of intermediate goods and will likely depress prices further. Beijing has also experimented with supply-side adjustments to counter falling prices, such as encouraging industrial consolidation and mergers. These were more effective in winnowing out unproductive private firms in the steel sector in 2016 and 2017. But reducing the importance of state-owned players in these sectors requires far more aggressive controls on output and expansion, which will certainly slow overall economic growth. If producer prices consistently decline, Beijing will probably be tempted to return to the same tools that had supported them in the past: driving additional property and infrastructure investment. But with limited demand for property (and more than enough housing built already) and a broader fiscal reform necessary to drive faster infrastructure investment, there are no easy measures available.

It is probable that China will face persistent disinflationary pressures with higher risks of deflation in the years ahead, given the ongoing decline in China's credit growth, and therefore investment activity. Falling prices or extremely slow price growth will reduce private sector incentives to invest and will add to debt burdens for most Chinese companies, requiring larger proportions of cash to reduce debt rather than increasing output. But the deflationary threat centers around a larger problem Beijing is confronting at present: declining confidence among Chinese private firms and entrepreneurs.

Private Firms Remain Cautious

One of the most important consequences of the slowdown in China's economy and the change in economic policymaking processes has been a significant deterioration in confidence and risk-taking by China's private firms and entrepreneurs. Official statistics point to the downgrade, although they likely underreport the magnitude of the change in private sentiment. Official fixed asset investment growth among private firms has averaged only 1.7 percent in nominal terms since 2020, compared to 12.3 percent over the previous decade (2012 to 2019).[26] Some of this decline in private investment is naturally linked to the collapse in the property sector, but this also impacted many state-owned property developers. Credit demand among private enterprises has certainly declined, along with the overall slowdown in credit growth. Other sources of finance such as venture capital and private equity have seen even more dramatic collapses. Official data are difficult to find, but technology analysts at Crunchbase claimed that venture funding in China in 2024 was the lowest since 2014, with the full-year level likely to be just above $20 billion.[27] The sharpest declines were evident in early-stage financing for new companies. For comparison, $20 billion in financing reflects only around two days of new credit produced by China's banks. Individual private firms may still be able to raise money for expansion, but in the economy as a whole, private firms are largely on their own.

For China to return to 4 to 5 percent GDP growth over the next decade, faster productivity growth than current rates will be essential. That productivity growth is unlikely to emerge from state-owned enterprises and LGFVs. Even China's industrial policy objectives depend heavily upon the innovative capacity of private companies. Therefore, the financing available for private enterprises to expand becomes an important influence on the capacity of the overall Chinese economy to increase productivity growth. Private firms are also the primary sources of employment in China, responsible for at least half of total employment in the country and a significant majority of new jobs created. Chinese officials frequently cite a powerful but oversimplified statistic that private firms represent 50 percent of national tax revenue, 60 percent of GDP, 70 percent of technological innovation, 80 percent of urban employment, and 90 percent of total registered enterprises.[28] Many of these enterprises, of course, are sole proprietorships in the services sector, involving small-scale retail operations.

China's private sector has suffered in recent years under both political pressure from the crackdowns on Internet platform companies and education and tutoring companies, as well as the impact of restrictions on movement under zero-COVID policies. Government assistance to private firms during COVID restrictions was generally limited to rolling over loans and promising new credit. Many smaller enterprises still struggled to keep the doors open given the on-again/off-again pattern of China's COVID restrictions from 2020 to 2022. In 2020 alone, a two-time survey of Chinese small and medium-sized enterprises revealed that 19 percent of corporations and 25 percent of sole proprietorships surveyed had closed during the year.[29]

An ongoing anti-corruption campaign within the financial sector is similarly creating problems for China's private firms.[30] Private companies have always struggled to access credit from China's banks. Chinese loan officers typically lend on the basis of government guarantees and fixed assets as collateral. In a banking system where most profits are generated by the volume of lending, it is far easier to lend large amounts to safe state-owned companies than smaller amounts to private firms. In some cases, private firms would pay fees to third parties for credit guarantees on their loans in order to make them attractive to banks. A loan officer would probably raise questions internally before making loans to private enterprises that might default, rather than loans to state-owned enterprises that were always going to be guaranteed, even if the underlying business was unprofitable. The current anti-corruption campaign in the financial sector, which has targeted banking system officials, regulators, and NBFIs, only introduces even more caution into China's financial system, making it even more difficult for private firms to access credit. The campaign may slow down in the future, but patterns of credit allocation tilting toward state-owned firms are entrenched and would require more fundamental changes in the financial system to shift those patterns.

The politically motivated crackdowns on technology firms had a far more chilling effect, as private entrepreneurs found themselves the targets of political campaigns, rather than simply being ensnared in regulatory disputes. In 2021, many of the founders of prominent Internet companies, such as Colin Huang of Pinduoduo and Zhang Yiming of Bytedance, resigned their formal positions as executives of the companies (but retained shareholding stakes), given the change in the political climate.[31] The message that China had sent to the founders of some of its prominent firms was that they were growing too powerful, and the government was intending to control their growth and potential influence. While the regulatory crackdown ended in 2022 and the leadership soon found themselves reaching out to private firms once again and encouraging their growth – with Xi Jinping publicly meeting with Jack Ma in February 2025 – the costs of these past crackdowns will linger, creating a significant problem in encouraging entrepreneurs to take risks and start new ventures.

The broader issue confronting private firms in China is the continued importance of state-owned firms to Beijing's development plans, and the clear statist tone to Xi Jinping's governance. It is always easy for Chinese leaders to argue that they want "both" state-owned and private firms to prosper in China's economy. In March 2023, Xi Jinping argued that private firms bear responsibility along with state companies to deliver prosperity to China.[32] In July 2023, following a weak recovery, the State Council unveiled multiple measures to make the private sector "bigger, better, and stronger," with pledges to protect property rights and support financing for these firms.[33] By August 2024, the National Development and Reform Commission, China's state planning agency, had updated a "17-point plan" to encourage private capital investment, mostly involving coordination between Beijing and local governments on key investment priorities.[34] The Central Economic Work Conference in December 2024 promised additional support for the private sector, including eliminating "cutthroat competition" and limiting the tax and fee collection practices of local governments.[35] By February 2025, Xi Jinping was meeting directly with the leaders of several private firms, including those that had previously been the targets of politically motivated regulatory campaigns, and was encouraging them to support China's economic recovery. None of these measures has addressed the fundamental problem facing China's private sector: if overall credit growth slows and fiscal revenues are declining, as long as the state sector retains implicit guarantees and the private sector does not, then state firms will continue to benefit from better access to a shrinking pool of financial resources. The problems facing China's economy are not simply linked to problems of confidence among private firms, but the basic capacity of the financial and fiscal systems to fund new investment, whether by private or state-owned enterprises.

Who Loses? The Politics of Writing Down Bad Debt

Given the continued decay of China's fiscal and financial systems, Beijing has stark choices ahead. China's leaders can either allow the decay to continue, reducing the effectiveness of policy in maintaining growth and potentially the risk of unexpected crisis, or they can embark upon structural reforms to the system. Those reforms would need to change the ways in which China's financial system allocates credit and how the fiscal system directs resources to Chinese households. The investment-led growth model is now producing rapidly diminishing returns, and the financial system cannot sustain it further. The problems that reformers will face are fundamental: Who will be cut off from credit and fiscal resources in the future? Whose claims on those defaulted companies and assets will be honored, and who will lose their investments or deposits? It is often mentioned that China's bad debt problems can be fixed by simply shifting resources around among state entities, since all of the debt is internally held. But the process involves cutting off those who had previously relied upon the financial system for credit, and they will naturally be angry about those decisions.

Decisions to cut certain firms off from new credit can become fraught with political implications. Most of China's bad debt has been generated by state-owned enterprises and local governments themselves. If their activities need to be controlled, what will be the future role of state-owned firms in the economy? Will they still receive implicit guarantees, or can SOEs actually fail? And if they do fail, what does this mean for the sectors they used to control, such as telecommunications and energy? If a local government can fail, what happens in terms of social service provision for the citizens of that jurisdiction? How do officials know what to prioritize?

Answering these questions is far from straightforward, particularly for Chinese officials who have only presided over a period of rising prosperity and growing levels of government wherewithal. When the Soviet Union's leadership faced similar questions in the late 1960s, the divides over these issues were ideological as well as economic, tied to the vision of the Soviet state and its role as an example of Communist political and economic organization for the world. The Soviets' inability to agree upon how to reform the state and to write down the capital stock of the Soviet Union ultimately produced the pushback against reform and the economic stagnation of the Brezhnev era, as Yakov Feygin's work has detailed extensively.[36]

For Beijing, the primary decisions that need to be made concern the fate of central SOEs and local government debt. Many countries have state-owned firms providing public goods, services, and utilities, even at the cost of persistent fiscal losses. There is nothing uniquely Chinese about SOEs as an important pillar of the structure of a modern economy. What is different in China is the scale of the financial support for the state sector.[37] China remains an investment-led economy in which most investment is not funded through direct fiscal allocations but via the state-owned banking system. Even though credit growth has slowed, new credit in China's economy averaged $4.9 trillion per year from 2020 to 2024, based on the PBOC's preferred measure of credit growth.[38] As detailed in chapter 2, over half of that credit likely flowed to the state sector.

In order to change these patterns, there are two critical decisions involved: changing the funding mechanisms for SOEs and local governments and shifting their uses of available financing toward more productive activities. Both decisions would probably slow economic growth sharply in the short term, by reducing investment. Curtailing credit growth to the state sector would drive bankruptcies, unemployment, and a sharp reduction in industrial output almost immediately. That would likely have secondary effects on household consumption as more employees of these enterprises lose their jobs. Replacing that credit growth entirely with direct fiscal outlays would involve a significant expansion in government borrowing from banks, and an unsustainable fiscal situation. The annual fiscal deficit would likely expand from its current level around 7.5 to 9 percent of GDP to close to 15 to 20 percent of GDP. While this could be financed internally, the banks that used to make loans to state-owned enterprises would essentially be extending the same financing to the central government, earning lower returns, and therefore limiting their capacity to add more assets in the future or to lend to the private sector. Without changing how SOEs and local government companies are investing, the debt levels would simply keep rising, but they would be held by the central government rather than banks.

Beijing has started the process of restructuring a portion of local government debt, without making any significant changes to the investment activities of local governments themselves. In late 2023, following a significant financial work conference held every five years, Chinese authorities issued an internal circular, known as Circular 35, which designated twelve provinces as "high-risk" regions for local debt.[39] Within those twelve provinces, the circular stipulated, the debts accrued by local governments would receive direct government and central bank support through the end of 2025. In exchange for that support, new borrowing would be limited. Banks were then encouraged to renegotiate debt with local governments and their LGFVs at lower interest rates. In late 2024, the Ministry of Finance went further and authorized a five-year plan to swap 10 trillion yuan of higher-interest local government debt for lower-interest local government bonds. The localities were still on the hook to repay the debt, but it would now bear lower interest rates. While leaving the system that had generated rising local government debt levels unchanged, these policy adjustments shifted more of the costs of local debt to China's banks, who would be forced to accept lower interest rates on loans to LGFVs and bonds issued by localities.

From the perspective of China's leadership, there is an internal logic to such an adjustment in costs. The banking system grew rapidly and profited from the expansion of credit to local governments. Now local governments are suffering from paying interest to banks. It may be persuasive to argue in internal discussions that banks should bear more of the costs of this local government debt for the sake of China's financial stability. The problem is that *someone* within China's political system will need to pay for the costs of the bad debt already accrued – there is no free lunch. Forcing this cost upon banks will reduce their profitability and their capacity to fund investment in the future. A local government fiscal crisis would then create additional risks of bank failures similar to those of Baoshang and Jinzhou in 2019. Forcing the costs upon the central government is not fundamentally different, as many trillions of yuan in bonds would need to be issued in order to either recapitalize China's banks or to buy the bad assets from China's banks without banks facing losses. Those bonds would need to be purchased by the same banks, which would also reduce their returns on the assets. Alternatively, they could be purchased by the central bank, effectively "monetizing" China's debt. The likely costs of these steps would be to either generate inflation (a debasement of the currency), or more probably, a sustained depreciation of the exchange rate and China's overseas purchasing power.

During the last banking system bailout following the Asian financial crisis, most of the costs of the bailout were borne by China's households, indirectly. By fixing deposit rates at low levels relative to lending rates, China ensured a high level of profitability for the banking system and continued investment growth. The costs of lower deposit rates were administratively imposed upon Chinese households. Effectively, if the market pricing of capital existed in China, households probably could have earned far more on their savings since interest rates were cut in 2002. The profitability of the banking system in the 2000s received a significant boost from the low funding costs offered due to administrative controls on deposit rates.

But imposing further costs upon Chinese households would be a political problem for Beijing. The restructuring of China's banking system in the late 1990s was largely a "bail-out" or an external injection of government funding to buy assets from banks. Another model for bank restructuring is a "bail-in" where investors or depositors are forced to accept some of the costs of restructuring. This is different from a straightforward default of a risky financial institution such as China's P2P lenders, in which high-risk loans produced losses and investors in the products offered by these platforms simply lost their money. There was no structured bailout or planned bail-in.

Another experience in Henan in the spring of 2022 offered a cautionary tale for Chinese authorities. Bank runs began in four small rural lenders when some investment products offered by the banks started to default. As depositors asked for their money back, banks tried to clarify that what their customers had purchased were not deposits, but investment products, meaning that customers should bear the investment risk.

Naturally, bank customers argued that since the bank sold the products, the bank should stand behind them. There were a series of demonstrations in the provincial capital of Zhengzhou and at the banks themselves, and eventually a solution was crafted in which customers with claims of 50,000 yuan or less would be paid first.[40] The Henan bank runs offered a real-time test of the public reaction to potential bail-ins of the banking system, and it was overwhelmingly toxic for the authorities trying to manage the public fallout.

China's leaders must decide not only who will bear the costs of the bad loans generated during the last round of investment expansion, but what the Chinese economy will look like after any restructuring of bad debts. A consumption-driven economy would likely grow at slower overall rates, because investment would slow more significantly, and investment still represents 42 percent of China's GDP every year. Local government infrastructure projects are currently in process, and some will need to continue construction, but how many? And how will they be financed if the banking system can no longer provide the same levels of lending? As tax revenues from investment-driven growth continue declining, China's households will likely need to pay more in taxes. But this would also reduce the household income levels necessary to drive faster household consumption growth. None of the choices facing Beijing is straightforward. But unless the choice is to continue the stagnation and decay of the financial and fiscal systems, Beijing will need to grapple with the question of who will lose in any structural reform of China's economy.

The System is Most Vulnerable When it is Being Reformed

For years, the long-term trends in China's economy and financial system have appeared unsustainable. But the short-term threats to financial stability remain under control. The question that invariably arises when confronting this set of conditions is "How long can this go on?" with the questioner usually suggesting that it is only a matter of time before financial crisis will hit. "Crisis" is a loaded word, meant to evoke a sudden panic or lack of credibility in financial markets or policy measures. Its invocation recalls events such as the panic over subprime mortgage-based securities in 2007 and 2008 and the currency devaluations across Asia in 1997 and 1998.

The more precise question to ask in China's case is: How long can these trends continue before China faces *the same economic outcomes as a financial crisis*? Here the answers are clearer, as these consequences are already apparent in China's economy, in the decay of the financial and fiscal systems. China has already seen a sharp slowdown in economic growth, led by its vitally important property sector and local government infrastructure investment. Private sector credit demand remains weak, similar to the effects of a shock to aggregate demand. The downshift in economic growth is structural in nature, as the economy is unlikely to recover to previous growth rates. Fiscal policy has been ineffective in maintaining growth, because of the debt levels among local governments and their related companies, which prevent a significant rebound in infrastructure investment. The problems within the financial system call out for more fundamental restructuring, as risks continue rising to the surface. Overall, these would be similar consequences to the effects of a widespread financial crisis in China.

The decay of China's fiscal and financial institutions has steadily eroded economic and policy performance, rather than producing a sudden shock or crisis. This is the result of explicit political choices. Injecting short-term funding to prevent local governments from defaulting on certain risky bonds can always prevent a crisis today. But unless the signal is communicated that all such bonds will similarly receive bailouts, nothing will prevent another local government from risking default tomorrow. In fact, local officials might actually want to threaten default in order to clarify that they will receive direct financial support from Beijing.

But that does not mean that Beijing has improbably avoided the risks of a financial crisis. Instead, China's system is ironically most vulnerable to crisis precisely when it is being meaningfully reformed. The possibility of crisis emerges when assets and institutions previously thought to be guaranteed are suddenly declared by the government to be risky, in order to allow Beijing to reduce risks in the system overall. At present, no individual LGFV has defaulted on its publicly traded bonds. But should Beijing see the need to manage systemic risks by introducing the prospect that local government-related companies could actually fail, then all such holders of these bonds will quickly rush to sell them, potentially starting a financial panic. As more of the government's implicit guarantees are lifted or questioned, the remaining guaranteed assets suddenly appear risky as well.

The possibility of a financial crisis *directly created by policymakers* during attempts to reform the system has produced the most acute episodes of panic in China's financial system over the past two decades. In June 2013, the PBOC signaling that the central bank was unlikely to extend additional liquidity to commercial banks to manage their WMP redemptions triggered a rapid withdrawal of lenders from China's money market and caused short-term interbank money market rates to rise to 20 to 30 percent. The crisis was averted only by the PBOC's complete reversal of its stance, by providing banks with the money they needed only days later. In a different context in November 2020, the Henan provincial government triggered a complete panic in China's corporate bond market by defaulting on bond investors in state-owned company Yongcheng Coal. Even though the provincial government had money available to repay the bond, market rumors suggested that local officials had redirected the funds away from bondholders and toward salaries for migrant workers in the firm. While there would be a clear political logic in making this choice, no companies in Henan could issue debt for a few months after the decision. Investors had previously considered the provincial government's support as a source of stability. But now local government support had become a new source of credit risk, as the local officials might just decide not to pay bondholders this month. Markets can quickly imagine the consequences if other localities attempted to follow this example.

As described in chapter 2, the slowdown in credit growth has created higher levels of financial risk in new types of asset classes, moving closer and closer to the center of China's financial system – its local governments and state-owned banks. In contemplating how to reform China's financial and fiscal system, it is probable that state-owned enterprises and local governments will default on loans and bonds and that Beijing's reform decisions will need to involve cutting these institutions off from new credit, leaving investors and lenders holding the bag. How China's leaders make these choices will determine the future trajectory of China's economy. But the fact that these reforms themselves pose the most significant risk of financial crisis in China can help to explain Beijing's long period of inaction so far. Decay is destructive and debilitating, but gradual, and therefore appears safer. If one risky choice could destabilize China's economy and financial system and produce a wave of negative coverage concerning the competence of China's leaders and political system, it becomes much easier to explain why decay has continued even as its long-term costs accumulate.

6

A Broken Chinese Economy and the Rest of the World

Many of the statistics about the unprecedented expansion of China's financial system are abstractions – large numbers that are difficult to conceptualize. But they have real-world consequences, often materializing in unexpected places. China's rapid credit expansion was unsustainable, but along with that lending growth came a dramatic surge in China's money supply, in newly printed RMB within China's domestic economy. China's money supply expanded to the equivalent of $43 trillion in 2024 at year-end exchange rates, around twice the size of the US money supply. With all of that new money created in RMB onshore in China and declining investment possibilities inside China from the property and equity markets, Chinese households and corporates have strong incentives to try to diversify their savings by moving money overseas. When authorities tightened capital controls following the depreciation of China's currency in 2015 and 2016, it became more difficult for Chinese citizens and businesspeople to move money abroad. But the massive size of China's money supply and the country's unprecedented onshore credit expansion produced global impacts in unexpected places, because of the strong demand from Chinese citizens to move money overseas.

One of these unanticipated venues has been international money laundering and drug trafficking. Recent reporting on trends in organized crime suggest that Chinese underground money laundering operations have dominated the illicit industry around the world in recent years, because of Chinese households' and corporates' demand to move money outside of China. This outsized demand for foreign currency – which is tied most directly to the political forces in China keeping credit growth and money creation at elevated rates – has been matched with one of the world's largest suppliers of illicit foreign currency: international drug cartels.[1] Through a series of mirror transactions between China, the United States, and Mexico, the profits that the drug trade generates in illicit cash often end up matched with the outsized demand for dollars created indirectly by China's unreformed financial system. When drug cartels need to move their cash revenues into the global financial system, it is now often Chinese syndicates who facilitate those flows. If capital outflows from China intensify as the economy continues to slow, this will likely be an even more prominent concern in the years ahead.

Moreover, the global emergence of Chinese money laundering operations in the late 2010s coincides directly with both the rapid growth of China's financial system and the depreciation of China's currency in 2015 and 2016. The depreciation of the RMB and newly tightened capital controls at the time generated new but unsatisfied demand for foreign currency from Chinese citizens and businesses. More interesting still, Chinese crime syndicates not only took over previously dominant drug money laundering operations, but also dramatically reduced costs to the cartels. A 2022 ProPublica report on the money laundering activities of Chinese syndicates quoted a retired US Drug Enforcement Administration agent, claiming that commissions on moving the cash into the financial system were falling from 13–18 percent under Colombian networks to only 1–2 percent under Chinese networks.[2]

As China's economy slowed, the world became increasingly concerned about overcapacity in China reducing profitability in several industries as exports of goods surged around the world, reducing prices. But in the criminal underworld, the exact same thing was happening in the money laundering industry. China's excessive credit expansion in RMB was producing too much money onshore relative to the growth in its productive uses in China's economy. That meant more Chinese wanted to move the money abroad but could not. That demand for foreign currency outside the formal financial system came from tens of thousands of Chinese households and businesses and was so strong that it presumably pushed the prices and margins of money laundering for international drug organizations lower and lower. The money demand was the primary driver of the illicit activity, as John Tobon of US Homeland Security Investigations argued in an article on the subject, "The laundering that occurs for the Mexican DTOs [drug trafficking organizations] is an ancillary activity, merely a means to an end for Chinese money brokers."[3] China's excess capacity in money creation and the slowdown in China's economy were indirectly contributing to forces that made the operations of the drug trade cheaper around the world. This is only one example of the effects of the expanding Chinese financial system and China's structural slowdown reverberating far beyond China's borders.

New Talking Points, Slower Adjustments in Thinking

It is difficult to overstate how quickly global perceptions of China's economic trajectory changed in 2023 and 2024, well before the US–China trade war intensified. One might assume that this change in China's fortunes would be welcomed in Washington, given the potential advantages to the United States in longer-term strategic competition with Beijing. But ironically, official Washington has been highly resistant to the message that China's macroeconomic conditions are deteriorating, if not openly hostile to that message. There are several reasons for this resistance. From a military and security perspective, the perceived risks from China's military modernization efforts are still rising, and a downturn in economic growth is seen as irrelevant to strategic competition, rightly or wrongly. Through the lenses of industrial modernization or technological competition, China is still competing with the United States despite its economic slowdown, and posting significant gains and achievements. The fervor over DeepSeek's activities in artificial intelligence is only one recent example. For many officials who tried for years to refocus US efforts on threatening behavior and capabilities from China, the message that China is weakening economically is unwelcome, and may be perceived as distracting from more targeted policies to address China-related threats. The Chinese state still appears capable in many areas of direct competition with the United States, and to be leading in several areas of global manufacturing. Widespread skepticism remains that the downturn in China's economy is severe, given several previous calls for China's economic demise over the past two decades. Economists have been very wrong about China before, and very few in Washington actively embrace the argument that China's structural slowdown should change US policy options.

Despite this resistance, the debate about China's economic future is shifting the foundations of strategic competition, both in Beijing and Washington. Part of this shift occurred because of how Chinese officials themselves started discussing the economy. Chinese officials and economists often travel to Washington to exchange views. Many of these conversations occur in public in the context of regular meetings of the International Monetary Fund and the World Bank in April and October, but others are more ad hoc and informal, or are protected by Chatham House rules, in which one can cite what was said at a meeting but not who said it. As a frequent participant in these conversations with Chinese contacts I had maintained from my years of research in Beijing, one learns to read between the lines and understand where the official talking points end and the analysts' real opinions begin.

In early 2023, for example, Chinese officials and economists were extremely optimistic about the prospects for a recovery after COVID restrictions had been lifted. Many expressed the view that obviously the COVID controls had created significant economic costs, and there would be a quick and substantial rebound in not only consumer spending but property sales and infrastructure spending as these controls were lifted and the economy recovered. Achieving 5 percent GDP growth was no problem at all in 2023, the official line emphasized, because economic activity had been so clearly deeply depressed in the previous year, when China had only officially claimed 3 percent GDP growth. (In reality, the economy likely contracted in 2022.) The Chinese economists at these meetings genuinely seemed to believe this line of argument in early 2023, even if they were somewhat skeptical about the strength of the rebound in household consumption. Many expressed concern that China would be perceived as contributing to global inflationary pressures – still an acute issue at the time – because the rebound in Chinese demand would occur much faster than the resumption of China's industrial output and supply of manufactured goods.

Of course, China's economic rebound fell far short of those expectations. The property sector continued contracting in 2023, and as China's most important industry, there was no other source of investment that offset the impact of that decline. Household consumption did recover, but at very slow rates, because unlike Western governments, Beijing had not provided additional support for household incomes during the pandemic. With limited savings and rising concerns about their jobs and incomes, the recovery in real household spending was modest, likely around 5 to 6 percent compared to 2022 levels, and contributing only around 2 percentage points to GDP growth.[4] Rather than Chinese demand contributing to global inflationary pressures, prices of consumer goods trended toward zero growth and producer prices remained in deflation. By October 2023, China's leaders reversed course, revealing that they were aware of the extent of the weakness in domestic demand, and revised the central government budget in the middle of the year for the first time since the Asian financial crisis, to provide additional fiscal stimulus and issue even more government bonds.

One of the signs that China's economic slowdown was becoming far more severe was the rise in China's trade surplus, with imports and domestic demand slowing considerably relative to China's exports. By early 2024, the term that started to circulate in overseas policy discussions of China's slowdown was "overcapacity." The concept was far from new, as Chinese economists had discussed excess industrial capacity in the country contributing to deflationary pressures in the domestic economy for several years. But it became a convenient and useful term for governments to discuss the problems that China's economic slowdown had created for the world.

China's economy remained driven by investment by 2024, but China's own sources of domestic demand – property and infrastructure spending – were slowing. This meant that the additional output from China's rapid investment growth ends up being exported to the rest of the world, usually at lower prices. Those lower prices in turn depress prices of the same goods elsewhere around the world. This process may help Chinese firms gain market share, but at the cost of competition with producers in other countries, with the threat to wipe out profits (and eventually employment) for several global industries. Because Chinese firms operate with indirect sources of state support and the backing of a financial system that continued to roll over credit to unproductive enterprises, even highly unprofitable firms in China could continue producing goods and gaining market share by offering lower and lower prices while overseas firms went bankrupt trying to compete with them. Unless domestic demand in China improves significantly, China's investment-led growth model now depends upon claiming a larger share of a shrinking pie of global demand, while forcing other countries to disinvest or shut down their own factories. In the current pattern of investment-led growth, China can only continue growing its economy if other countries reduce their own investment, economic growth, and employment.

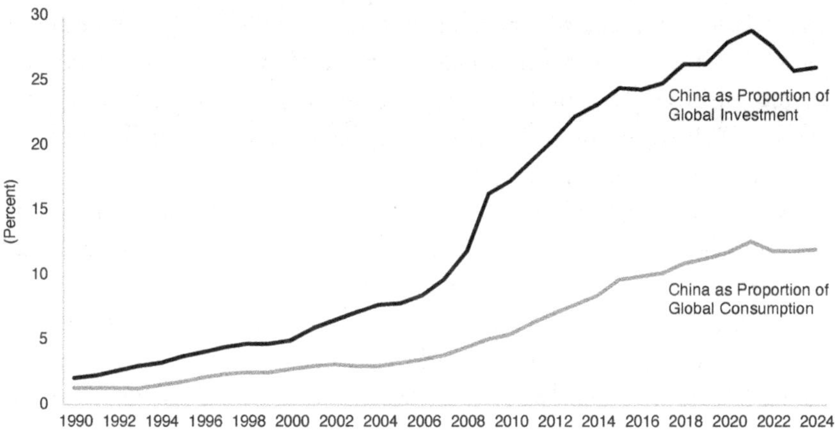

Figure 6.1 China as proportion of global investment and consumption, 1990–2024.
Data source: World Bank.

Even though overcapacity has no precise economic definition, the concept effectively described the problems that rising Chinese trade surpluses were creating for the rest of the world. The threat of "de-industrialization" in competition with Chinese firms became far more pressing and politically salient, particularly in Europe. By 2023, China was responsible for around 27 percent of global investment, but only around 12 percent of global consumption (figure 6.1).[5] In the context of rising trade imbalances, the world was looking for China's leaders to finally commit to reducing these gaps between production and consumption and to emphasize the importance of promoting domestic demand and rising household consumption.

But the policy response from Beijing in 2024 was tone deaf to these concerns. The two most significant policy documents that China released that year – the government work report at the National People's Congress and the results of the Third Plenum meeting in July – both clearly prioritized industrial policy and the need for advanced manufacturing investment to boost productivity growth. The rest of the world saw only more industries in which China would attempt to export its output abroad rather than consuming at home. Fundamentally, a manufacturing-led economy can only grow as fast as the demand for those manufactured goods, and most of that demand existed outside of China. Chinese economists themselves had discussed overcapacity problems within Chinese industry for years, but in the spring of 2024, Beijing's propaganda authorities started pushing back publicly against the term, after foreign governments had highlighted its salience as a potential justification for tariffs and trade defenses against Chinese imports.[6]

When informal discussions with Chinese officials resumed in Washington in late 2024, the tone of economists' comments had suddenly turned distinctly downbeat. Chinese economists who had previously been optimistic about the scope of the post-COVID recovery now argued that the rest of the world needed to understand that China's demand would remain weak after such a dramatic adjustment in the property sector, as every other economy that had seen such a property bubble burst needed years to emerge in a healthier state. China was aware that the steps that had been taken to prop up domestic demand were only getting started, but the hope was that this would build momentum if the initial measures were successful. In one meeting I joined in the winter of 2024, when asked for comment on the prospect of structural fiscal reforms to improve domestic demand, one of China's most prominent economic thinkers simply shook his head.

The economic technocrats realized the conundrum that China faced. The choices that Beijing needed to make were structural in nature, and there was no political momentum to take these difficult decisions. Trade tensions with the rest of the world were inevitable as long as China's leaders emphasized more production and exports, and China's own domestic demand lagged. Washington still viewed China as a competitive threat. China could only hold back the global political pressure for trade restrictions and de-risking for so long. In 2025, that global pushback accelerated significantly, starting with new tariffs from the United States.

The World Confronts a Slowing China

This chapter discusses what a broken Chinese economy means for the rest of the world, and how the world will confront the consequences of a slowing China. A structural slowdown in China's economy means that China will continue to rely upon export manufacturing, even if China's rising output of goods reduces prices in the rest of the world. China will be fighting to increase its share of a shrinking pool of global demand, rather than expanding that pool.

- Global political resistance to China's export-oriented economic model will intensify in the years ahead, regardless of changes in global political leadership.
- One of the consequences of sustained capital outflows from China will likely be a weaker Chinese exchange rate. That should widen China's trade surpluses by further reducing China's imports and overseas purchasing power.
- With a slowing economy at home, China will be under greater pressure to find investment opportunities abroad through continuing its Belt and Road Initiative, but the appetite among developing economies to borrow from China will likely weaken.
- Liberal democratic governments should reconceptualize the risks that China poses. Rather than foundational risks that China's economic model might prevail in a larger systemic competition, the threat from China is narrower but still dangerous, likely emerging over shorter timeframes.
- Confronting a slowing China, de-risking should be more targeted at preventing specific risks from security threats or technological competition, with less resulting concern that China's economy will continue expanding.
- Most of the risks resulting from China's control of global manufacturing supply chains depend upon Beijing's actual behavior, which relates to China's political incentives.

The pushback against China's slowing economy and rising exports has already begun. How China responds to the change in global public perceptions of its economic trajectory will influence the scale and scope of restructuring in the global economy in the years ahead.

China's Rising Trade Surplus and Overcapacity

One of the most important economic impacts of China's slowing economy is exporting overcapacity to the rest of the world. Overcapacity has no precise economic definition. Several economic phenomena are indicative of excessive industrial capacity, including low capacity utilization rates for existing factories or facilities, declining prices and profits within the industry, or a high degree of dependence upon exports relative to domestic demand. But none of these factors individually is sufficient to identify that a sector or industry is facing persistent overcapacity. In China, however, the primary evidence of overcapacity has been the continued growth of investment in several industries despite declining profits and sales prices, as well as the persistent rise in China's manufactured goods trade surplus in recent years.

China's trade surplus has risen significantly since the economy has slowed. In 2022, the surplus rose to $838 billion from only $352 billion in 2018, and surged to an astonishing $992 billion in 2024.[7] Given that China still runs a trade deficit in services, the rise in China's trade surplus is almost entirely a byproduct of manufactured goods trade, with China's overall trade surplus reaching almost 1 percent of global GDP in 2024 (figure 6.2). This represents a significant proportion of global demand for manufactured goods that must be absorbed outside of China and generally places downward pressure on prices and profits in multiple industries.

Importantly, overcapacity in China is a system-wide problem, with multiple policy incentives contributing to expansions of output and industrial capacity, without considering whether that capacity can be matched with domestic demand. Local governments collect value-added tax on production within their own jurisdictions, which creates incentives

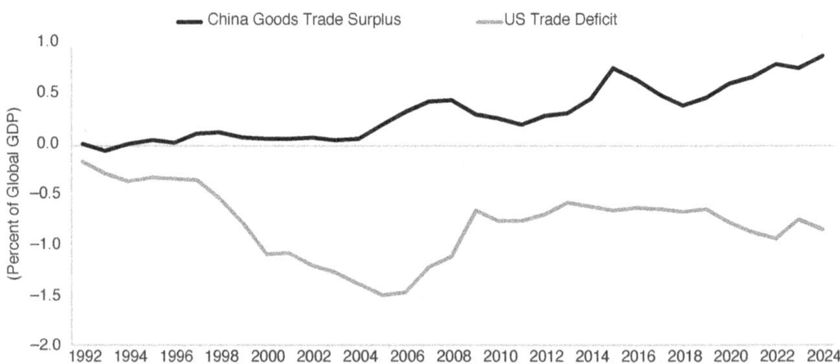

Figure 6.2 China's rising goods trade surplus, 1992–2024.
Data source: World Bank; China General Administration of Customs.

to expand investment simply to generate tax revenues, even if this investment is ultimately unprofitable. Often, Chinese firms benefit from below-market prices for land, energy, or critical intermediate inputs. The financial system continues to extend loans to state-owned enterprises and local governments, even if those loans cannot be repaid, which allows unprofitable enterprises to operate and continue producing long after they would be forced to exit the market in a system without these financing guarantees. In several important industries, government subsidies and investment funds directly provide financing for new investment, as these are designated as strategic objectives of the state.[8] All of these factors make it difficult to identify a single cause of China's industrial overcapacity, as the system of implicit state guarantees and government support both initiate new investments that might not otherwise occur in market economies and extend the lifespans of unprofitable firms.

For companies around the world competing against Chinese firms, these types of system-wide incentives encouraging additional output at lower prices create significant disadvantages. Trade policy has long focused on the prospect of firms "dumping" goods below cost to gain market share. In China's case, the accusation is more difficult to make directly, because the entire cost structure of Chinese firms has been impacted by system-wide policy incentives that encourage production without consideration for final demand.[9] As China's trade surpluses have expanded, many governments have broadened their search for remedies against China's exports, by seeking to identify individual policy distortions that are producing cost advantages. But the search for such remedies remains difficult, as many Chinese firms may have benefited initially from subsidized costs early in their development, but no direct subsidies after they had already achieved a certain level of market share.

The system-wide nature of China's policy distortions in manufacturing is primarily evident when looking at the broadest levels of trade activity. China is the world's leading exporter by value and volume, representing around 14 percent of global exports by value, but the breadth of China's export dominance is far more remarkable. Analyzing individual export products using the Harmonized System (HS) codes, China represented over half of total imports of developing economies in an astonishing 20 percent of product categories by 2022 (up from 15 percent in 2019), and 8 percent for developed economies.[10] No other economy in history had established this type of broad-based dominance of export manufacturing across multiple industries, besides perhaps the United States at the end of World War II.

The larger concern that emerges from China's overcapacity is the threat of outright de-industrialization in the rest of the world. Competitive pressures from rising productivity exist in several industries, but rapidly declining prices caused by investments made without consideration for final demand do not. As China remains committed to investment-led growth, China can only expand its own economy relative to the rest of the world by increasing export market share, or forcing other countries to reduce investment, and likely employment. The solar photovoltaic (PV) industry is a case in point. For most of the 2000s and 2010s, Chinese firms were important players but not the only firms active in producing solar panels and polysilicon for PV modules. But by 2020, China had a dominant position across virtually all components of the solar PV supply chain. As a report from the International Energy Agency on the industry claimed, "During 2010–2015, China expanded its manufacturing capacity twice as quickly as the rest of the world, leading to a major global supply glut and causing polysilicon prices to plummet 70 percent, pushing many producers out of the market."[11] At the same time, the report noted, additional Chinese investments since 2020 caused plants to close in Japan, Korea, and the United States. Chinese investment in the solar PV industry occurred primarily because of government incentives to expand output early in the industry's development. Even though prices remained under pressure, Chinese firms continued to add capacity.

The threat of de-industrialization in the solar industry has already materialized, but the threat to global auto manufacturing, along with its associated political sensitivities, is still developing. China's efforts to develop a domestic electric vehicle (EV) and battery industry started as an attempt to reduce dependence upon imported energy. Years of subsidies for both producers and buyers of electric vehicles and batteries, including indirect measures such as easing application requirements for license plates in major cities, helped China's electric vehicle industry grow rapidly throughout the 2010s. Now, the large number of players in the industry has led to a crippling price war, dramatically reducing profits and the potential attractiveness of new investments in the industry, both inside and outside China. Even as China's domestic demand for automobiles in volume terms peaked in 2017, China's capacity to produce electric vehicles continued expanding at the expense of facilities for traditional internal combustion engine (ICE) vehicles.

This also naturally encouraged China's automobile exports to expand as well, with domestic firms seeking to export EVs at higher prices in overseas markets, particularly in Europe. By 2023, China had suddenly become the world's largest exporter of automobiles, overtaking Japan. Most of the initial gains in international markets were the result of exports of traditional vehicles to Russia and Mexico, but the rising cost competitiveness of Chinese EV exports created the prospect that Chinese EVs would also displace global manufacturers in Southeast Asia, Latin America, and Europe. The rise in Chinese exports amidst falling prices has raised new concerns about the displacement of auto manufacturers around the world. Several German automakers and auto suppliers started reducing output and laying off workers in 2024, including Volkswagen, Porsche, ZF Friedrichshafen, Bosch, and Continental.[12] The head of Brazil's automotive industry association commented in January 2025 that the country was becoming a "dumping market" for China's surplus output.[13] The Biden Administration enacted 100 percent tariffs on imports of Chinese EVs in 2023, well before the recent surge in overall US tariffs on Chinese imports.

The surprising element of China's surge in auto exports was the speed with which conditions in the industry changed, spurred by the slowdown in China's domestic demand. Not only were Chinese firms becoming more cost competitive, but weaker consumption in China left the country with nowhere else to send surplus production. The change has been readily apparent in industries such as solar PV production and the auto sector, but it extends to many other industries as well.

For several developing economies in Southeast Asia, the pressures created by Chinese overcapacity are multifaceted. Many countries in the region are becoming more and more dependent upon China for imports of critical intermediate goods, while also competing more directly with Chinese firms in manufacturing of mid-tech goods. As a result, their exports to China have declined. Most of the surge in China's trade surplus since 2022 has occurred in Asia, largely because of declining Chinese imports of intermediate components and consumer goods from

Southeast Asia. This reflects both weakening Chinese domestic demand and rising Chinese investment in vertical integration of supply chains. At the same time, these countries are on the front lines of de-risking and diversification of supply chains away from China, which includes investments by Chinese firms attempting to reduce costs and avoid China-specific trade and regulatory restrictions. Chinese overcapacity means that the benefits Southeast Asian economies gain from trade with China are eroding, even as these countries become more dependent upon China for their own efforts to develop more resilient supply chains and independent industrial capabilities.

The rising concentration of global manufacturing supply chains in China is a peculiar development. Should China develop a dominant market share in export manufacturing industries, Beijing could try to reverse deflationary trends in prices by artificially stifling competition, pushing up global prices using China's near-monopolies on production. As economist Brad Setser argued about the consequences of liberalized trade in the twenty-first century, "Free markets appear to favor a country that hasn't freed its own market."[14] As a result, China's overcapacity has raised new questions about the tradeoffs involved in a purely cost-based assessment of the benefits of trade with China. Other considerations such as national security are becoming far more important in the political calculations of China's trading partners.

The downgrade in China's economy has produced a sharp acceleration in China's trade surplus, caused primarily by weakness in China's domestic demand and China's imports. But the persistence of China's investment-led growth model and industrial policies, along with all of the indirect subsidies that are implied, have also fed the rapid growth of China's exports in a variety of sectors at lower prices. For the rest of the world, these two trends have dramatically changed the costs and benefits of trading with China, which will implicate the outcome of trade conflicts between China and the rest of the world, including the United States. There are far fewer benefits to attempting to develop China as a market for any country's exports if growth in China's domestic demand will continue to slow, and prices within China appear likely to continue falling. Similarly, while cheap Chinese goods can be attractive to countries that do not have industries vulnerable to direct competition, for most countries, the risks of de-industrialization will only become more acute in the years ahead. Even if China pares back support for prioritized sectors, only a surge in domestic demand will reduce the export of excess capacity and narrow China's trade surplus.

The Peculiar Case of China's Exchange Rate

Ironically, China's ongoing economic slowdown may cause its global export market share to expand further rather than shrink, because of the response of China's exchange rate. Conventional economic wisdom would suggest that a country with a sharply rising trade surplus would see its currency appreciate in value in response, reducing the competitiveness of its exports and eventually narrowing the trade surplus. In China, however, the exchange rate of the RMB has remained under pressure to *depreciate* against the US dollar and most other currencies, even as the trade surplus has expanded over the past five years. This is because China faces large volumes of capital outflows from Chinese households, corporates, and foreign investors, which have been even larger than the inflows from China's trade surplus most of the time. As a result, there has been more demand for foreign currency in Chinese markets than for domestic currency, and the People's Bank of China has been forced to intervene in the foreign exchange market by directing state banks to sell US dollars to meet this demand and to prevent the value of China's currency from depreciating further.

There are many reasons for this unusual situation, but the net result is that China's currency is more likely to face pressure to depreciate against the dollar than appreciate in the years ahead, even if China's trade surplus continues expanding. That would make China's exports even more attractive in global markets and likely increase China's global export market share for most manufactured goods.

China's rapid economic expansion and capital controls have created a situation in which around 98 percent of Chinese savings are held in domestic currency, in RMB. This is an abnormally high level, and if even 10 percent of those savings were converted into foreign currency, this would create around $3.2 trillion in capital outflows. The rapid expansion of China's financial system since the global financial crisis has similarly facilitated a huge expansion of China's RMB money supply, from the US dollar equivalent of $7 trillion in 2008 to $43 trillion in

2024.[15] This is the largest single-country money supply in US dollar terms in the world, far outpacing the US money supply of $21.5 trillion.[16] Because this money supply is created in domestic currency, in RMB, and makes its way into corporate and household deposits in the banking system, an expansion of $3 to 4 trillion in the equivalent value of new RMB every year creates powerful incentives for Chinese households and corporates to diversify their holdings into foreign assets. After all, US interest rates have been significantly higher than Chinese interest rates since the Federal Reserve started raising rates to fight inflation in early 2022. Anyone in China with access to foreign capital markets has an incentive to buy US dollar-denominated assets, which will provide higher interest rates than RMB-denominated assets. Even with the US economic outlook deteriorating during the trade war, these conditions are likely to persist, as Chinese interest rates will need to keep moving lower to manage China's domestic debt pressures. Capital controls can certainly slow these outflows, but they are unlikely to completely bottle them up inside China's borders.

The consequences of these dynamics in China's exchange rate for the rest of the world are surprising. One of the mechanisms often discussed to reduce the global imbalances between countries running trade deficits and countries running trade surpluses is an orderly depreciation of the US dollar, and an appreciation of other countries' currencies against the dollar. For any such global currency arrangement to work – similar to the Plaza Accord or Louvre Accord in the 1980s – China would have to be involved, as the country running the most significant trade surplus in the world. But given persistent capital outflows producing depreciation pressure on China's currency, Beijing simply cannot commit to a stable exchange rate for an extended timeframe and has no chance of committing to a stronger currency against the dollar, which would only kickstart further capital outflows. China would likely engage in such discussions with the United States if it were possible to avoid additional tariffs or trade barriers, but the reality is that Beijing cannot credibly make commitments concerning the stability of its exchange rate. Even though China has $3.2 trillion in foreign exchange reserves (and likely more ammunition through the foreign assets of state banks), that is very small relative to the size of China's $43 trillion money supply, which continues growing. The best that Beijing can promise is that they will intervene selectively to attempt to maintain the currency's stability, using their reserves at critical moments to prevent China's trade surplus from widening further.

Similarly, the chance that China can develop the RMB as a credible alternative to the US dollar is highly remote, if not infinitesimal. With China running a persistent trade surplus, RMB will remain scarce outside of China's borders. Only the countries that export more to China than they import from China are likely to receive persistent flows of RMB into their markets. Most of these countries are in Southeast Asia or are commodity exporters. The other mechanisms for RMB to leave China are through outbound lending in RMB (via the Belt and Road Initiative or other mechanisms), which is slowing, or through capital outflows from individuals, which mostly involve conversions into foreign exchange at Chinese banks.

Moreover, China has consistently prioritized the stability of the exchange rate against the dollar over the potential international role of the currency. This involves maintaining systems of capital controls that prevent outflows from China, even though these controls also reduce the attractiveness of foreign countries holding RMB. When the currency faces pressure to depreciate, China typically tries to further restrict the supply of offshore RMB, tightening liquidity offered via offshore Chinese banks. This makes it more attractive to move the offshore RMB back onshore where it can fetch higher prices, but it also reduces the possibilities of using RMB outside of China. This is the exact opposite of what the Federal Reserve does with the US dollar in a crisis, by making more dollar liquidity available to central banks around the world when global financial conditions tighten.

China's rapid expansion of its trade surplus will always raise questions about how Beijing is managing the exchange rate. Starting in 2022, China has generally acted to stabilize the currency against the dollar and other currencies, which is also in the world's interest. A managed depreciation of the currency against the dollar started in response to US tariffs in April 2025 but then stopped a few weeks later, while the RMB continued to depreciate against the euro. China is often charged with "manipulating" its currency, but there have been far more days over the past decade in which China has tried to stop its currency from *weakening* than days in which the central bank has resisted the currency strengthening. As a result, while many call for China's currency to be market-determined, the central bank withdrawing from regular intervention in the foreign exchange market would likely cause the currency to depreciate significantly over time, widening China's trade surplus. This makes it far more difficult to contemplate external measures that would meaningfully reduce China's trade imbalances. The effective remedies all start at home in Beijing.

Tariffs and Global Trade Defenses

As China's trade surpluses have expanded in recent years, the world has searched for policy options to reduce Chinese imports into several markets. Given that a market-based exchange rate adjustment is not likely to reduce China's trade imbalances, other blunter measures restricting trade have surfaced in global policy discussions. First and foremost among these are new tariffs, or taxes on imports administered at the border. Throughout the escalation of trade conflict with China in 2018 and 2019, the United States raised tariffs on Chinese imports incrementally, adding 25 percent to the cost of many categories of imports. The Biden Administration added to those with targeted tariffs on electric vehicles, batteries, and semiconductors. In October 2024, the European Union imposed tariffs on Chinese EV imports. Brazil similarly added to existing tariff levels on Chinese steel products, fiber optic cables, and a slew of additional products in October 2024.[17]

But the actions taken by the second Trump Administration reset the bar entirely. After raising new tariffs on all Chinese imports by 20 percent in two increments in February and March 2025, a rapid series of escalations following the April 2 "Liberation Day" announcements quickly saw tariffs on Chinese imports to the US raised to 145 percent. After additional retaliation, China raised tariffs on US goods to 125 percent. These levels of tariffs were essentially prohibitive of bilateral trade flows. A series of negotiations between the United States and China then paused these extreme tariff levels, while leaving most of the previous tariffs at pre-April levels.

The logic of tariffs is to incentivize domestic production relative to imports, by raising the price of imports, making domestic production more profitable and competitive. Raise tariffs high enough – and enforce them – and flows of Chinese imports will decline. The problem is that the theory breaks down quickly when reacting to globalized supply chains, a country facing depreciation pressure on its currency, and an extreme concentration of global manufacturing capacity in a single country. Restricting imports from China may mean that there is no immediate alternative supplier in another country capable of producing enough to satisfy consumer demand in a short timeframe. Placing extremely high tariffs on imports from China can simply result in trans-shipments of goods through third countries, such as Vietnam, as occurred during trade conflict with the United States during the first Trump Administration. Tariffs on individual goods can be circumvented through relabeling, deliberate undervaluation, and other means of subterfuge. When tariffs were coming down around the world during periods of trade liberalization, it made little sense to invest significant resources in tariff enforcement. But a world of much higher tariffs incentivizes exporters to actively test these controls.

Higher tariffs on all Chinese goods would likely result in pressure on China's exchange rate to depreciate, which can offset the effects of tariffs. This is what happened in the first round of the US trade conflict with China in 2018 and 2019, and there was little change in China's overall export activity despite the rise in tariffs. But there is no easy way for Beijing to offset the effect of a completely prohibitive tariff of 145 percent, or even a higher level such as 50 or 60 percent, without a collapse in the value of its currency.

Similarly, while China's economy has become more reliant upon exports as domestic demand has slowed, it is also less dependent upon exports to any individual country, including the United States. That means that any successful effort to combat the effects of Chinese overcapacity globally requires a coordinated approach to raising tariffs on Chinese imports, and political alignment on the objectives of doing so. Not all countries have the same political sensitivities to rising Chinese import levels, and some have been recipients of Chinese investment, with China-financed production of goods within their borders. Under these circumstances, it is far from a straightforward decision to raise tariffs on Chinese imports in line with US actions, delivering higher costs to domestic consumers for uncertain long-term benefits, even if there are growing political concerns about China's concentration of global manufacturing capacity. Many European countries found themselves in this difficult position in early 2025, with little desire to cooperate with the United States and raise tariffs on Chinese goods, while also seeking some other way to prevent a flood of Chinese imports.[18] Ongoing trade tensions and negotiations with the United States only make such Europe–US alignment against Chinese imports even more unlikely.

Trade policy decisions often revolve around findings related to government subsidies or dumping of products below cost, and this can generate a case for countervailing duties on individual products or industries, protecting those industries from overseas competition that allegedly benefits from unfair practices. But the case for combating rising Chinese imports with across-the-board tariffs is more difficult to make while sustaining domestic political support for these restrictions. For developed economies, the impact will be felt by domestic consumers paying higher prices or reducing consumption in the absence of alternative suppliers of some goods. For developing economies, tariffs on Chinese intermediate goods will only make it more expensive to finance the buildout of alternative manufacturing supply chains. Tariffs may also potentially weaken emerging market currencies relative to the dollar, as they are likely to depreciate along with the RMB to the extent that they are competitive with Chinese exporters. This may be helpful in supporting their own exports in the short term but can also catalyze capital outflows and require tightening domestic financial conditions.

Restricting global trade alone – through tariffs or non-tariff barriers such as security-related restrictions on imports – will likely weaken the economies of the countries imposing the tariffs by destroying consumer demand. The evidence of these direct economic costs was already mounting in the United States shortly after the "Liberation Day" tariffs were announced in April 2025, leading to the Trump Administration's sharp reversal of many tariffs a week later. The missing step is to empower and facilitate new investment into alternative sources of supply to satisfy consumer demand, behind a tariff-enabled wall. But even though these needs are obvious, the process of developing these alternative supply chains in a globalized economy where China has a dominant position in manufacturing is far from straightforward. New investments can quickly be undercut in price if China's exchange rate depreciates enough, or if Chinese firms continue to practice predatory pricing to retain market share. Beijing can and did respond with export controls on critical raw materials needed to build out alternative supply chains, raising the costs of these alternatives.[19]

Chinese firms will continue to finance their own investments outside of China in order to reduce their sensitivity to China-specific tariffs. Those Chinese firms can enmesh developing economies more tightly within China-centric manufacturing supply chains by continuing to import Chinese intermediate goods. For several countries, the choice of whether to invite Chinese firms to invest in domestic manufacturing within their borders is a difficult one. Some European countries are willing to host Chinese investment assuming it comes with transfers of advanced technology, similar to the requirements China made in attracting foreign investment throughout its development. Developing economies may be far more open to Chinese investment, with the hopes of building their own manufacturing bases. The United States is likely to cast a far more skeptical look at Chinese investment in any industry that potentially involves consumer data or critical infrastructure. As the world readjusts currently China-centric manufacturing supply chains, Chinese firms will be part of that process of diversification, and different countries will perceive the costs and benefits of those investments differently.

A more effective path toward changing the structure of the global economy would be a two-tiered trade regime, with low or minimal trade barriers for those inside, including the world's primary sources of consumer demand, and higher tariffs or trade barriers for countries outside, including China. Even the trade skeptic former United States Trade Representative Robert Lighthizer endorsed a version of this idea in a *New York Times* opinion piece early in the second Trump Administration.[20] While this is theoretically simple, it is extremely complex to negotiate among multiple trading partners. But the key insight from Lighthizer's concept is that, in order to reduce reliance upon Chinese manufacturing, countries need incentives to invest in alternative suppliers, including greater market access to the key sources of consumer demand in G7 economies. Tariffs alone that weaken consumer demand would arguably reduce those incentives to invest, as the overall global economy would likely contract. This is exactly the risk that has materialized from US tariffs imposed over the course of 2025.

However, despite the volatility in tariff implementation by the United States under the Trump Administration, de-risking from China is increasingly seen as a strategic imperative in both the United States and Europe. As a result, tariffs and other trade restrictions on Chinese exports are likely to continue to emerge in the years ahead. But individually, these steps may not provide a significant restructuring of the global economy or reduce China's influence on global export markets – only a coordinated approach to tariffs will do so.

Similarly, Beijing will find itself in an increasingly adversarial position relative to the rest of the world as long as domestic demand in China remains weak. Even if Beijing is successful in slowing global alignment with tariffs and other trade restrictions by offering temporary concessions to countries in Europe and Southeast Asia, political opposition to Chinese imports will not disappear. The structural imbalances in the Chinese economy are driving the world's response to Chinese imports, rather than the politics of individual nations. China can only alter this reality with meaningful steps toward rebalancing its economy, but all of these will slow growth further in the short term.

External Lending and Debt Relief in Developing Countries

An entirely different set of consequences emerges when considering the future of China's external lending activity, broadly organized under the Belt and Road Initiative (BRI). Launched formally in 2013, the BRI was an attempt to rebrand and organize China's already significant volumes of external lending to developing countries into a more formal political structure. By acting as a large sovereign lender for infrastructure projects in developing countries while other multilateral financial institutions such as the World Bank and International Monetary Fund imposed stricter criteria before lending, the BRI was meant to boost China's reputation as a champion of developing economies. The BRI was also an attempt to clean up the image of the China Development Bank, which had already generated widespread losses on some of its external lending from 2006 to 2012, including billions of dollars of loans to Venezuela's faltering government under Hugo Chavez and investments in Zambia's copper belt that became a lightning rod for local political opposition.

The definition of the BRI was always fluid, as there was never a clearly established list of countries that fit within the initiative. But as the research group AidData has unearthed in painstaking detail, BRI-related loans to infrastructure projects overseas were made to the host government on largely commercial terms, usually involving conditions that the proceeds were spent with specific Chinese firms to complete construction activity.[21] Most of the loans were made in US dollars, rather than RMB. The net result of most of these loans was that the host country received the financing and a completed infrastructure project, usually involving some sort of large-scale public work that would otherwise be difficult to finance, while a Chinese state-owned enterprise and its subcontractors would receive most of the business of completing the project and would import significant volumes of labor and intermediate goods from China to do so. The resulting debt would be owed by the developing country's treasury to a Chinese bank, usually the China Development Bank or Export–Import Bank of China.

China's policy banks had made similar loans before the BRI was formally launched. But the establishment of the BRI allowed Chinese state-owned enterprises and banks to formally court developing countries for this type of business. The total expansion of lending was generally estimated to exceed $1 trillion over a decade.[22] Naturally, many of these loans were never likely to be repaid, as they were far beyond the capacity of developing countries to service the debt. When the defaults started accumulating, Chinese lenders took multiple different paths. In one circumstance in Sri Lanka, the Chinese bank took possession of the infrastructure of a major port when the government could not repay the loan, and China's demands in renegotiations focused on equity in the port itself.[23] But this was a relatively rare occurrence, and in many cases Chinese banks had no recourse and simply extended the terms of the loans, without providing more money.

The problems for many developing countries came when US dollar interest rates began rising in 2022 and they risked defaults on loans to China, but also loans to private creditors. Rhodium Group found $78 billion of Chinese external loans in default or in renegotiation from 2020 to March 2023 alone.[24] This touched off a wave of negotiations over debt restructuring, which essentially involved the difficult question of who would be repaid first, and at what levels, among Chinese banks, private lenders, and multilateral development banks (MDBs). There were several rounds of discussions to try to bring Chinese lenders into existing multilateral processes for debt renegotiations, including those managed by the Paris Club group of lenders, which had successfully restructured several developing countries' debt in the 1970s and 1980s. As calls for relief came from Zambia, Sri Lanka, Ghana, Suriname, Chad, and Ethiopia, China found itself in a difficult position of appearing publicly as an obstacle to more efficient debt relief. Without China offering relief, many individual countries were unable to restructure their other claims with private creditors or MDBs, as the concern was that any new payments would simply be made to existing Chinese loans.

Simply put, these were not situations in which China had established regular practices for its actions, precisely because China had only been a significant external lender for just over a decade. Lower-level Chinese officials negotiating the claims presumably did not have authorization to make broad-based concessions on lending terms that would then set a potential precedent for all of China's other sovereign borrowers. Offering a 10 percent haircut on debt to one borrower might help to resolve a short-term logjam but those losses would multiply over more than $1 trillion in lending. Any Chinese official would be loath to take the internal blame for setting such a precedent with implications for such a large volume of China's sovereign lending. Over time, Chinese officials did adapt to the demands of multilateral lenders and began offering solutions that would allow debt renegotiation processes to proceed, so that developing countries could access private capital markets again. But while China did provide enough concessions to make progress, the moves were far from sufficient to provide meaningful debt relief to the countries demanding it or to others that had not yet started negotiations with China and private creditors.[25]

With China's economy slowing, and billions of dollars in external loans in default, the surge in BRI-related lending is over and will not be repeated in the future, which will impact a critical instrument of China's external economic engagement. China will likely come under pressure to offer more significant debt relief to emerging economies. But the BRI will not disappear entirely, and China will double down on providing additional financing for countries willing to borrow from its banks. In September 2024, just as China was acting aggressively to prop up the domestic economy, Xi Jinping pledged an additional $51 billion (360 billion yuan) in lending to African nations over three years at the Forum on China–Africa Cooperation Summit, including $30 billion via credit lines and $9.8 billion in new infrastructure investment.[26] Even with significant volumes of external loans potentially in default, the domestic pressures on China's banks are far larger in scope than non-performing overseas lending, and China's loans to developing countries were made by state-owned policy banks with explicit state guarantees. The slowdown in China's economy will reduce China's ongoing external lending activity, but this remains a second-tier problem compared to the decay within the broader financial system.

Defense Spending and China's Military

One of the questions that surfaces most frequently when discussing the implications of a structural slowdown in China concerns the impact on China's military activity and defense spending. On the surface, one would assume China's defense spending should decline along with the economy, or at the very least growth rates of military spending should slow. But China's leaders can always simply prioritize defense spending and run larger domestic budget deficits, even if the economy is slowing. Those larger budget deficits can still easily be financed internally in China without concern about pressure from external creditors. That has been the broad pattern in recent years, with China's budgeted defense spending rising 7.2 percent in nominal terms in both 2024 and 2025, while the estimated budget deficit has expanded sharply. China's planned defense spending officially reached 1.81 trillion yuan ($250 billion) in 2025, although a more comprehensive view of defense spending using industry-specific purchasing power parity adjustments places the 2024 level at $471 billion and would therefore imply a 2025 level closer to $505 billion.[27] Even at these adjusted estimates, China would still be spending less than 3 percent of its GDP on defense, which is a relatively low level; Beijing could easily raise it over time. China's overall defense spending would still be far below comparable measures of US defense spending, but importantly, planned spending on China's military continues growing, while the economy has reached the slowest rates of expansion in China's recent history.

For many analysts, these facts alone are sufficient to demonstrate that the economic slowdown in China should have no impact at all on perceptions of China's military and security threats, especially China's Taiwan-related military buildup and modernization efforts. But those arguments can only extend so far. Obviously, a Chinese economy that is growing at 7 or 8 percent per year sustainably poses a far greater threat in successfully developing its military than a Chinese economy growing at 2 or 3 percent per year. Therefore, the downgrade in Chinese growth in recent years should also change perceptions of Beijing's capacity to fund multiple policy objectives, including defense.

Nominal growth rates are important here, along with China's exchange rate relative to the US dollar. If China is struggling with deflationary pressures, nominal GDP growth rates are likely below real GDP growth rates. But it is nominal GDP that forms the foundation for actual fiscal spending on China's military, and wages to the armed forces. Similarly, if China's currency depreciates against the US dollar, this may not impact the purchasing power of the budget for China's domestic defense industry, but every imported component for that industry, including energy, will become more expensive.

The reality of China's fiscal decay is that the era of budget trade-offs is already here, and it is difficult to see how defense spending can remain immune from these pressures and continue current growth rates. China officially expected only 0.1 percent fiscal revenue growth in its 2025 budget, even while targeting 5 percent real GDP growth. In 2024, total tax revenues declined by 3.4 percent. If economic growth slows below China's targeted levels in the future, it is plausible that total fiscal revenues will decline in outright terms in the years ahead, without a significant restructuring of China's tax system. Including both the central government and local government accounts, the total fiscal deficit has risen from 1 to 2 percent of GDP in 2014 and 2015 to 7.7 percent of GDP in 2024, and around 9 percent in 2025. These deficits can be financed internally, as domestic banks will buy the necessary government bonds, even if that means they will also make fewer loans to Chinese companies. But overall deficits of this size alongside outright declines in nominal fiscal revenues suggest a time-limited surge in China's defense spending ahead, not a sustainable one that would ever approach US spending levels.

No one can predict the year that "guns versus butter" tradeoffs will finally be internalized among Chinese fiscal planners, reducing the growth rate of defense spending. In the event that China engages in a military conflict, Beijing could certainly expand the scope of defense spending in wartime, just as a beleaguered Russian state has continued to prioritize its military. But most analyses of China's military spending tend to assume that straight-line projections will continue into the future, without considering the fact that fiscal resources are declining outright at present. Those projections should likely be reconsidered in light of China's structural slowdown.

It would be complacent and wrong for Western policymakers to assume that China's slowing economy automatically reduces China's military and security threats. China's military buildup continues and could even accelerate in some scenarios. But that does not mean that the risks are the same as during the years of China's rapid economic growth. The range of potential expectations for China's defense spending should shift lower, along with the downgrade in China's overall fiscal capacity.

Thinking Differently About De-Risking from China

China's economic slowdown should also change how the world thinks about de-risking from China. A slowing China presents an entirely different set of risks from a China growing at high and sustainable rates, as outlined in this chapter. When most discussions of de-risking occur, analysts tend to conflate three different sets of "risks" associated with ongoing economic engagement and interaction with China. Importantly, while global perceptions of all of these risks have risen over the past decade, particularly since China's centralization of power under Xi Jinping and the exercise of control over global manufacturing during the pandemic, the three types of risks should diverge in the next five to ten years.

The first set of risks is military and security-related, as China is continuing to develop its military capabilities and test them in military exercises, particularly Taiwan-specific conflict scenarios. These perceived risks are likely to increase in the future, even if there are widespread disagreements about their significance and China's economic capacity to accelerate its military buildup. The second risk is related to industrial and technological competitiveness with Western firms and governments, particularly in industries such as semiconductors, artificial intelligence, or quantum computing, which all have some potential military applications. Here the outlook is less certain, as China has significant capabilities in multiple industries and has deployed its financial system aggressively toward its industrial policy objectives, but US technology controls have also weakened China's capacity in some sectors. Risks from China's competitiveness in strategic industries are likely to fluctuate in the years ahead.

But the third set of risks is related to economic or systemic rivalry, and the risk that China would overtake the United States as the world's largest economy, thereby allowing it to build capabilities and economic influence over time. That risk will decline in the years ahead, for all of the reasons outlined in this book. China cannot maintain the same pace of economic growth given the decay of its fiscal and financial systems and repairing those systems would entail significant short-term costs. But even as these three types of risks are likely to evolve in different directions in the years ahead – military and security risks rising, industrial competitiveness risks fluctuating, and systemic rivalry risks declining (as depicted in figure 6.3) – most calls for de-risking from China's economy have not adjusted to the emerging reality of a weakening Chinese economy in the years ahead.

The prevailing narrative surrounding China's economy used to be that the country was a rising economic power growing in strength and

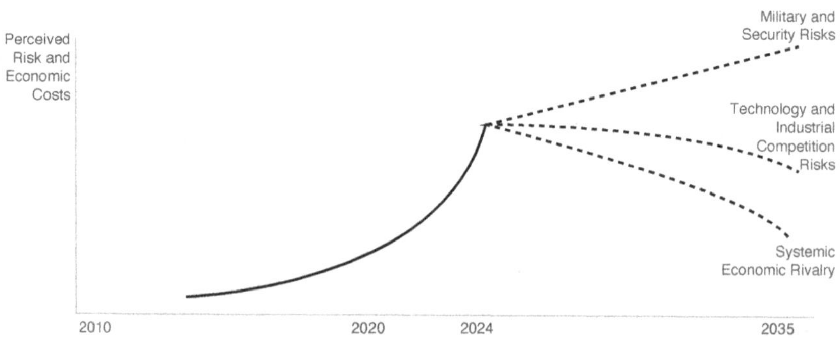

Figure 6.3 Diverging risks from China in the next decade.
Source: Author's own schematic.

global influence. That conventional wisdom is now shifting rapidly, but those changes will still take years to unfold. This book has argued that China is now a declining economic power, albeit one with considerable ongoing strengths and capabilities. Beijing is now being forced to fight over a shrinking pie of global demand via its export manufacturing sector without a straightforward path to restore past rates of economic growth. Even if there is more productive and efficient investment in advanced technologies within China, that does not change the fact that demand from Chinese households is insufficient to support this investment, and China still needs to sell its manufactured products abroad.

Different perceptions of China's future trajectory should require different policies in response. Confronting a rising and revisionist economic power requires immediate and significant steps to counter the sources of the revisionist power's economic strength. Under this scenario, even if separating from China-centric supply chains is extremely costly, there is a stronger case to act quickly to cut off multiple economic linkages with China, because continuing on the current path means that China's relative influence may continue to expand. A rapidly expanding Chinese economy should grow China's capabilities on multiple fronts, from military modernization to technological competitiveness with Western firms. As a result, when facing a rising China, it is reasonable for Western governments to consider asymmetric steps to deter the usage of Chinese economic statecraft tools, even if these measures disrupt the operations of existing international rules and institutions.

In contrast, a declining economic power presents an entirely different set of policy options and choices. Most importantly, acknowledging China's economic slowdown allows Western governments a wider range of policy tools to counter China. Focusing on China's building economic strength requires policy options to immediately respond to those broader strengths and capabilities. Given a slowing China, policy steps can become more focused. There is no need to weaken China's economy overall, as economic growth is already decelerating. Measures to counter China's economic statecraft can be targeted toward those specific policy tools, with a focus on deterring specific Chinese actions. China can always threaten to cut off exports of rare earths (or place controls on some other industrial component) as an instrument of coercion in economic negotiations, as Beijing has done in 2025. But the rest of the world can push back by restricting Chinese access to Western demand for critical exports, while also demonstrating a commitment to developing alternative supplies of rare earth minerals over time. These actions do not deprive Beijing of economic statecraft tools, but they can make it more costly for Chinese leaders to use them.

Moreover, strategic competition with a declining economy should incorporate the fact that time is an important ally. Early options should be focused on how to constrain China's behavior and increase the costs of Beijing initiating gray zone military actions in the Taiwan Strait or the South China Sea, export controls on critical materials, investigations into foreign companies, arbitrary detentions, and other actions from China that Western democracies are trying to prevent. Increasing the economic costs of those actions in the short term will only make them even costlier for Beijing in the long term, given that China's degree of influence will decline over time along with the size of its economy. A declining economic power that is still engaging in a military buildup and aggressive economic statecraft is a contingent threat, not a foundational threat to Western liberal democratic systems.

Moreover, de-risking from dependence upon Chinese manufacturing can be more targeted and specific, without concern about the large volume of trade with China that has little strategic significance and can continue. Beijing's dependence upon global demand for a large volume of its manufacturing sector can be used as a point of leverage for the US and its allies, rather than being targeted via across-the-board tariffs, which will only redirect shipments to third countries in the absence of a coordinated multilateral response. The focus should be on changing Beijing's perceptions of the costs of aggressive economic and military actions and their probability of success, given China's need to keep global markets open for its manufactured goods. China depends upon the rest of the world for economic growth, which limits how aggressive Beijing's economic statecraft can be over the long term.

A declining economy that is more dependent upon exports for growth has few long-term strategic options in a sustained systemic competition. China must keep overseas markets for its goods open, but the only tool it has to do so is to continue reducing prices, usually by producing more, which threatens overseas industries and raises protectionist walls further. Beijing must also keep capital flowing into its markets to stabilize its exchange rate and preserve its overseas purchasing power and corresponding economic influence. De-risking and removing China from global manufacturing supply chains is a significant threat to Beijing's primary drivers of growth. China's most important priorities will be slowing the foreign retreat from investment in China and the process of supply chain diversification. Beijing can take steps to raise the costs of separating Chinese components from global manufacturing. But even if Beijing succeeds at keeping global export markets open for a few more years, its problems do not disappear. Reducing political opposition to rising Chinese imports around the world is a far more difficult proposition, even if Beijing can successfully highlight the costs of American tariffs.

The conventional hindsight concerning US policy toward China alleges that American policy was far too slow to adapt to rising risks from China's economic power, territorial ambitions in the South China Sea, and the increasingly authoritarian turn in domestic politics. The pivot in US policy toward China started in the late Obama Administration around 2015 or 2016, and the Trump Administration took far more aggressive steps in systemic competition and trade conflict over the following four years, with most of the political forces traditionally pushing for engagement with China on the back foot throughout the late 2010s.

But with perfect hindsight, if the change in US approach to Beijing was far too slow, when should it have occurred? Here the alternative answers are revealing. Those focused on human rights concerns in China would argue that Tiananmen Square in 1989 marked a fundamental breaking point, while others focused on trade imbalances would claim that WTO membership for China was a mistake. But in economic policy, there was a clear track record of reform and steps toward convergence with international economic norms and practices developing in China in the 2000s. The clearest break with that pattern of convergence arguably occurred somewhere between the political instability in China in the leadership transition in 2012 and the reversals of the Third Plenum reform agenda that began in 2015. Was there a clear political case for breaking off engagement with China in 2008 immediately after the global spectacle of the Olympic Games, which were a significant step toward demonstrating the potential for China to join the rest of the world? Should it have occurred in 2011 or 2012, even before Xi Jinping's eventual political tendencies were known? The conventional wisdom argues that the US adjusted to China's changing reality far too late, after the global economy was far too dependent upon China's role in global manufacturing. But it still remains unclear how the results might have been different had the US taken alternative decisions in 2013 or 2014, rather than starting to adjust a few years later.

More importantly, the question about when US policy should have changed focuses on the most important issue: When did China change? And when was there sufficient evidence to demonstrate to Western democracies that China was no longer committed to economic reform and convergence with global norms? The shifts in China's political character and behavior were the more important drivers of US policy, and rightly so. In other words, it was Beijing's changing goals and actions that compelled US policy changes. China shifted from a path of eventual convergence with international economic norms and practices to a far more divergent course. US policy may have been slow to adjust to those changing Chinese objectives and behavior, but focusing on any mistakes in US timing misses the point. The centralization of authority in Beijing, the pursuit of import-substitution efforts, and the reversal of promised structural economic reforms compelled a change in approaches toward China in the United States, but also in Europe, Latin America, and Southeast Asia.

But just as Beijing shifted direction in the past, it can do so again. Beijing's break from a reformist path was not inevitable. There was no long-term plan in Beijing to launch a market-based structural reform program to great fanfare in 2013 and then walk it back piece by piece when it became too difficult to implement. There was nothing inevitable about Xi Jinping's consolidation of authority and capacity to serve a third and potentially a fourth term as general secretary after the intra-Party instability that was revealed during the Bo Xilai incident in 2012. And there was no long-term plan to unleash a risky shadow banking system and then dramatically rein it in, slowing the economy and breaking implicit guarantees.

The questions animating Western debates about strategic competition with China should focus on how to change Beijing's calculus about the rising costs and limited benefits of continuing to pursue their current policy course of military coercion of Taiwan and Southeast Asia along with economic mercantilism. That requires new strategies of economic deterrence in the short term and the coordinated usage of economic leverage to expose the limited benefits of Beijing's approach in the medium term.

Future plans for de-risking from China must consider the contingent nature of China's recent economic and political developments. De-risking is not correcting a historic mistake; it is strategically necessary because of Beijing's concentration of influence over global manufacturing and because of China's behavior in wielding statecraft tools based on that control. Beijing's behavior and objectives may change in the future. The purpose of de-risking from a declining economic power should be to alter Beijing's cost-benefit calculus in pursuing systemic competition with liberal market democracies and therefore constrain China's actions and behavior.

Changing Beijing's Calculus

De-risking from China reflects an attempt to provide economic security in a world of strategic competition. As Edward Fishman argues persuasively in his recent book on the history of modern economic statecraft, the world cannot prioritize economic security, economic integration, and geopolitical competition at the same time.[28] Only two out of three are possible. During the Cold War, there was less economic integration between the Warsaw Pact and the West, which allowed both sides to focus on economic security amidst strategic competition. Now, the United States and China are pursuing greater economic security in an economically integrated world, while also engaging in strategic competition. The only offset to this search for security will be a decline in economic integration, and the dissolution of trade linkages between China and the rest of the world. Importantly, China is far more vulnerable to this reversal in global economic integration than the United States, given that China's tools to drive domestic demand are impaired and Beijing depends upon global demand for growth.

Given the extent of China's investments in its export manufacturing supply chains, there is no automatic level of production outside of China at which the world will suddenly feel secure from Beijing's coercion. Raising one's imports from destinations other than China by 10 percent may provide some level of security, and by 40 percent may provide more, but ultimately Beijing will retain some degree of influence over global markets. China can always act more aggressively than they are currently acting, using the tools that they have available. De-risking will only be considered successful when the world no longer considers the risks from Chinese economic influence to be unmanageable. Beijing's behavior and actions are arguably the most important variable in that calculation of whether de-risking strategies are improving economic security. The key question for any de-risking strategy from a slowing Chinese economy should be how to deter Beijing from coercion and induce Beijing to become more cautious rather than acting aggressively, in military or economic terms.

Therefore, de-risking efforts should focus on changing China's incentives. Rather than a broad-based effort to reduce China's involvement in all manufacturing supply chains, using across-the-board tariffs, those efforts should be focused where China's potential economic coercion could have the largest effects, such as in critical minerals, components for global semiconductor manufacturing, or other areas important for national defense. Beijing continues to rely upon the goodwill of global markets to absorb its exports. That leverage should be preserved in some areas that pose few direct security risks and then used to deter China's deployment of other instruments of economic coercion. It is not difficult to envision a scenario in which the credible threat of broad-based de-risking from China drives Beijing to reduce its own reliance upon export controls, capricious customs inspections, and investigations into foreign firms in an effort to retain its existing share of global trade and prevent it from declining further.

The recent patterns in China's economic development were not inevitable. Beijing made concrete choices to walk away from structural economic reform and convergence with global economic practices in the 2010s. Strategic competition and trade conflict between China and the United States are underway, but China's future choices are still in the balance. How Beijing responds to the reality of a broken financial and fiscal system and slowing economic growth will have significant consequences for the rest of the world. Beijing – under Xi Jinping or another leader after Xi – may choose to discard or downplay systemic competition with the United States in order to maintain domestic stability. Or China could choose to double down on its existing policies and accelerate de-risking activity from the rest of the world, raising the possibility of new global trading blocs. The key point is that the outcomes are contingent, and not inevitable.

All of this reinforces the importance of speaking forthrightly and accurately about the nature of the threat and risks from China's current pattern of economic development: it is now a contingent risk dependent upon China's behavior and actions, and not a foundational risk to the United States or Western democracies resulting from China's continued growth. Framing the problem appropriately makes it easier to address and widens the range of policy options available to the United States and its allies. There are few appropriate courses of action to limit a rapidly growing Chinese system, and it is increasingly costly and difficult to sustain a domestic political consensus around their necessity. But maintaining an international coalition for de-risking from China is much easier if the benefits of accessing China's domestic economy are seen as declining over time rather than growing. Accurately describing China's economic weakness advances the international political space for de-risking strategies, which is one reason Beijing forcefully resists the idea that China is slowing. To counter a slowing China, there are far more low-risk steps targeting individual industries rather than the entire economy that can still deliver meaningful improvements in the US strategic position, while time plays its own healing role. Importantly, those steps can be sustained more easily on a multilateral basis.

Changing the narrative around China's economic development is a critical first step in expanding Western policy options to manage threats from China. The intellectual bubble surrounding China's growth will take many years to completely burst. But reframing the threat from China's economic slowdown can help to reduce the most significant risks market democracies face: undermining the foundations and demonstrated benefits of the market-based international system. Unfortunately for the United States, this is exactly the scenario that is materializing at present, with high tariffs being used and threatened against US allies and partners in addition to Beijing and seemingly disconnected from any broader US de-risking strategy focused on China. Policy choices matter, and as China's experience over the past decade has amply demonstrated, waiting too long to adjust can place hard ceilings on the economy's future.

Epilogue

Another Shift in China's Economic Narrative

By the summer of 2025, Donald Trump's presidency had provided China's leaders with new reasons for optimism about China's long-term political and economic prospects. The arbitrary imposition of tariffs on US allies, the capricious destruction of years of expertise within the US civil service under the guise of "efficiency," government interventions into corporate decision-making, government investments in private companies, and cuts to funding for scientific research all undermined critical US strengths in strategic economic competition against China. After a series of bilateral US–China negotiations in Geneva and London brought both countries' tariff rates back from the trade-prohibitive levels of 145 and 125 percent, Beijing was able to use the threat of withholding exports of rare earth elements and magnets from global industry to reduce the scope of future economic retaliation by the United States. While tariffs had been expected to trigger economic pressure on countries running global trade surpluses, the net result of the US threats in April 2025 was a surprisingly sharp weakening of the US dollar, and financial flows out of US assets.

As a result of these developments early in 2025, the global media narrative surrounding China's economy and capacity for strategic competition shifted once again, in Beijing's favor. Edward Luce, editor of the *Financial Times*, wrote in early August, "The year is barely halfway done but China is 2025's runaway winner."[1] Renowned economics commentator Adam Tooze added, "The contrast between the turmoil in Donald Trump's America and the mood of calm progress exuded by Beijing is striking both in style and substance."[2] The advances in artificial intelligence and large language models announced by DeepSeek in January had rekindled interest from both Chinese and global investors in the prospect of additional innovations and profits within China's technology sectors. As Xi Jinping shook hands with Jack Ma once again in February, the political campaigns against technology firms seemed to be a thing of the past, and investors were happy to move on.

The weakness of the US dollar resulting from Trump's tariffs also gave global investors a reason to reconsider bets on Chinese assets. Hedging against US policy unpredictability requires putting money somewhere outside of US markets. European companies and markets were beneficiaries, but China no longer appeared nearly as "uninvestable" in 2025 as it had during the previous three years. The weakness of the dollar also took depreciation pressure off China's currency and allowed the PBOC to manage the exchange rate during the trade war without generating shocks or surprises. In only a few months, much of the gloom surrounding China's long-term economic prospects appeared to be lifting.

This was the third time that Trump's presidency had provided China with additional breathing room in strategic competition with the United States. The first such episode occurred in 2017 with the US withdrawal from the Trans-Pacific Partnership trade agreement and the US drawdown in overall economic engagement in Asia, which allowed China to expand its regional influence. As loans from the Belt and Road Initiative were still flowing, China was able to make the argument that the US was withdrawing from the world while Beijing was offering deeper economic engagement and additional investment. The second such episode occurred in the early responses to the COVID-19 pandemic in 2020, when China's draconian controls on the spread of the virus, along with a haphazard US response, limited the early spread of the disease and the deaths that accompanied it far more effectively in China than in the United States. This provided Beijing with fuel for a global propaganda effort surrounding the superiority of China's political system relative to Western democracies. While Chinese vaccines were not nearly as effective as the later mRNA innovations developed in Western countries, Beijing also proactively engaged in diplomatic efforts to distribute Chinese vaccines in several countries, generating some goodwill in the absence of other alternatives.

But the damage the Trump Administration's actions inflicted upon the US strategic position vis-a-vis China in 2025 was far more severe, and some of the consequences for the United States are likely to be irreversible. Rather than cooperating with the United States in developing new investments in global manufacturing capacity that excluded China, US allies were instead scrambling to negotiate to minimize tariffs on their own exports to the US, while also developing hedging strategies to reduce their reliance upon the United States in the future. For countries such as India who had been leaning toward the United States because of concerns about Beijing's actions, US tariffs only rekindled interest in restarting diplomatic engagement with China, casting aside years of US diplomacy designed to deepen cooperation with New Delhi.[3] As immigration is the only driver of US population growth, the Trump Administration's attempt to reduce immigration over time while accelerating deportations undermines one of the core demographic advantages the US economy enjoys over China. Firing the nonpartisan commissioner of the Bureau of Labor Statistics in August after evidence emerged that tariffs were hurting the US economy similarly undermined a core US advantage relative to Beijing. Until that moment, there was no legitimate reason to suspect that US economic data might be distorted for political reasons, even while evidence that Beijing was engaging in patterns of economic data manipulation was growing. Defunding US scientific research will reduce the probability of productivity-enhancing innovations and technological breakthroughs in the future, with implications for US economic growth and competitiveness in several industries.

These changes in the globally prevailing narratives surrounding China's economic prospects and US policy credibility are consequential for US–China strategic competition. The strong growth of the US economy and its consumer markets is arguably the most important source of support for US economic statecraft, along with the institutional strengths of the US legal system. US sanctions and export controls are generally respected because of the potential threat of losing the US consumer market or losing access to the dollar-based financial system. Undermining the long-term health of the US economy in the future can reduce the effectiveness of US economic statecraft tools and compliance with US rules in the present. China needs the perception of stable and strong economic growth to not only attract foreign capital, but to mitigate the impact of US sanctions and export controls, as argued earlier in this book. How the world perceives the relative trajectories of the US and Chinese economies directly impacts the tools that both sides can use in strategic competition.

The bulk of this book was written in the last quarter of 2024 and the early months of 2025, before many of the events described above had occurred. The consequences for the US strategic position are already dire and will be difficult for US policymakers to manage in the future. But even considering these US mistakes, China's strategic position is still likely to deteriorate in the next five to ten years, for many of the reasons outlined in this book. China's current policy choices and economic strategy are simply incompatible with growing economic power and global influence. China wants to become less dependent upon the rest of the world for its industrial and technological development, while becoming even more dependent upon the rest of the world for economic growth. Beijing's strategies can change fundamentally, but until they do, China's current policy choices will generate both rising international pushback against Chinese exports and weakening domestic demand in China itself. The US can retreat from the world temporarily behind tariff walls and unilateral actions, but Beijing is unlikely to boost its global economic or political influence in response.

Success Produces Failure

The recent shift in the global narrative surrounding China's economy is unlikely to last, simply because none of the factors temporarily improving global perceptions of China will have a meaningful impact on long-term economic performance. Inflows into China's stock market are likely to be temporary and still insufficient to offset large-scale capital outflows from China's households and corporates. The exchange rate will likely remain under pressure to depreciate, and Chinese interest rates will need to remain below US interest rates to manage China's large domestic debt burdens. China's strategic usage of rare earths and other critical industrial materials as political leverage will be limited over time by trading partners' responses and the fact that China needs to keep global export markets open for its own economic growth.

Meanwhile, China's economy continues to face the same pressures described in the early chapters of this book. Deflationary forces have deepened in 2025, with producer prices falling by more than 3 percent per year as of this writing and consumer prices trending around zero growth. The deflation problem has become so severe that Beijing's strategy has returned to controls on supply in heavy industrial sectors, in the name of fighting "involutionary competition." Even if these controls on supply are successful, they will slow industrial output and economic growth further. The property sector remains a drag on the economy, even if it is now a smaller one. Infrastructure investment continues slowing despite government efforts to expand fiscal stimulus. Through the first half of 2025, China's fiscal revenues were still declining outright, reducing government wherewithal to fund its industrial policy ambitions. Consumer confidence hit new lows in PBOC surveys and consumer spending was supported primarily via increasingly costly government subsidies. And most significantly, credit growth continued to trend toward all-time lows of around 6 percent, slowing China's investment growth over time and contributing to all of the economic pressures listed above. The necessary structural reforms to China's fiscal and financial systems are not even remotely visible on the horizon.

China's achievements in electric vehicles, artificial intelligence, and advanced manufacturing techniques raise different questions about China's economic development strategy at present. What if this strategy succeeds? Strangely, even runaway success in China's chosen objectives to achieve technological and supply chain dominance in strategic industries would not resolve any of the most important problems in China's economy, although it may indirectly help Beijing find more resources to do so. GDP growth via investment may improve temporarily, and fiscal revenues may also recover if Beijing can figure out how to tax these industries effectively. But improving manufacturing efficiency and productivity in capital-intensive industries is unlikely to benefit China's labor force or improve prospects for domestic consumption without some dramatic shift in China's fiscal system. Newly graduated job seekers are more likely to be college-educated and less interested in working in the manufacturing sector. Services sector and consumer activity remains limited by the constraints in China's existing growth model. Without the property sector and its rising asset prices, it will be difficult for Beijing to outline a plausible path to wealth and upward mobility for most Chinese households.

Moreover, many of the industries China has targeted as its growth engines for the future are already facing deflationary pressures, and declining prices and profits. In July 2025, Xi Jinping made a pointed comment about the excesses already created by China's industrial policies, criticizing local governments for duplicating capacity in several industries, "When it comes to launching new projects, it's always the same few things: artificial intelligence, computing power, new-energy vehicles [. . .] Should every province in the country be developing industries in these areas?"[4] Chinese regulation in these sectors will likely tend toward mergers and consolidation, rather than encouraging significant new investments. In either scenario, they seem unlikely to deliver investment growth sufficient to offset China's current economic slowdown.

Without strong domestic demand growth, China will need to continue exporting most of the products and services generated from its advanced high-technology industries. China will become even more dependent upon the rest of the world for economic growth and will therefore be required to gain global export market share and accelerate disinvestment overseas. This type of export-led expansion is already generating global pushback, and the political energy behind trade defenses among China's trading partners is only likely to intensify. Beijing will be able to argue that China's rising export competitiveness is a byproduct of market efficiencies and productivity rather than weaker domestic demand, but politically, most workers within China's trading partners will care less about why they are losing their jobs than the fact that they are losing them.

From a macroeconomic perspective, there are clear limits to how fast China can grow by continuing to rely upon export-led manufacturing, even if China's technological innovation is world-leading. Ultimately, this model implies that China can only grow as fast as its export markets themselves, which will limit any relative gains in Beijing's global economic influence. In terms of political influence, the more likely result will be a rising global pushback against China's exports and attempts to leverage its control over critical inputs for political purposes. Even success in China's chosen path of economic development will likely produce failure for Beijing's longer-term political objectives of expanding global economic and political power or overtaking the United States as the world's largest economy.

Critiquing China's current economic strategy is one thing, but actually changing it is a far more difficult proposition. China's fiscal and financial resources to support its industrial policy ambitions are finite and will not expand forever. But even if Xi Jinping decided tomorrow that China's current path to development was only likely to generate deflationary pressures domestically and political resistance abroad, the industrial capacity that China has already built would still exist. Companies would still have incentives to export production at lower prices, and only deliberate export restrictions or quotas from China would likely prevent them from doing so. Even if China limits direct support for advanced manufacturing industries in the future, Beijing is unlikely to actively restrict economic activity in those sectors.

Even this scenario of limiting policy support appears far-fetched. Xi Jinping and the Chinese bureaucracy have committed to a manufacturing-led growth strategy for several years. Reversing course or changing this approach would require as dramatic a shift as occurred during the sudden relaxation of zero-COVID policies, and it would need to be led by Xi himself. More often, course corrections to Chinese policymaking tend to be incremental adjustments, while preserving the larger objectives of the previous approach. It seems highly unlikely that Xi Jinping will suddenly decide that the policy direction he has set for China is simply incorrect and needs to be abandoned. Beijing is almost certainly going to pursue an economic development strategy that produces weaker domestic demand at home and rising trade tensions in the rest of the world.

The Supply and Demand of De-Risking from China

In the wake of the Trump Administration's trade war against allies and adversaries alike, the prospect of a global coordinated response to China's overcapacity and industrial policy appeared more remote than ever. Most countries could no longer rely upon the United States to lead such an effort against China, given the capriciousness of US policy changes and growing concerns about the US commitment to shared liberal democratic values. China's control over rare earth minerals appeared to provide a powerful form of leverage that Beijing could use to discourage the US from imposing further export controls or raising tariffs. In the first half of 2025, China's exports rose by 5.9 percent in US dollar terms, while imports fell further, boosting China's trade surplus and the export sector's contribution to economic growth. Exports had shifted away from the US to other markets, at least temporarily. China was more vulnerable to a coordinated pushback against its trade practices, but US actions undermined the probability that this unified effort would take place.

However, none of these trends means that de-risking from China will lose momentum, and Beijing will have smooth sailing ahead. US actions under Trump's second term have temporarily impacted the *supply* of de-risking policies around the world. It appears unclear where a coalition to change China's concentration of global manufacturing capacity will arise. However, the *demand* for de-risking from China remains extremely strong, and is nearly certain to increase in the years ahead. Should China succeed in expanding its global export market share and diversifying its export destinations, the response is likely to be new sources of political opposition to rising Chinese imports, and more political energy behind trade defenses and coalition-building against Beijing. The supply of de-risking policies can still reconstitute in different forms in response to rising global demand for limits to China's exports and a change in China's economic practices.

The only factor that might delay the global push to reduce China's scope of economic influence and control would be a "grand bargain" between the United States and China that would pledge to reintegrate the economies of the world's largest exporter and the world's largest importer. However, the forces working against such a lasting trade-focused grand bargain are much stronger than the forces that would keep it intact. China cannot offer much to the United States at this point, primarily because its own domestic markets are unlikely to grow at the same rates as in the past. Beijing can pledge to increase investment for the manufacturing of electric vehicles, batteries, advanced robots, or other technologies in the United States, but such investments will not bring significant quantities of new jobs and will certainly invite new political resistance from both state governments and Washington. National security hawks will question the data transfers and other security vulnerabilities that could arise from Chinese-owned firms supplying US consumers and businesses. Nor will Beijing likely feel comfortable limiting its own economic influence over developing countries by redirecting significant volumes of its imports to US producers. As former US Treasury officials Brendan Kelly and Michael Hirson argued in March 2025 in an article skeptical of a US–China trade deal, "The underlying security, economic, and ideological imperatives that have driven the United States and China to reduce their reliance on each other for a decade remain in place."[5]

China's continued slowdown in domestic demand and its dependence upon investment-led growth make trade tensions with the rest of the world inevitable. The current tendency to interpret China's rising export levels as indicative of stronger competitiveness rather than a much weaker domestic economy will fade over time. Most trading partners will focus less on why China is driving disinvestment in their own economies, and more on how to respond to those disinvestment pressures.

The question now facing the world is how to assemble a coalition for de-risking from China, coordinate trade defenses, and develop alternative sources of manufacturing, while also factoring in a less important role for the United States within such an arrangement. One path forward is a limited coalition to develop alternative sources of critical minerals and rare earth elements and magnets, combining investments from countries with mining experience and expertise and then building upon that limited scope to develop investments in other industries. Another would be for Europe and China's other trading partners to establish tariff levels that match those of US levels on China, coordinating informally with Washington on this issue even without a concrete agreement to do so. Another pattern of de-risking may be the institutional development of alternative trade arrangements that deliberately exclude or limit trade with China. For many developing countries, defenses of their own export industries will likely involve non-tariff barriers and other restrictions on trade, along with requirements for local content within operations funded by Chinese investments. Other ideas will surely emerge in the years ahead.

The demand signal for some global response to China's trade imbalances appears certain, even if the form of the de-risking approach is still undetermined. Beijing's response will be to try to leverage its control over manufacturing capacity in several industries within bilateral trade discussions to slow or delay trade restrictions, while also using threats or inducements of new investment to prevent a coordinated response to China. But delays in these negotiations are only Pyrrhic victories for Beijing, because another year of rising imports from China likely redoubles efforts among most trading partners to take even more forceful measures the next time.

China's push into auto exports is a case in point. Even near-dominance of electric vehicle and battery manufacturing in such an important industry has generated antibodies in multiple markets, leaving only around one-sixth of global auto markets completely open to Chinese exports, and a further third of the global market open only if Chinese automakers commit to local production.[6] In the recent negotiations surrounding the EU–China summit, Beijing was unable to roll back EU tariffs on electric vehicle imports from China, despite the fact that European politicians appeared far more open to reducing their own alignment with the United States on trade issues. Global demand for de-risking from China is driven by the weakness of China's own domestic economy. If China's economy were actually expanding by around 5 percent per year, as Beijing claims, there would not be nearly the same level of global concern about surging Chinese exports, falling prices, and disinvestment. As this book has argued, the ultimate cause of that domestic slowdown has been the overextension of China's financial system, and the consequences of years of unproductive lending continuing for political reasons. US mistakes may prolong China's window to maintain its current economic strategy, but only marginally. Diversifying China's trade flows will also diversify trade conflict. Restructuring the financial and fiscal systems to change China's growth patterns and produce additional demand, while seeking the world's patience during this transition, is Beijing's only long-term solution to the economic and political bind China faces. These reforms are obviously nowhere on the horizon at present. A shift away from China's control of global manufacturing and industrial supply chains will emerge and accelerate, even if the price of de-risking trends higher.

Logan Wright
August 2025

Acknowledgments

Any book like this one is the unanticipated and cumulative byproduct of years of learning, conversation, reflection, and above all, hope. My thanks and appreciation to so many people for these influences extend far beyond the few that can be listed here. Correspondingly, any mistakes and inaccuracies in the book are solely my responsibility.

Thank you to all of my colleagues at Rhodium Group for your constant insight and guidance, and for creating the intellectual environment in which projects like this are possible. A sincere debt of gratitude to my editors, Louise Knight and Ian Malcolm at Polity, for seeing the opportunity available for this book and guiding a first-time author through the process. I greatly appreciate the efforts of my friends and colleagues who read early drafts of chapters on short notice, particularly Joseph Dickson, Martin Chorzempa, Barry Naughton, Jude Blanchette, and Stephanie Jose. I especially want to thank Kate Aitken for the original idea for the title.

I have been extremely fortunate to have been placed in circumstances where inspiration has emerged from the sheer power and force of the example of others around me. Being surrounded by my brilliant and dedicated housemates and friends from Georgetown for more than two decades now has shaped my intellectual and emotional development in more ways than I could have ever imagined. This book is only one small manifestation of the pervasive influence this group has had on my education and my life. My highest respect and appreciation to David Wilder and Allen Feng for their knowledge, camaraderie, and humor throughout my years in Beijing and afterward. Sincere thanks to Michael Pettis (and so many of his talented students) for years of wide-ranging conversations in Beijing on these topics, and for introducing me to so many people who would end up supporting my work. Thank you to Mark Crotty, Dan Kasten, and Christine Eastus for first teaching me about the English language and the process of writing, and to Ward McCarthy and the late John Carter for their early professional mentorship.

Above all, I would like to thank my parents Sharon and Perry Wright, and more than anyone else, my wife Bridget, for your patience, support, understanding, and love, as well as being by far my most thorough and diligent reviewer and editor. The results of this book and the long process of finishing it are for you.

Glossary

Financial Terms

CNY, RMB, CNH, and *yuan* – These are various names or labels for China's currency. For domestic usage, the currency is typically called the renminbi ("people's money") or RMB. In international foreign exchange trading, the typical abbreviation is the CNY (Chinese yuan). The "yuan" itself is the unit measure of the currency and is basically interchangeable with RMB. The CNH is the designation of CNY held and traded offshore, primarily in Hong Kong, rather than in mainland China.

GDP – Gross domestic product, or the total value of final output of goods and services within an economy. This is the most commonly used measure of the size of an economy in cross-country comparisons.

Implicit or *explicit guarantees* – Explicit guarantees on assets are direct promises to investors from a third party, usually a local or central government, that the investor bears no risk and any losses will be absorbed by the third party. Implicit guarantees were far more common in China, in which this promise that government would absorb any losses was widely assumed but never directly stated.

Interbank rates – These refer to the interest rates or the costs that banks would charge one another for funding in China's money market. The most commonly used interbank rates in China's money markets are the overnight and seven-day pledged repo rates. Interbank rates are significant because they can provide early signals of financial stress. If banks are suddenly charging higher rates to other banks, it is usually indicative of funding stress throughout the financial system.

LGFVs – Local government financing vehicles are platform companies used by local governments to borrow and finance infrastructure projects within their jurisdictions. They proliferated in China in the years following the global financial crisis.

NBFIs – Non-bank financial institutions. In China, these were the institutions that received money from commercial banks to lend to riskier borrowers such as property developers or local governments, or who held assets temporarily for commercial banks in exchange for a fee. They can include trust companies, asset management companies, brokerages, credit guarantee companies, peer-to-peer lenders, and other types of financing companies. These institutions flourished and expanded quickly as shadow banking activity grew.

P2P – Peer-to-peer lenders were among the riskiest forms of shadow banking activity, offering high returns to individual investors and then lending funds at even higher interest rates to borrowers, often with little credit evaluation. These institutions were among the first to default within the shadow banking system after regulations tightened, breaking the common perception that nothing in China's financial system could fail, as Beijing would always have incentives to offer bailouts.

Presales – This refers to pre-construction sales by property developers, in which these firms could collect most or all of the sales revenues from a property sale before construction was complete. Presales were effectively a form of borrowing, with credit extended from homebuyers to property developers. The rising volumes of presales created a significant political headache for Beijing when developers ran short of liquidity to complete construction of houses already purchased.

Repo rates – This refers to the financing cost or interest rate to enter into a repurchase agreement for a security pledged as collateral within the agreement. The most frequently traded rates in China's interbank money market are the overnight and seven-day rates in the pledged repo market (meaning collateral is pledged but does not need to actually change hands).

Shadow banking – This is a broader term describing several forms of unregulated or lightly regulated financial transactions and institutions. Shadow banking activity expanded rapidly in China from 2012 to 2016, and was the primary target of Beijing's deleveraging campaign from 2016 to 2018.

Trust companies – Trust companies were non-bank financial institutions usually owned primarily by local governments, borrowing from high-net worth individuals and lending to property developers and infrastructure projects. Trust companies are often the first to default during times of financial stress in China, as occurred in the late 1990s and in 2020, before the worst of the property market crisis.

TSF – This refers to "total social financing" or the People's Bank of China's revised label of "aggregate financing for the real economy," and reflects a broader measure of monthly new credit extended by China's banks and non-bank financial institutions. The coverage and definition of TSF have been revised several times over the past decade, to include or exclude certain types of credit.

WMPs – This refers to wealth management products, which were the most common form of shadow finance offered to individual bank depositors or investors. These were deposit-like investments promising higher returns than official deposits for a few months or a year. They were targeted directly in regulatory changes under China's deleveraging campaign.

Institutions

CBRC or *CBIRC* or *NFRA* – The China Banking Regulatory Commission (2003–2018), the China Banking and Insurance Regulatory Commission (2018–2023), and the National Financial Regulatory Administration (2023–present) have all been names for China's primary banking system regulator, with the latter two institutions including an expanded jurisdiction over insurance companies and other financial firms.

PBOC – The People's Bank of China is China's central bank. It is not an independent central bank and takes direction from the State Council for monetary policy decisions, but can also shape those decisions through the options offered to China's political leaders. The PBOC has long been among the most reform-oriented institutions within China's bureaucracy.

Politburo and *Politburo Standing Committee* – The Political Bureau of the Central Committee of the Chinese Communist Party includes twenty-four members (recently reduced from twenty-five) and is the highest level of Communist Party leadership, usually meeting around once per month. The Politburo Standing Committee is an even more select group of top political leaders within the Politburo that now includes seven members, led by Xi Jinping, and can make decisions when the full Politburo is not in session.

State Council – The highest-level leadership of the state administrative bureaucracy in China, which implements decisions made by the leadership of the Chinese Communist Party. The leader of the State Council is the premier, who also sits on the Politburo Standing Committee of the Communist Party.

Notes

Introduction

1 Description of a photo of the demonstration from David Kirton, "Disgruntled China Evergrande Investors Crowd Headquarters in Protest," *Reuters*, September 13, 2021. Photograph by David Kirton.

2 Alexandra Stevenson and Cao Li, "Evergrande Gave Workers a Choice: Give Us Cash or Lose Your Bonus," *New York Times*, September 19, 2021.

3 *China Digital Times*, "Evergrande Protesters Become Target of Stability Maintenance," September 15, 2021.

4 Joe McDonald, "Explainer: Chinese Builder's Debt Struggle Rattles Investors," *Associated Press*, December 7, 2021.

5 Stevenson and Li, "Evergrande Gave Workers a Choice."

6 Quoted within Cyrus Sanati, "Prince Finally Explains His Dancing Comment," *New York Times Dealbook*, April 8, 2010.

7 See Yakov Feygin, *Building a Ruin: The Cold War Politics of Soviet Economic Reform* (Harvard University Press, 2024).

8 Subbaraman quoted within Evelyn Cheng and Yen Nee Lee, "New Chart Shows China Could Overtake the U.S. as the World's Largest Economy Earlier than Expected," *CNBC.com*, January 31, 2021.

9 *Washington Post*, "What Just Happened: Storm Clouds Loom for China's Economy," August 18, 2023.

10 See Elizabeth Economy, *The Third Revolution: Xi Jinping and the New Chinese State* (Oxford University Press, 2018).

11 See Michael Pillsbury, *The Hundred-Year Marathon: China's Secret Strategy to Replace America as the Global Superpower* (St. Martin's Griffin, 2015).

12 See, for example, James McBride, Noah Berman, and Andrew Chatzky, "China's Massive Belt and Road Initiative," Council on Foreign Relations, February 2, 2023.

13 See Henry Kissinger, *On China* (Penguin Press, 2011).

14 Andreea Brînză, "No, China Doesn't Think Decades Ahead in its Diplomacy," *The Diplomat*, October 7, 2020.

15 See Daniel Rosen, "China's Economic Reckoning," *Foreign Affairs*, July/August 2021.

Chapter 1: The Promise of China's Economic Development

1 Joerg Wuttke, interview by author, Washington, DC, April 4, 2025.

2 See Joe Studwell, *The China Dream: The Quest for the Last Great Untapped Market on Earth* (Grove Press, 2002), chapters 4 and 5.

3 James McGregor, phone interview by author, April 2, 2025.

4 See Aaron Friedberg, *Getting China Wrong* (Polity Press, 2022).

5 Wuttke, interview.

6 See the discussion of the importance of the direction of reform within Huang Yasheng, *Capitalism with Chinese Characteristics: Entrepreneurship and the State* (Cambridge University Press, 2008), 35–40.
7 For an extensive discussion of the importance of the 2001 decision to admit private entrepreneurs into the Party, see Bruce Dickson, *Red Capitalists in China: The Party, Private Entrepreneurs, and Prospects for Political Change* (Cambridge University Press, 2003).
8 McGregor, interview.
9 Liu Shiyu, Wu Yi, and Liu Zhengming, "The Lessons Learnt from the Development and Reform of China's Banking Sector," in *The Banking System in Emerging Economies: How Much Progress Has Been Made?* (Bank for International Settlements, 2006), BIS Papers No. 28, 181–7.
10 Technically foreign exchange reserves cannot be used to meet domestic currency liabilities. The placement of foreign reserves as capital provided a signal to foreign investors that these banks would remain capitalized at high levels, since they could not sell the reserves.
11 Nicholas Lardy, "Issues in China's WTO Accession," Brookings Institution, May 9, 2001.
12 For discussion of this argument, see Jennifer Hillman, "China's Entry into the WTO – A Mistake by the United States?" in *China and the WTO: A Twenty-Year Assessment,* ed. Henry Gao and Damien Raess (Cambridge University Press, 2023).
13 William Jefferson Clinton, "Full Text of Clinton's Speech on China Trade Bill," *Federal News Service*, March 9, 2000.
14 McGregor, interview.
15 Pang Zhongying, "The Beijing Olympics and China's Soft Power," Brookings Institution, September 4, 2008.
16 Ibid.
17 Congressional Research Service, "China's Economy and the Beijing Olympics," August 6, 2008.
18 *Reuters*, "Factbox – World Leaders to Attend Opening Ceremonies," August 7, 2008.
19 Henry M. Paulson Jr., *On the Brink: Inside the Race to Stop the Collapse of the Global Financial System* (Business Plus, 2010), cited within Krishna Guha, "Paulson Claims Russia Tried to Foment Fannie-Freddie Crisis," *Financial Times*, January 29, 2010.
20 Wuttke, interview.
21 Zhou Xiaochuan, "Reform the International Monetary System," People's Bank of China, March 23, 2009.
22 *New York Times*, "China Announces $586 Billion Stimulus Plan," November 9, 2008.
23 Erica Downs, "China Development Bank's Oil Loans: Pursuing Policy and Profit," *China Economic Quarterly*, December 2011: 43–7.
24 Benjamin Kang Lim and Ben Blanchard, "China Ex-Security Chief Warned Bo Xilai He Would Be Ousted – Sources," *Reuters*, April 15, 2015.
25 Christopher Johnson, "Xi Jinping Disappears From View," Center for Strategic and International Studies, September 14, 2012.
26 Nicholas Kristof, "Looking for a Jump-Start in China," *New York Times*, January 5, 2013; Robert Lawrence Kuhn, "Xi Jinping: A Nationalist and a Reformer," *South China Morning Post*, June 6, 2013.
27 Daniel Rosen, *Avoiding the Blind Alley: China's Economic Overhaul and its Global Implications* (Asia Society, 2014), 8–12.
28 Ibid., 5.

29 Arthur Kroeber, "Xi Jinping's Ambitious Agenda for Economic Reform in China," Brookings Institution, November 17, 2013.
30 Eric Mu, "Yu'ebao: A Brief History of the Chinese Internet Financing Upstart," *Forbes*, May 26, 2014.
31 Stella Xie, "More Than a Third of China is Invested in One Giant Mutual Fund," *Wall Street Journal*, March 27, 2019.
32 See Martin Chorzempa, *The Cashless Revolution: China's Reinvention of Money and the End of America's Domination of Finance and Technology* (PublicAffairs, 2022), introduction and chapter 2.
33 Steven Liao and Daniel E. McDowell, "No Reservations: International Order and Demand for the Renminbi as a Reserve Currency," *International Studies Quarterly* 60 (June 2016): 272–93.
34 Nicholas Watt, Paul Lewis, and Tania Branigan, "US Anger at Britain Joining Chinese-Led Investment Bank AIIB," *The Guardian*, March 12, 2015.
35 See Edwin Truman, "The Chinese Renminbi is Not a Freely Usable Currency Yet," Peterson Institute for International Economics, August 7, 2015; Ho-fung Hung, "RMB Inclusion into SDR: Hyperbole and Reality," *Columbia University Press Blog*, December 1, 2015.
36 Paul Krugman, "China's Naked Emperors," *New York Times*, July 31, 2015.
37 Tom Orlik, *China: The Bubble that Never Pops* (Oxford University Press, 2020), 216.
38 Wuttke, interview.

Chapter 2: The Rise and Stall of China's Financial System

1 Yuan Yang and Xinning Liu, "Police Lock Down Beijing's Financial District to Thwart Protests," *Financial Times*, August 6, 2018.
2 *Bloomberg News*, "China Unleashes $483 Billion to Stem the Market Rout," July 17, 2015.
3 Measured using data from the People's Bank of China, "Balance Sheet of Other Depository Corporations," multiple years.
4 Data cited from National Bureau of Statistics, "Gross Domestic Product," accessed via Bloomberg terminal.
5 Calculations based on data from the People's Bank of China, "Balance Sheet of Other Depository Corporations," multiple years.
6 Data from Bank for International Settlements, BIS Data Portal, "Credit-to-GDP Gaps Dashboard: United States."
7 Charles Calomiris and Stephen Haber, *Fragile by Design: The Political Origins of Banking Crises and Scarce Credit* (Princeton University Press, 2014), 35.
8 Lin William Cong, Haoyu Gao, Jacopo Ponticelli, and Xiaoguang Yang, "Credit Allocation Under Economic Stimulus: Evidence from China," *Review of Financial Studies* 32 (September 2019): 3412–60.
9 Yiming Cao, Raymond Fisman, Hui Lin, and Yongxiang Wang, "SOEs and Soft Incentive Constraints in State Bank Lending," *American Economic Journal: Economic Policy* 15 (February 2023): 174–95.
10 Data on the Shanghai Composite Index sourced from the Bloomberg terminal, code SHCOMP.
11 Kyoungwha Kim, "China Margin Debt Shrinks First Time in a Month Amid Stock Rout," *Bloomberg News*, June 21, 2015.

12 Lingling Wei, "China's Response to Stock Rout Exposes Regulatory Disarray," *Wall Street Journal*, August 4, 2015.
13 Calculated using the two line items, "Claims on other depository corporations" and "Claims on other financial institutions" from December 2010 to December 2016 within People's Bank of China, "Balance Sheet of Other Depository Corporations," multiple years.
14 Bank of Jinzhou, *2015 Annual Report*, 2016.
15 Bank of Jinzhou, *2018 Annual Report*, 2019. Official GDP data for Liaoning province from National Bureau of Statistics, "Gross Regional Product-Liaoning," 2012 to 2017, accessed via China Economic Information Center (CEIC).
16 *Bloomberg News*, "China's Great Ball of Money is Rushing into Commodities Futures," April 22, 2016.
17 *People's Daily*, "Asking About First Quarter Big Trends – An 'Authoritative Person' Discusses China's Economy," May 9, 2016.
18 Selection translated by author, *People's Daily*, "Asking About First Quarter Big Trends."
19 Ibid.
20 Interest rates cited from Bloomberg terminal, securities codes CNRE01 and CNRE07.
21 See Logan Wright, *Grasping Shadows: The Politics of China's Deleveraging Campaign* (Center for Strategic and International Studies, 2023), chapter 5.
22 Data cited from online platform Wangdaizhijia, in Lauren Gloudeman and Bart Carfagno, "Fintech Crunch: Deleveraging Hits P2P," Rhodium Group, July 24, 2018.
23 Neil Gough, "Online Lender Ezubao Took $7.6 Billion in Ponzi Scheme, China Says," *New York Times Dealbook*, February 2, 2016.
24 Gabriel Wildau and Yizhen Jia, "Collapse of Chinese Peer-to-Peer Lenders Sparks Investor Flight," *Financial Times*, July 22, 2018.
25 Logan Wright, "Beijing's Credibility and the Baoshang Bank Dilemma," Rhodium Group, July 18, 2019.
26 *Bloomberg News*, "China's First Bank Seizure in 20 Years Sets Investors on Edge," May 27, 2019.
27 Logan Wright, "China's Slow-Motion Financial Crisis is Unfolding as Expected," Center for Strategic and International Studies, September 21, 2022.
28 *Reuters*, "China's Liaoning Province to Merge 12 Local Banks to Defuse Regional Risks," January 28, 2021.
29 Kim Gittleson, "Chaori Solar in Landmark Chinese Bond Default," *BBC.com*, March 7, 2014.
30 Data on corporate bond defaults sourced from Rhodium Group's proprietary database on China's corporate bond defaults. Annual totals cited within Allen Feng, "The Party's Over in China's Corporate Bond Market," Rhodium Group, March 26, 2020.
31 Longmei Zhang, "Credit Bonds," in *The Future of China's Bond Market*, ed. Alfred Schipke (International Monetary Fund, 2019).
32 Amanda Lee, "China's 'Grey Rhino' Debt Risk Highlighted by Bond Defaults," *South China Morning Post*, November 23, 2020.
33 Mark Landler, "Chinese Investment Trust Defaults on Bond Payment, Stirring Fear," *New York Times*, October 28, 1998.
34 *Bloomberg News*, "Key Part of China Shadow Banking Faces Doubling of Defaults," April 14, 2020; *Bloomberg News*, "China's Sichuan Trust is Latest to Miss Payments in Trust Market," June 16, 2020.

35 Gan Li's China Household Finance Survey cited within Tamim Bayoumi and Yunhui Zhao, "Incomplete Financial Markets and the Booming Housing Sector in China," International Monetary Fund Working Paper 20/265, December 2020; Jonathan Kemp, Anirudh Suthakar, and Tom Williams, "China's Residential Property Sector," *Reserve Bank of Australia Bulletin,* June 18, 2020; Kenneth Rogoff and Yuanchen Yang, "Peak China Housing," National Bureau of Economic Research Working Paper No. 27697, August 2020.

36 Marriage data are reported quarterly from China's Ministry of Civil Affairs.

37 Data from National Bureau of Statistics, "Floor Space Sold: Residential: House in Advance," accessed via CEIC.

38 Data from the People's Bank of China, "Sources and Uses of Credit Funds of Financial Institutions (RMB)," multiple years; US data from Federal Reserve Bank of New York, Center for Microeconomic Data, Household Debt and Credit Report, multiple quarters. Calculations using December 31, 2021 exchange rate for USD-CNY.

39 Wang Jing et al., "Developers Face New Debt Limits as Property Crackdown Continues," *Caixin Global,* September 2, 2020.

40 Data from National Bureau of Statistics, "Main Developer: Land Acquisition: Land Area: Overall," accessed via CEIC.

41 Data cited within Baldwin Cheng, David Li, and Sophie Lyall, "China's Real Estate Sector Shows the Beginning Signs of Recovery," White & Case, Debt Explorer, October 10, 2024.

42 Li Yao and Zhou Na, "China's Mortgage Boycotts Signal Deeper Problems in its Real Estate Sector," National University of Singapore, East Asian Institute Commentary No. 57, August 24, 2022.

43 See, for example, Shawn Yuan, "China's Cash-Strapped Local Governments Can't Pay Workers on Time," *Al Jazeera,* May 11, 2023.

44 Logan Wright and Allen Feng, "Tracking Credit Events at LGFVs," Rhodium Group, September 26, 2022.

45 Data sourced from National Bureau of Statistics, "Gross Domestic Product by Expenditure Approach," accessed via CEIC.

46 Rogoff and Yang, "Peak China Housing."

47 Allen Feng and Logan Wright, "Tapped Out," Rhodium Group, June 1, 2023.

48 Data from National Bureau of Statistics, "Retail Sales-Catering," accessed via Bloomberg terminal.

49 Data from the People's Bank of China, "Sources and Uses of Credit Funds of Financial Institutions (RMB)," 2022.

50 Land sales revenues are paid by developers to local governments with up to a one-year lag, and are reported by China's Ministry of Finance.

51 Cheng Leng and Ryan McMorrow, "Beijing Seeks to Curb 'Shakedown' Detentions of Chinese Executives," *Financial Times,* December 28, 2024.

52 Logan Wright and Allen Feng, "City-Level Financial Stress Rising," Rhodium Group, December 18, 2019.

53 Feng and Wright, "Tapped Out."

54 Data from Ministry of Finance, multiple series on government revenues, accessed via the Bloomberg terminal.

55 Aggregate export data reported from China's General Administration of Customs, multiple years, accessed via the Bloomberg terminal.

56 International Monetary Fund, "People's Republic of China: 2021 Article IV Consultation," January 28, 2022, 13–14.
57 Harry X. Wu, "China's Institutional Impediments to Productivity Growth," Reserve Bank of Australia, Conference Volume 2016, 5–29.
58 Martin Wolf, "China's Excess Savings Are a Danger," *Financial Times*, March 5, 2024.
59 Logan Wright et al., "No Quick Fixes: China's Long-Term Consumption Growth," Rhodium Group, July 18, 2024.
60 See Matthew Klein and Michael Pettis, *Trade Wars Are Class Wars: How Rising Inequality Distorts the Global Economy and Threatens International Peace* (Yale University Press, 2020).
61 Wright et al., "No Quick Fixes."
62 Data from the People's Bank of China, "Sources and Uses of Credit Funds of Financial Institutions (RMB)," multiple years; National Bureau of Statistics, "Gross Domestic Product."
63 *Xinhua News Agency*, "China Auto Industry Revenue Rises 4 Percent, Passes 10 Trillion Yuan Mark in 2024," February 11, 2025.
64 Andrew Hayley, "China Clean Energy Sector Was Biggest Driver of 2023 GDP Growth – Research Report," *Reuters*, January 25, 2024.
65 Data from National Bureau of Statistics on "Value: Building Sold: Residential," accessed via CEIC.
66 Based on data from the People's Bank of China, "Aggregate Financing to the Real Economy (Flow): Loans Written Off," multiple years.
67 Guonan Ma, "Who Pays China's Bank Restructuring Bill?" *Asian Economic Papers* 6 (2007): 46–71.
68 *Bloomberg News*, "China to Recapitalize Four Big Banks with $69 Billion," March 30, 2025.
69 Alexis Brown, "China's Anti-Corruption Efforts Gain Momentum in Finance and Healthcare," *Jamestown Foundation China Brief*, October 6, 2023.
70 *Straits Times*, "China to Cut Pay by Half for Staff at Top Financial Regulators, Sources Say," January 15, 2025; Rebecca Feng and Chun Han Wong, "China Reins in its Once-Freewheeling Finance Sector with Purges and Pay Cuts," *Wall Street Journal*, January 13, 2025.
71 Quoted within Feng and Wong, "China Reins in its Once-Freewheeling Finance Sector."

Chapter 3: Policy Mistakes and Indecision

1 Jing Yang and Serena Ng, "Ant's Record IPO Suspended in Shanghai and Hong Kong Stock Exchanges," *Wall Street Journal*, November 3, 2020.
2 Liyan Chen, Ryan Mac, and Brian Solomon, "Alibaba Claims Title for Largest Global IPO Ever with Extra Share Sales," *Forbes*, September 22, 2014.
3 Raymond Zhong, "In Halting Ant's I.P.O., China Sends a Warning to Business," *New York Times*, November 6, 2020.
4 Tiffany May, "Jack Ma Appears in Public for the First Time Since Challenging Beijing," *New York Times*, January 20, 2021.
5 Lingling Wei and Keith Zhai, "Chinese Regulators Suggested Didi Delay its U.S. IPO," *Wall Street Journal*, July 5, 2021.
6 The function of Party leading groups was first detailed extensively in Carol Lee Hamlin, "The Party Leadership System," in *Bureaucracy, Politics, and Decision Making in Post-Mao*

China, ed. Kenneth G. Lieberthal and David M. Lampton (University of California Press, 1992), 95–124.

7 See Minxin Pei, *China's Trapped Transition* (Harvard University Press, 2006), introduction and chapter 1.

8 Li Cheng, "The New Bipartisanship within the Chinese Communist Party," *Orbis* 49 (Summer 2005): 387–400.

9 Barry Naughton, "The General Secretary's Extended Reach: Xi Jinping Combines Economics and Politics," *China Leadership Monitor* 54 (September 2017): 7.

10 Chris Buckley and Keith Bradsher, "China Moves to Let Xi Stay in Power by Abolishing Term Limit," *New York Times*, February 25, 2018.

11 Austin Ramzy, "Ousted Chinese Official is Accused of Plotting Against Communist Party," *New York Times*, October 20, 2017.

12 *The Economist*, "Communist Party Members Must Study Xi Jinping's Thinking," April 13, 2023.

13 Xingqiang (Alex) He, "Top-Level Design for Supremacy: Economic Policy Making in China Under President Xi," Center for International Governance Innovation Papers No. 242 (May 2020), 6.

14 Ibid., 7.

15 Minxin Pei, "Rewriting the Rules of the Chinese Party-State: Xi's Progress in Reinvigorating the CCP," *China Leadership Monitor* 60 (June 2019): 1–4.

16 Minxin Pei, "Xi Jinping's New Economic Team and Government Re-Organization," *China Leadership Monitor* 76 (June 2023): 8–9.

17 *Communiqué of the Fifth Plenary Session of the 19th Central Committee of the Communist Party of China*, October 29, 2020.

18 Zichen Wang, "The 'Spirit' of the 5th Plenum," *Pekingnology* (newsletter), February 24, 2021.

19 Sui-Lee Wee, "China Says it Will Allow Couples to Have 3 Children, Up From 2," *New York Times*, May 31, 2021.

20 Xiaopu Zhang and Hongming Zhu, *The Puzzle of Finance: A Comparative Study of the German Financial System* (China Finance 40 Forum Books, 2021), referenced within Allen Feng and Logan Wright, "Common Prosperity and Rethinking Chinese Capitalism," Rhodium Group, August 25, 2021.

21 Samuel Shen et al., "China Launches Antitrust Probe into Tech Giant Alibaba," *Reuters*, December 23, 2020.

22 Ibid.

23 Julie Zhu et al., "China's Ant to Hive Off Credit Data in Revamp; Sees IPO in 2 Years – Sources," *Reuters*, February 4, 2021.

24 Tony Munroe, "China Extends Crackdown on Jack Ma's Empire with Enforced Revamp of Ant Group," *Reuters*, April 12, 2021.

25 *Reuters*, "Meituan to Change Delivery Algorithm Rules as China Urges Labour Protection," September 13, 2021.

26 Elles Houweling, "'Common Prosperity' Contributions: The New Cost of Doing Business in China, Explained," *Verdict*, September 7, 2021.

27 Eamon Barrett, "Chinese Tech CEOs Just Keep Quitting," *Fortune*, November 1, 2021.

28 Zheping Huang, "China Warns 34 Tech Firms to Curb Excess in Antitrust Review," *Bloomberg News*, April 13, 2021.

29 Celia Chen and Iris Deng, "Tencent, Didi Chuxing, Other Internet Firms Slapped with

Fine by Antitrust Authorities for Failing to Disclose Deals," *South China Morning Post*, April 30, 2021.

30 *Reuters*, "China Investigates Didi Over Cybersecurity Days After its Huge IPO," July 2, 2021.

31 Iris Deng and Xinmei Shen, "Chinese Newspaper Labels Gaming 'Spiritual Opium' and Calls Out Tencent, Fanning Fears of a Crackdown," *South China Morning Post*, August 3, 2021.

32 Donny Kwok and Scott Murdoch, "Beijing's Regulatory Crackdown Wipes $1.1 Trillion off Chinese Big Tech," *Reuters*, July 12, 2023.

33 Keith Zhai, "China Plans to Ban U.S. IPOs for Data-Heavy Tech Firms," *Wall Street Journal*, August 27, 2021.

34 *Bloomberg News*, "China Bans For-Profit School Tutoring in Sweeping Overhaul," July 24, 2021.

35 Ibid.

36 Daniel Rosen and Logan Wright, "Masks Off," Rhodium Group, July 27, 2021.

37 *Reuters*, "China's Efforts to Calm Investor Jitters Help Markets Rebound," July 29, 2021.

38 *Bloomberg News*, "Xi Unleashes a Crisis for Millions of China's Best-Paid Workers," September 18, 2024.

39 Data from National Bureau of Statistics, cited within Guo Jinhui, "China's College, University Graduates to Likely Exceed 11.7 Million This Year, Gov't Report Shows," *Yicai Global*, March 5, 2024; *China Daily*, "China's College Graduates to Exceed Two Million in 2003," March 27, 2002.

40 Li Yuan, "As Beijing Takes Control, Chinese Tech Companies Lose Jobs and Hope," *New York Times*, January 5, 2022.

41 *Bloomberg News*, "China's Daily Covid Cases Top 20,000 as Isolation Expands," April 5, 2022.

42 Stephen McDonnell, "Shanghai Covid Lockdown Extended to Entire City," *BBC.com*, April 5, 2022.

43 *Bloomberg News*, "Anger Erupts at Xi's 'Big White' Army of Lockdown Enforcers," April 26, 2022.

44 Liza Lin and Liang Jie, "Shanghai's Covid Lockdown Leads to Logistics Disarray, with Quarantined Truckers, Piled-Up Containers," *Wall Street Journal*, April 21, 2022.

45 Sonya Yuan, "Shanghai's Censors Can't Hide Stories of the Dead," *Wired*, June 13, 2022.

46 Logan Wright, "Rethinking China's Economic Future," Rhodium Group, May 31, 2022.

47 Data mentioned in Wright, "Rethinking China's Economic Future," and sourced from National Bureau of Statistics, "Floor Space Started: Commodity Building: Residential," and monthly auto sales from China Association of Automobile Manufacturers, accessed via CEIC.

48 Data from Alibaba, Taobao, and Tmall monthly sales totals, mentioned in Wright, "Rethinking China's Economic Future."

49 Hong Kong Census and Statistics Department, "Mid-Year Population for 2022," Press Release, August 11, 2022.

50 Brenda Goh and Ryan Woo, "COVID-Hit Shanghai to End Two-Month Lockdown on June 1," *Reuters*, May 30, 2022.

51 Quoted within Edward White, Sun Yu, and Cheng Leng, "China Claims Covid Victory in Shanghai Despite Recession Risks," *Financial Times*, June 2, 2022.
52 *Xinhua News Agency*, "CPC Leadership Analyzes Economic Work, Reviews Disciplinary Inspection Report," July 29, 2022.
53 *Bloomberg News*, "Xi's Covid Zero Strategy Faces Make-or-Break Test in Chengdu," September 6, 2022.
54 Chris Buckley, Alexandra Stevenson, and Keith Bradsher, "From Zero Covid to No Plan: Behind China's Pandemic U-Turn," *New York Times*, December 19, 2022.
55 Zhanwei Du et al., "Estimate of COVID-19 Deaths, China, December 2022–February 2023," Centers for Disease Control and Prevention, *Emerging Infectious Diseases* 29 (October 2023): 2021–4.
56 Data cited within Logan Wright, "China's Economy Has Peaked: Can Beijing Redefine its Goals?" *China Leadership Monitor* 81 (September 2024).
57 All data cited within Wright, "China's Economy Has Peaked."
58 Evelyn Cheng, "China Signals More Support for Real Estate with a 'Big Change' in Tone," *CNBC.com*, July 26, 2023.
59 Data from National Bureau of Statistics, "Output of Main Industrial Products," and retail sales data from Bloomberg, cited within Wright, "China's Economy Has Peaked."
60 Data from National Bureau of Statistics for 2023, "Nationwide Per Capita Income and Consumption Expenditure," accessed via Bloomberg terminal.
61 Data from China's Ministry of Finance for 2023, "Main Items of the General Public Budget Revenue of Central and Local Governments: Individual Income Tax," accessed via Bloomberg terminal.
62 Logan Wright, "Beijing's Silence is Deafening," Rhodium Group, February 2, 2024.
63 Feygin, *Building a Ruin*, chapter 5.

Chapter 4: A Contested Story of China's Economic Future

1 Joe Leahy, Edward White, and Cheng Leng, "Why Xi Jinping Changed His Mind on China's Fiscal Stimulus," *Financial Times*, October 22, 2024; Mia Nulimaimaiti, Ralph Jennings, and Sylvia Ma, "Xi Jinping Tones Down Focus on China's Growth Targets as Headwinds Mount," *South China Morning Post*, September 13, 2024.
2 Keith Bradsher, "China Eases Overall Monetary Policy Stance for First Time in 14 Years," *New York Times*, December 9, 2024.
3 Kevin Yao and Ellen Zhang, "China Unveils $1.4 Trillion Local Debt Package But No Direct Stimulus," *Reuters*, November 8, 2024; *Reuters*, "China Gives Government Workers First Big Pay Bump in a Decade to Boost Economy," January 3, 2025.
4 Central Economic Work Conference statement in 2023, quoted within Neil Thomas, "Xi Signals More Growth but Same Strategy at China's Central Economic Work Conference," Asia Society Policy Institute, December 14, 2023.
5 The story is related in footnote 47 of Lucian Pye, "An Introductory Profile: Deng Xiaoping and China's Political Culture," *The China Quarterly* 135 (September 1993): 437.
6 Mentioned within Carsten Holz, "Quality of China's GDP Statistics," Stanford Center for International Development Working Paper No. 487 (November 2013), 5–6.
7 Eric Eckholm, "China Reports 7.8% Growth, Close to Goal it Set for '98," *New York Times*, December 31, 1998.

8 Thomas Rawski, "What is Happening to China's GDP Statistics?" *China Economic Review* 12 (2001): 347–54.
9 *Xinhua News Agency*, "Premier: China 'Able to Achieve' About 8% Growth," March 5, 2009.
10 My paraphrasing, as the conversation took place in 2009.
11 Daniel Rosen and Beibei Bao, *Broken Abacus: A More Accurate Gauge of China's Economy* (Center for Strategic and International Studies, 2015).
12 International Monetary Fund, "Press Release: The People's Republic of China Subscribes to the IMF's Special Data Dissemination Standard," October 7, 2015.
13 Prices quoted from Bloomberg, "Iron Ore Spot Price Index 62% Import Fine Ore CFR Qingdao USD," 2014 to 2015, accessed via Bloomberg terminal.
14 Count of negative word choices based on a Rhodium Group analysis contained within Logan Wright and Daniel Rosen, "China's GDP: The Costs of Omerta," Rhodium Group, August 2019.
15 Ibid.
16 Holz, "Quality of China's GDP Statistics"; Tom Orlik, "Lies, Damned Lies, and Chinese Statistics," *Foreign Policy*, March 20, 2013.
17 Wei Chen, Xilu Chen, Chang-Tai Hseih, and Zheng Song, "A Forensic Examination of China's National Accounts," Brookings Papers on Economic Activity, Spring 2019, 77–141.
18 William Barcelona, Danilo Cascaldi-Garcia, Jasper J. Hoek, and Eva Van Leemput, "What Happens in China Does Not Stay in China," Board of Governors of the Federal Reserve System, International Finance Discussion Papers No. 1360, November 2022.
19 Scott Kennedy and Qin (Maya) Mei, "Measurement Muddle: China's GDP Growth Data and Potential Proxies," Center for Strategic and International Studies, September 13, 2023.
20 John Fernald, Eric Hsu, and Mark Spiegel, "Is China Fudging its GDP Figures? Evidence from Trading Partner Data," Federal Reserve Bank of San Francisco Working Paper 2019-19, August 2019.
21 Calculation using the methods outlined in Rogoff and Yang, "Peak China Housing."
22 Lingling Wei, "Xi Jinping Muzzles Chinese Economist Who Dared to Doubt GDP Numbers," *Wall Street Journal*, January 8, 2025.
23 *Washington Post*, "China Says its Economy Grew 5 Percent Last Year. It Probably Didn't," January 26, 2025.
24 Greg Ip, "Why You Shouldn't Trust China's Growth Data," *Wall Street Journal*, March 6, 2024.
25 *Billions*, Season 2, Episode 2, "Dead Cat Bounce," directed by Anna Boden and Ryan Fleck, written by Wes Jones, aired February 26, 2017, on Showtime.
26 Kennedy and Mei, "Measurement Muddle."
27 Hunter Clark, Maxim Pinkovskiy, and Xavier Sala-i-Martin, "China's GDP Growth May Be Understated," National Bureau of Economic Research Working Paper No. 23323, April 2017.
28 Charles Goodhart, "Problems of Monetary Management: The UK Experience," in *Inflation, Depression, and Economic Policy in the West,* ed. Anthony S. Courakis (Barnes and Noble Books, 1981), 116.
29 Rosen and Bao, *Broken Abacus.*

30 Roberto Aragao and Lukas Linsi, "Many Shades of Wrong: What Governments Do When They Manipulate Statistics," *Review of International Political Economy* 29 (2022): 88–113.

31 Anirban Nag and Ronojoy Mazumdar, "India Has Been Accused of Overstating its Growth Statistics," *Bloomberg Businessweek*, July 24, 2019.

32 I may be somewhat naive in making this point, as some initial discussions with India-focused economic analysts suggested the Modi administration in India was highly sensitive to the political implications of economic data revisions.

33 See Joe Studwell, *The China Dream: The Quest for the Last Great Untapped Market on Earth* (Grove Press, 2002).

34 See Robert Schiller, *Narrative Economics: How Stories Go Viral and Drive Major Economic Events* (Princeton University Press, 2019), preface and chapters 3, 7, and 8.

35 Laura He, "China Silences Prominent Market Analyst as Economic Slump Deepens," *CNN.com*, May 2, 2022.

36 Sun Yu, "Chinese Economists Told Not to Be Negative as Rebound Falters," *Financial Times*, August 5, 2023.

37 Ji Siqi, "China Censors Economic, Financial Writer Wu Xiaobo for 'Hyping Up Unemployment Rate' Amid Economic Slowdown," *South China Morning Post*, June 27, 2023.

38 CNN Staff, "Prominent Chinese Business Analysts Are Starting to Disappear from Social Media," *CNN.com*, December 22, 2023.

39 Minxin Pei, "Do Chinese Leaders and Elites Think Their Best Days Are Behind Them?" *China Leadership Monitor* 81 (September 2024).

40 John Burn-Murdoch, "China's GDP Blackout isn't Fooling Anyone," *Financial Times*, October 21, 2022.

41 *Bloomberg News*, "China is Hiding More and More Data From the Rest of the World," August 15, 2023.

42 *Bloomberg News*, "China to Stop Publishing Daily Global Stock Flows in Mid-August," July 29, 2024.

43 *Bloomberg News*, "China is Hiding More and More Data."

44 Colleen Howe, "China Stops Publishing Data that Showed Falling Renewable Power Plant Usage," *Reuters*, July 1, 2024.

45 Sidney Leng, "China Power Firms Suspend Publication of Coal Data, Frustrating Analysis of Industrial Production," *South China Morning Post*, July 8, 2020.

46 People's Bank of China, "PBOC Officials Answer Press Questions on the Revision of the Statistical Coverage of Narrow Money (M1)," December 2, 2024.

47 Thomas Hale, "China's Data 'Black Box' Puzzles Economists," *Financial Times*, July 23, 2023.

48 Data components from Logan Wright et al., "China Q1 2023 Macro Data Recap," Rhodium Group, April 18, 2023.

49 *Reuters*, "Chinese Data Provider Tightens Some Information Access for Offshore Users," May 3, 2023.

50 *Bloomberg News*, "China is Hiding More and More Data."

51 International Monetary Fund, "Press Release: Statement by the IMF Executive Board on Argentina," Press Release No. 13/33, February 1, 2013.

52 International Monetary Fund, *People's Republic of China: 2016 Article IV Consultation*, August 2016, 29.

53 Zhang Zhengxin statement in International Monetary Fund, *People's Republic of China: 2022 Article IV Consultation*, January 12, 2023 (report published February 2023), 124.

54 International Monetary Fund, *People's Republic of China: 2013 Article IV Consultation*, July 2013, 15.

55 See Rush Doshi, *The Long Game: China's Grand Strategy to Displace American Order* (Oxford University Press, 2021).

56 For an extensive discussion of how China uses these narratives strategically, see Peter Mattis, "'Changes Unseen in a Century': Seeking American Partnership in US Decline," *Jamestown Foundation China Brief*, November 21, 2023.

57 Samantha Custer et al., "Winning the Narrative: How China and Russia Wield Strategic Communications to Advance Their Goals," Gates Global Policy Center, AidData, Global Research Institute, and William & Mary, November 2022.

58 Ibid.

59 For just one example, see the history described in Edward Fishman, *Chokepoints: American Power in the Age of Economic Warfare* (Portfolio Press, 2025).

Chapter 5: What a Prolonged Economic Slowdown Means for China

1 Yan Zhuang, "Dejected Social Media Users Call 'Garbage Time' Over China's Ailing Economy," *New York Times*, September 13, 2024.

2 David Bandursky, "The 'Lying Flat' Movement Standing in the Way of China's Innovation Drive," Brookings Institution, July 8, 2021.

3 *South China Morning Post*, "From 'Lying Flat' to 'Letting it Rot:' Why China's Frustrated Youth are Embracing 'Bailan' Way of Life," October 4, 2022.

4 *Bloomberg News*, "Young Chinese Take Slacking Off to New Heights as 'Rat People,'" April 17, 2025.

5 Calculations made over multiple years using the methods of Rogoff and Yang, "Peak China Housing," by multiplying the relevant input-output table coefficients for construction and investment, and then adding the value-added component for housing within tertiary sector GDP calculations.

6 Allen Feng and Logan Wright, "The Long-Term Fundamentals of China's Property Market," Rhodium Group, December 12, 2022.

7 Data from China's Ministry of Finance, "Main Items of General Public Budget Expenditure of the Central and Local Governments," accessed via Bloomberg terminal.

8 Based on total level of central government bonds outstanding (33.8 trillion yuan) relative to nominal GDP at the end of 2024 (134.9 trillion yuan). Data from National Bureau of Statistics via CEIC.

9 Logan Wright and Rogan Quinn, "The Myth of China's Fiscal Space," Rhodium Group, August 29, 2023.

10 Hannah Miao, "China's Local Governments Hold Back Wages in Desperate Scrape for Cash," *Wall Street Journal*, November 29, 2024.

11 *Reuters*, "Chinese Provinces Spent at Least $51.6 Billion on COVID Curbs in 2022," February 15, 2023.

12 Clarence Leong, "Hundreds Protest in China as Government Cuts Medical Benefits," *Wall Street Journal*, February 17, 2023.

13 Stella Yifan Xie, Yoko Kubota, and Cao Li, "China's Cities Struggle Under Trillions of Dollars of Debt," *Wall Street Journal*, March 6, 2023.

14 Laura He and Berry Wang, "Starving Zoo Animals and Cucumber Fines: China's Indebted Cities Are Desperate for Cash," *CNN.com*, September 20, 2023.
15 Cheng and McMorrow, "Beijing Seeks to Curb 'Shakedown' Detentions."
16 Ding Jingjing, "Truck Fined 275,000 Yuan in Two Years, Neihuang County, Henan Province Launched an Investigation," *Jiemian News*, May 17, 2023.
17 *Wall Street Journal*, "China Dismisses Tax Crackdown Speculation," June 18, 2024.
18 This is approximate, but reflects a calculation based on the official fixed asset investment totals for infrastructure investment in 2017, compounded using the official growth rates for infrastructure investment in nominal terms through 2024, and then multiplied by a related coefficient for construction activity within the official input-output table.
19 Richard Koo, *The Holy Grail of Macroeconomics: Lessons from Japan's Great Recession* (Wiley, 2009), 39–51.
20 Hiroshi Nakaso, "The Financial Crisis in Japan During the 1990s: How the Bank of Japan Responded and Lessons Learnt," Bank for International Settlements, BIS Papers No. 6, October 2001, 6–9.
21 Joint Statement by Minister of Finance and Governor of the Bank of Japan, November 26, 1997.
22 Data from US Federal Reserve, "Population – Total for Japan," and "Working Age Population Total – From 15 to 64 Years for Japan."
23 Lingling Wei, "Xi Digs in with Top-Down Economic Plan Even as China Drowns in Debt," *Wall Street Journal*, December 23, 2024.
24 Data cited from National Bureau of Statistics, "Retail Sales" and "Per Capita Disposable Income Growth" (using urban households before 2014).
25 Sheng Zhongming, "Rethinking CPI and Real Interest Rates," China Finance 40 Research, August 28, 2024.
26 Data from National Bureau of Statistics, "Non-Governmental Investment in Fixed Assets," accessed via Bloomberg terminal.
27 Chris Metinko, "Venture Funding to China-Based Startups Dries Up," *Crunchbase News*, August 27, 2024.
28 For just one example, Yin Yeping and Deng Xiaoci, "Xi Urges Healthy, High-Quality Development of Private Sector," *Global Times*, February 18, 2025.
29 Ruochen Dai et al., "The Impact of COVID-19 on Small and Medium-Sized Enterprises (SMEs): Evidence from Two-Wave Phone Surveys in China," *China Economic Review* 67 (June 2021).
30 Laurie Chen, "China Anti-Graft Body Vows Crackdown on Finance Sector Corruption," *Reuters*, February 23, 2023.
31 Li Yuan, "What China Expects From Businesses: Total Surrender," *New York Times*, July 19, 2021.
32 Yew Lun Tian, "China's Xi Urges Private Firms to 'Be Rich and Loving' in Pursuit of Prosperity for All," *Reuters*, March 6, 2023.
33 Ella Cao and Kevin Yao, "China to Increase Support for Private Firms to Bolster Recovery," *Reuters*, July 19, 2023.
34 Milton Ezrati, "Beijing's Planners Offer Guidance to Inspire Private Investment," *Forbes*, August 1, 2024.
35 Frank Chen, "China Makes Space for Private Sector, Vows Spending to Boost Demand," *South China Morning Post*, December 12, 2024.
36 See Feygin, *Building a Ruin*, chapters 5–6.

37 Camille Boullenois, Agatha Kratz, and Daniel Rosen, "Far From Normal: An Augmented Assessment of China's State Support," Rhodium Group, March 17, 2025.
38 Measured via total social financing (TSF) or the "Aggregate Financing for the Real Economy (AFRE)," reported via People's Bank of China and the Bloomberg terminal. US dollar value calculated using end-year exchange rates from 2020 to 2024.
39 The circular itself remains unpublished but is referenced extensively in Chinese state media in late 2023 and early 2024. Logan Wright, "Beijing's Silence is Deafening."
40 Andrew Mullen and Amanda Lee, "What You Need to Know About the Henan Banking Crisis," *South China Morning Post*, July 13, 2022.

Chapter 6: A Broken Chinese Economy and the Rest of the World

1 Sebastian Rotella and Kirsten Berg, "How a Chinese American Gangster Transformed Money Laundering for Drug Cartels," *ProPublica*, October 11, 2022.
2 Ibid.
3 John Tobon, "Black Market Foreign Exchange," Indo-Pacific Defense Forum, March 24, 2022.
4 Official retail sales growth in China was 7.2 percent in nominal terms in 2023. The retail sales data were flattered by unorthodox adjustments to 2022 growth rates that boosted headline retail sales growth in 2023. After the adjustments were removed, this did not change the year-on-year growth rates, suggesting actual retail sales growth was weaker than the official data implied.
5 Calculations based on data from the World Bank on global investment, consumption, and GDP, "World Bank Group Data."
6 See, for example, Xin Ping, "Excess or Shortage? The 'Overcapacity' Smear Against China Must Stop Now," *Xinhua News Agency*, June 13, 2024.
7 Data from China's General Administration of Customs, "International Trade in Goods," accessed via Bloomberg terminal.
8 For a more extensive discussion of the systemic distortions involved, please see Boullenois, Kratz, and Rosen, "Far From Normal."
9 Ibid.
10 Camille Boullenois and Charles Austin Jordan, "How China's Overcapacity Holds Back Emerging Economies," Rhodium Group, June 18, 2024.
11 International Energy Agency, *Special Report on Solar Global PV Supply Chains*, August 2022, 22.
12 Nette Nostlinger, "Germany's Industrial Bloodbath Leaves Politicians Fumbling for Answers," *Politico*, November 27, 2024.
13 Igor Patrick, "China Carmakers Merit Dumping Probe and Tariffs: Brazil Auto Industry Group," *South China Morning Post*, January 30, 2025.
14 Brad Setser, "The Surprising Resilience of Globalization: An Examination of Claims of Economic Fragmentation," in *Strengthening America's Economic Dynamism*, ed. Melissa S. Kearney and Luke Pardue (Aspen Institute, 2024), 76.
15 Data from the People's Bank of China, "Money Supply."
16 Data for 2024 from the US Federal Reserve Bank of St. Louis, FRED Economic Data, "M2."
17 Igor Patrick, "Brazil Imposes New Tariffs on Imports from China in Bid to Fight Dumping," *South China Morning Post*, October 19, 2024.

18 Camille Boullenois and Agatha Kratz, "If Not Tariffs, then What?" Rhodium Group, April 7, 2025.

19 Gracelin Baskaran and Meredith Schwartz, "The Consequences of China's Rare Earths Export Restrictions," Center for Strategic and International Studies, April 14, 2025.

20 Robert Lighthizer, "Want Free Trade? May I Introduce You to the Tariff?" *New York Times*, February 6, 2025.

21 See Anna Gelpern, Sebastian Horn, Scott Morris, Brad Parks, and Christoph Trebesch, *How China Lends: A Rare Look into 100 Debt Contracts with Foreign Governments* (Peterson Institute for International Economics, Kiel Institute for the World Economy, Center for Global Development, and AidData at William & Mary, 2021).

22 Keith Bradsher, "China Invested $1 Trillion to Gain Global Influence. Can That Go On?" *New York Times*, October 16, 2023.

23 Maria Abi-Habib, "How China Got Sri Lanka to Cough Up a Port," *New York Times*, June 25, 2018.

24 Matthew Mingey and Logan Wright, "China's External Debt Renegotiations After Zambia," Rhodium Group, June 29, 2023.

25 Gregory Makoff, Theo Maret, and Logan Wright, "Sovereign Debt Restructuring with China at the Table," Harvard Mossavar-Rahmani Center for Business and Government, Associate Working Paper No. 248, January 2025.

26 Laurie Chen and Joe Cash, "China Offers Africa $51 Billion in Fresh Funding, Promises a Million Jobs," *Reuters*, September 5, 2024.

27 M. Taylor Fravel, George Gilboy, and Eric Heginbotham, "Estimating China's Defense Spending: How to Get It Wrong (and Right)," *Texas National Security Review* 7 (Summer 2024): 40–54.

28 Fishman, *Chokepoints*, 424.

Epilogue

1 Edward Luce, "Trump is the Gift That Keeps on Giving to China," *Financial Times*, August 5, 2025.

2 Adam Tooze, "'Alligator Alcatraz' Policymaking Leaves the Field Clear for China," *Financial Times*, July 4, 2025.

3 Helen Davidson, "India and China Amid Trump-Induced Geopolitical Shakeup," *The Guardian*, August 20, 2025.

4 *Bloomberg News*, "Xi Questions Local Officials on EV, AI Plans in Rare Rebuke," July 17, 2025.

5 Brendan Kelly and Michael Hirson, "The Limits of a US–China Deal," *Foreign Affairs*, March 7, 2025.

6 Gregor Sebastian and Endeavour Tian, "From Fast Lane to Gridlock: Have Chinese Car Exports Peaked?" Rhodium Group, January 23, 2025.

Index

Page numbers in italics refer to figures.